Planning Cities for the Future

Planning Cities for the Future

The Successes and Failures of Urban Economic Strategies in Europe

Peter Karl Kresl

Bucknell University, USA

Edward Elgar

Cheltenham, UK • Northampton, MA, USA

© Peter Karl Kresl 2007

Published by
Edward Elgar Publishing Limited
Glensanda House
Montpellier Parade
Cheltenham
Glos GL50 1UA
UK

Edward Elgar Publishing, Inc.
William Pratt House
9 Dewey Court
Northampton
Massachusetts 01060
USA

A catalogue record for this book
is available from the British Library

Library of Congress Cataloging in Publication Data

Kresl, Peter Karl.
  Planning cities for the future : the successes and failures of urban economic strategies in Europe / Peter Karl Kresl.
      p. cm.
  Includes bibliographical references and index.
  1. City planning—European Union countries. 2. Europe—Economic conditions—1945– I. Title.
  HT395.E85K74 2006
  307.1′216094—dc22   2006023673

ISBN: 978 1 84542 530 2

Typeset by Cambrian Typesetters, Camberley, Surrey
Printed and bound in Great Britain by MPG Books Ltd, Bodmin, Cornwall

Contents

About the author

Peter Karl Kresl is Charles P. Vaughan Professor of Economics and Professor of International Relations at Bucknell University (USA), where he has taught since 1969. His Ph.D. was from the University of Texas (Austin) and he has a BA from Roosevelt University and an MA from Northern Illinois University. His teaching and research interests are in international economics, Canadian-American relations, the European integration process, cultural policy, and urban and regional economics. He has been visiting professor or researcher at the Norwegian School of Economics and Business, Lund University (Sweden), Carleton University (Canada), the University of Vermont and McGill University (Canada), where he was Seagram Visiting International Researcher. His articles have appeared in many journals, including Urban Studies, the Journal of European Integration, the American Review of Canadian Studies, and his books include, with Sylvain Gallais, *France Encounters Globalization* (Edward Elgar, 2002) and, with Earl Fry, *The Urban Response to Internationalization* (Edward Elgar, 2005); *The Urban Economy and Regional Trade Liberalization* (Praeger, 1992); and he has co-edited, with Gary Gappert, *North American Cities and the Global Economy* (Sage, 1995). He is, with Ni Pengfei, co-founder and currently director of the Urban Competitiveness Project. The research for this book was largely conducted while he was visiting researcher at the International Center for Economic Research, in Turin, Italy.

Preface

The research for this project was done during the winter–spring of 2005 in Turin, Italy, at the Department of Economic Geography of the University of Turin. This was made possible with a research fellowship from the International Center for Economic Research. For these excellent facilities and support I am deeply grateful to Professor Enrico Colombatto, Director of the International Center, and to Professor Sergio Conti, Dean of the Faculty of Economics at the University of Turin. I must also acknowledge the welcome I received from the faculty and staff of the Department and from Alessandra Calosso at the Center.

In each of the ten cities I interviewed individuals from government, and entities such as the chamber of commerce, as well as journalists and academics, both in 2005 and earlier in the early 1990s. My conversations with them and the access they gave me to documents and to data provided the informational basis on which this research was based. I am grateful to each of them for the gracious cooperation they gave to me. I can only hope that this book will be of interest to them as they and their colleagues in other cities chart the courses for the economic future of their economies and that they may gain some insight into best practices in this important area of public policy.

The people at Edward Elgar, Catherine Elgar and Alex O'Connell, have been most accommodating and congenial to work with, as always. Finally, I must express my thanks to my wife, Lois Svard, for putting up with my absence for a longer period of time than either of us found pleasant.

1. The urban context and the need for economic–strategic planning

We have all seen the satellite photographs of Europe at night, with the European geographic space filled with bright dots, larger or smaller, indicating the concentrations of human beings in towns and cities. Another feature of this photograph is, not surprisingly, the absence of national borders or of anything else that would suggest that Europe was anything other than a 'network of cities.' This is, of course, the conceptualization that many activist city leaders[1] sought to promote beginning with the establishment of the Eurocities Movement in 1988. This photograph is also a static, one frame image. In 1990, the year in which this study begins, things may not have been all that comfortable for those who were unemployed or in jobs which underutilized their skills, but at least things were generally predictable for Europe's citizens in this global economy. The state welfare systems are healthy enough so that those in real need are generally able to get by. Not at all like those living in market-driven, Anglo-saxon economics in which the unfortunate are left to fend for themselves.

Looking back on Europe as it was in 1990, it is clear that it was between two periods of crisis. The period the French refer to as '*les trentes glorieuses*,' the period of strong reconstruction or recovery based growth and unemployment rates of less than 5 per cent, had been brutally brought to its end by the oil price hikes of 1973 and 1979. Growth slowed, unemployment rates became double-digit, and European societies began to be afflicted by the variety of social pathologies, faced by cities in the US, which they had largely escaped during the post-Second World War period. Europhoria and Europtimism became replaced by expressions of Europessimism and Eurosclerosis. But by 1990 much of this OPEC-induced anxiety had run its course and the member countries of the European Community (EC) were occupied with the need to realize the potential inherent in the just adopted Single European Act (SEA). Markets of all sorts would be liberalized in the near future, the European economy would be dominated by new technologies and efficiency, but still within the comforting context of European social welfare structures. As a consequence of the SEA, incomes were predicted to rise by an additional one percentage point for each of five or six years.[2] Things did not look to be as rosy as they were during the ultimately heady years of 1945–1975, but the future did appear to be promising.

What Europeans did not know was that the decade of the 1990s and the beginning of the first decade of the new century were to be years in which Europe's response to the SEA would be dominated by powerful forces over which they had no control. What became known as 'globalization' was a collection of liberalizing changes that meant that it could no longer be said that *'plus ça change, plus c'est la même chose.'* Things would not be the same in a world that was gradually moving toward one in which each entity would have to look after its own wellbeing.

Tariffs and other trade barriers were lowered, in some cases to zero, or at least made subject to international scrutiny and regulation. Financial markets were slowly being pried open. Capital moved across national borders by telecommunications links that gave tangible evidence of a 'world without borders.' Cheap air fares made it possible for people to move relatively easily between nations and continents. Access to knowledge was greatly enhanced for all through application of new technologies of informatics and telecommunication. Producers who had heretofore felt secure in their assured position in the regional or national market in which they marketed their goods woke one morning to discover that a competitor hundreds or thousands of miles distant had begun to penetrate their market with goods that were lower in price and equal in quality. But they did not know this in 1990.

As is usually the case, what was a threat to some was an exciting opportunity to others. As appeared on the satellite photograph, each dot was to varying degrees disconnected from the pre-SEA structure of national protectionist and supportive laws, regulations, subsidies, and spatial barriers they had enjoyed. It was the national governments that had created this less structured environment in which they had, on their own initiative, given up their capacities to intervene in the interest of beleaguered national constituents. It was they who had met for decades in rounds of trade liberalization under the General Agreement on Tariffs and Trade, they had negotiated agreements on subsidies and other protectionist policies, and they had begun to open financial and other markets. And, of course, in Europe it was heads of governments of the member nations who pushed the economic integration and liberalization agenda. So when we look at the satellite photograph it seems apparent that each dot is on its own; some will in all probability do very well and become more prominent, while others will become dimmer as they shrink in population and in economic significance.

The point of this is to demonstrate that around 1990 the environment for European cities changed fundamentally. As this decade progressed it would become clear to many of the leaders of these urban economies that their economic future was increasingly going to be something for which they had new responsibilities, and it would be up to them to both gain control over the levers they needed to use in management of their economies and to design the strategies that would indicate the specific actions that would be most effective and beneficial. Two Danish researchers have noted that: 'Internationalization, change into a society where information and creativity are of importance, and rising weight of network position alter the risk pattern and thereby create new demands for active urban policy of marketing and strategic planning . . . Only localities that actively fight for their future will have one.'[3] This proactivity of city leaders in the economic context of the 21st century is the subject of this book.

It should be noted that most of the urban experience with strategic planning has had to do with land use, industrial sites, housing, transportation and other such physical dimensions of a city. Economic planning has tended to focus on tax rates and structures, the adequacy of communications and transportation infrastructures and education. These forms of planning are usually done for some specific objective that has nothing to do with urban competitiveness, although any such change has an impact on the competitiveness of the city's producers and on the attractiveness of the city as a place to locate economic activities. Tax changes often are purely ideological in their justification. Infrastructure projects often have more to do with the egos and political clout of certain individuals than with a rational effort to enhance competitiveness. In this book the subject is what can be rather awkwardly referred to as strategic–economic planning (SEP), that is, economic planning but from the specific standpoint of the enhancement of the relative competitiveness of an urban region.

Strategic planning is in the air everywhere these days. Companies, universities, and now even governments are doing it. Essentially, SEP is designed to make a more efficient use of a city's assets – its factors of production, amenities, infrastructure, and human capital, toward the objective of assuring the residents of the city that they will have the combination of jobs, incomes, leisure, environment, urban spaces, and so forth to which they aspire. This will be discussed in greater detail in the next chapter, but we can note a few things of general interest about SEP. First, it should be done without the end-objective having been specified in advance. Often, city leaders are tempted to demand that the city become a bio-technology or research and development or headquarters city when, in fact, neither the assets possessed by the city nor the aspirations of the city's residents would suggest that be the objective. What they are demanding may be nothing more than the consultants' flavor of the day. Cities may, of course, be successful as high-technology centers, but they may also succeed, in the sense just given, as tourism or transportation or government/administration or financial service or specialized manufacturing centers. SEP is about the efficient utilization resources and this leads one down a path without an end being defined prior to the exercise. Second, for it to be successful SEP should be done with a sufficiently broad, democratic participation so as to ensure both an objective that is attainable and desired and the enthusiastic engagement by city residents. As we shall see, a lack of democracy and public participation has made some city initiatives less effective than would otherwise have been the case, or totally ineffective. Third, SEP must be done with full awareness as to the assets and plans of all other important competitor cities. There is a clear difference between implementing policies or infrastructure projects that just keep a city on a par with its competitors and those that enhance the city's position in relation to those other cities. Congress centers, sports facilities, airports and the like are examples of this. Keeping up and moving ahead are two different things and city leaders must be aware of what their initiatives are accomplishing. A final introductory comment is that an honest and objective appraisal of the comparative strengths and weakness of the city is essential. Being clear as to what is holding a city back is as important as discovering what could generate positive movement. Often an outsider's eye is required for this, but local analysis of whatever comparative data is available – some form of benchmarking – can also generate a realistic understanding.

THE WIDER INTEREST IN URBAN ECONOMIC–STRATEGIC PLANNING

City leaders and those who work and live in urban regions are, of course, intensely interested in the future for their local economy. But the interest in effective economic–strategic urban planning must go far beyond these directly affected individuals to the rest of European society. The economic malaise of the EU as a whole and of most of its member economies has bedeviled economic managers since the adoption of the SEA. So much was supposed to go so well, yet so little of this has come to pass. Hence, the overriding question of the day is: How can the EU economy be made more competitive so it can generate more employment, higher growth, and better performance in international commerce? The consensus view is that the EU economy lacks flexibility and adaptability, it is rule- and regulation-bound, investment in high technology sectors is below what it should be, and government, trying to push economic actors to the right actions, on net basis tends to get in the way. This is all true, but there is another approach one can take that is equally useful.

Since the late 1980s economic geographers in collaboration with various civil servants and private sector planners have asked us to think of Europe as a network of regions or as a network of cities. This can appear to be little more than self-serving hyperbole, but it has the essence of a powerful truth. The fact is that a strong EU economy or strong member country economies must be built upon a structure of urban economies that are competitive, dynamic, forward-looking, and imaginative – and be effectively planning in an economic strategic way. Close to 70 per cent of Europeans now live in large cities. These urban economies account for 80 per cent of output, and 90 per cent of production in high tech sectors that will provide the high value added economic growth of the future EU economy. Some of the cities in this study, specifically Copenhagen, Amsterdam and Barcelona, have explicitly made the argument to their sub-national or national governments that without a strong principal city the economy of the entire sub-national or national economy will be weak and will become marginalized. Their argument was valid, and it is clear that this same argument should be made with regard to the EU economy as a whole. Nations are made up of urban and rural regional economies. It is of little comfort to a declining region to learn that the national economy of which it is a member is one of Europe's most successful and competitive.

Even in the famous Michael Porter 'diamond of competitiveness,' to be discussed in Chapter 3, two or even three of the four points of the diamond are the responsibilities of, or are powerfully affected by, actions taken at the level of the city or the urban region. Investments in the future strong sectors of the economy are made sites located in urban economies; jobs are created locally; the national government's monetary and fiscal policy instruments are blunt tools with uncertain impacts. Increasingly, national governments are giving up or are losing use of other policy tools such as commercial or trade policy, competition policy, labor policy, and the list goes on. Sub-national governments are often ineffective in introducing policies that are beneficial to urban economic development and competitiveness because of the need to respond to the political strength of rural and agricultural districts – this tension between urban and rural demands on national and sub-national government is observed in virtually every nation.

More will be said about this justification for focusing on urban economic–strategic planning throughout this book. But in this introductory chapter it will suffice simply to have made this point and to have stressed its importance to the economic wellbeing of potentially all residents in EU member countries.

THE RAPIDLY CHANGING GLOBAL ECONOMIC ENVIRONMENT

Central to all of these changes is the evolving specialization of all countries in the global division of labor. Formerly, there was a clear demarcation between 'industrialized' and 'less developed' economies. Europe, North America and Japan produced the manufactured goods and traded services; while the economies of Asia, Latin America and Africa provided the raw materials and many food products, as long as they did not provide competition to producers in the industrialized world. In this world, city leaders had a good sense of what their economies would be producing well into the future – whatever they had been producing in the past. Some cities were steel or automobile cities, some were centers of chemical products or machine tooling, and so forth. Basically, what was needed was a steady hand on the tiller to chart a steady course with no significant changes. Beginning in the 1950s, however, movements of national liberation began to break the colonial bonds that had constrained Third World economies in their development. New leaders began to assert themselves, individually as well as in organizations such as the United Nations Conference on Trade and Development, the non-aligned movement, the Group of 77 and so forth. This desire for change was buttressed by the dramatic rise in the price of a barrel of oil from $3 in 1972 to $30 in 1979, accomplished with the support of some industrialized nations, such as the United States and some European countries, for global political reasons.

With the rise in oil prices, we began to see the erosion of industrial production in traditionally strong areas such as the English Midlands, the Ruhr, the Belgian-French border, northern Italy and the industrial heartland of the United States, which took on the sobriquet 'the Rust Belt.' In the US, cities such as Cleveland, Buffalo, Chicago, Pittsburgh and Detroit, as well as cities in the European industrial areas encountered very difficult times. These developments brought home to city leaders, perhaps for the first time in recent history, the understanding that the economic futures of their cities and the urban regions in which they were situated had shifted very significantly into their hands. As we shall see, some city leaders responded and others did not; some who responded did this effectively while others were not successful in this respect. The events of turbulence which dominated the decades from the OPEC price hikes to today have only made more clear to all how crucial effective action at the municipal and urban regional levels has become.

More will be said about this later in the book, but for now we should simply note that during the 1990s and the first half of the present decade the economic context in which urban economies function and in which urban leaders have had to formulate and implement policies has been marked by considerable economic and political turbulence, both at the regional and the global levels. During this period, policy makers have had to contend with:

- The enhanced role of the World Trade Organization and the constraints this has imposed on government policy responses.
- Financial markets are progressively being opened, large flows of capital can be generated within minutes of some news or event.
- In Europe, the macro-economic situation has been one of stagnation or recession in most of the EU member countries.
- The EU has initiated the opening to Central Europe with both positive and negative implications for many urban economies.

- The emergence of China, India and other Third World economies has developed from competition to labor intensive, low wage activities to more skill-related areas of the services sector.
- The opening of borders and improvements in the flows of accurate, and not so accurate, information about living conditions and employment in other countries has resulted in migratory flows that are perceived by many in the EU as being more significant and negative in impact than is actually the case.
- The capacities of various levels of government to intervene in ways that alleviate economic distress in national economies have been markedly affected.
- Manufacturing sectors in industrialized nations throughout the world have been affected by outsourcing, restructuring and de-industrialization, which are powerfully negative on economies which are able effectively to plan their responses to these forces of globalization.
- The presumably positive transition in industrialized economies from manufacturing to services continues at a rapid pace.
- The comparative advantages of all economies in the global economy have been evolving at a pace which required flexible and effective policy response at some level of government.

One of the objectives of this study is evaluation of the policy response of leaders and decision-makers in a selection of the major, and representative, urban regions of the EU.

THE NEW POSITION OF CITIES IN THIS CONTEXT

The contemporary industrial situation is quite different from that which went before. In the Fordist period, the major areas of industrial production were industries such as steel, automobiles and chemicals. In these industries the capital investment was, by the standards of the day, extraordinarily large, and economies of scale were very important. Therefore, the facilities were very large and the industries tended to be oligopolistic in structure. In most countries there was room for only a small number of production sites. Hence, only a very small number of cities could be steel or automobile or chemical production centers. National governments adopted policies that ensured that almost every country would have some share of this industry, even if the production was inefficient and had to be protected from foreign competition. It simply was not possible for the leadership of a city to decide that their city would become a center of, say, steel production. Today, however, in industries such as bio-pharmaceutical, or information-communications technology, or nanotechnology, or medical research there is not a standard product. As a consequence each industrial sector is broken up into many smaller niches, each of which may be done in a different city and in more than one city. So today when one sees many city leaders declare that their city will become a center of bio-engineering, it is no longer just an unachievable pipe dream – many cities can specialize in virtually the same activity. Of course, each niche will have its own demands with regard to inputs, factors of production, and so forth, so careful decision-making is still required on the part of city leaders and their private-sector colleagues.

WHY THESE TEN CITIES?

The selection of the ten cities that are included in this study is largely dependent upon the decision to visit nine of them in 1990–1991 in relation to another project on the subject of the response of urban economies to regional trade liberalization.[4] The adoption of the Single European Act (SEA) in 1987 should have been seen by leaders in major European cities as a clarion call to become more proactive in the economic management of their urban regions, since the SEA reconfigured the economic space in which each of them functioned. At that time, some responded well while others did not respond or, for various reasons, were not effective in their response. For a good comparative analysis the cities chosen should have some similarities in terms of size and international engagement; furthermore, none of them was a national capital, with the exception of Copenhagen, since the economies of capital cities usually operate according to economic forces that are also political in nature. In the 1992 study, Manchester and Stuttgart were included but for reasons of time and interest to the current project they were replaced by Dresden and Milan.

In the early 1990s, the 1987 study done by Roger Brunet of DATAR which highlighted the high economic activity core of the EU, which was shortly to be designated by the French publication *La nouvelle observateur* as the 'blue banana,' had greater standing among economists and geographers than it does today; notions of centrality and peripherality have been challenged by multi-polarity and other conceptualizations that take into account the consequences of application of recent advances in the technologies of communication, transportation and production on the spatial characteristics of EU economic activity. Hence, in this study I have included four cities that are in the core, Amsterdam, Lyon, Milan and Turin, and six that are on the periphery, Barcelona, Copenhagen, Dresden, Hamburg, Munich and Seville. While multi-polarity may have a certain intellectual attractiveness to researchers, in practical matters the geographic locations of Amsterdam and Barcelona or of

Lyon and Dresden still do have their impacts on what is being and can be done by city leaders in each metropolitan area.

Finally, the cities chosen represent a variety of urban functions. Amsterdam and Hamburg have histories of commercial and logistical activity, while Barcelona, Dresden and Turin have been manufacturing or industrial centers. Milan is a city of fashion and of, perhaps fading, financial importance, Munich and Lyon have emphasized their city centers and cultural activity, while Seville and Copenhagen are far from the center of things, situated in regional economies in which agriculture and food processing feature prominently, from which both are attempting to transform themselves into more technology-related activities. The challenges that are posed by the SEA, the (Maastricht) Treaty of European Union (TEU), rapidly changing technology, and regional and global economic and political turbulence and their responses to these should be of interest to all who are interested in the possibilities of policy initiatives to globalization on the part of city leaders.

THE PLAN OF THE BOOK

The logic behind the organization of the book is, in essence, that it is necessary first to examine what theory and research findings can tell us about our subject, then to review the actual experiences of the ten cities included in the study, and finally to draw some lessons about urban strategic–economic planning that will be useful to other city leaders. Consequently, Chapter 2 presents various conceptualizations and approaches to both urban competitiveness and urban strategic planning. Chapter 3 presents the research findings of economists and economic geographers with regard to the roles in urban competitiveness of various spatial or relational structures of economic activity, of infrastructure and factors of production, and of technical change; and it considers the question of regional divergence or convergence within the EU. The next three chapters present the SEP experiences of the ten cities of this study, with Chapter 4 discussing the strategic planning, if any, that was being done around 1990. Even if there was no formal planning in place, city leaders did have aspirations for their urban economies and some idea as to how they intended to realize those aspirations. In Chapter 5, we will examine the experiences of these cities during the turbulent decade of the 1990s and the first years of the present century. Implicitly, it poses the question as to whether it is feasible to plan strategically at the level of the city or urban region. Then, in Chapter 6, we will review the strategic planning that is being undertaken by these cities today. What have they learned from the past 15 or so years? Are effective planning processes being used? Chapter 7 distills from these experiences some factors that have contributed to the success or failure in urban strategic planning that should be of use to city leaders, not just in Europe but throughout the world. In this rapidly globalizing world all cities are in the process of becoming confronted by the same challenges, threats and opportunities; clearly, they can learn from one another. In this concluding chapter, we also draw some lessons from these experiences and take a look to the future. It is hoped that this book will be of interest not only to researchers but most importantly to city officials, planners, and leaders, and their private sector counterparts, all of whom care about the cities in which they live.

A FINAL COMMENT

As a final introductory comment, it should be noted that the contemporary EU economy and those of most of its individual member countries are virtually stagnant and have been for the better part of a decade. The response to economic crisis in Europe is invariably the call for some new policy at the level of the national governments. Since adoption of the SEA, the TEU and the Euro, as well as constraints on action imposed by international agencies such as the World Trade Organization, the capacity of national governments to respond positively is no longer what it once was. Their relative impotence is compensated for, to some degree, by the increased capacity on the part of the EU and its agencies, but the policy instruments at the level of the EU are indeed blunt and inefficient tools for having macro-economic impacts on national or sub-national economies. EU monetary or fiscal policies cannot be targeted at both a surging Austrian economy and a Portuguese one which may be in recession, and so forth. Hence, when it comes to the economic lives of residents in the urban regions throughout the EU an increasing burden, responsibility and capacity are now lodged in the hands of leaders of these urban regions. So for the economic health of the EU and its member countries, the effective and flexible processes of policy implementation at the urban level are of great interest and essential to the maintenance and enhancement of economic competitiveness. The health and dynamism of the EU rests largely in the hands of urban leaders. The efficiency of urban strategic–economic planning is therefore of crucial importance to all.

NOTES

1. Throughout this book the term 'city leader(s)' will be used. This is because of the varying institutional structures in the different cities being studied. In some cities the mayor is all important, in others the legal mandate for urban economic policy rests with some other sub-national level of government, or a non-governmental organization such as the chamber of commerce, or some metro-wide planning council. Usually there is a cooperative structure which includes both public and private sector participants.

2. Michael Emerson et al., *The Economics of 1992*, Oxford: Oxford University Press, 1988, p. 218.
3. Hans Thor Anderson and Christian Wichmann Matthiessen, 'Metropolitan Marketing and Strategic Planning: Mega Events. A Copenhagen Perspective,' *Danish Journal of Geography*, Vol. 95, 1995, p. 72.
4. Peter Karl Kresl, *The Response of Urban Economies to Regional Trade Liberalization*, New York: Praeger, 1992.

2. The literature on urban competitiveness and strategic–economic planning

It is clear to many city leaders that specific actions must be taken by them and by the primary economic, social and political actors in their urban region if the residents of their city are to have the satisfying economic lives – employment, income, leisure time, and so forth – that it is their potential to have. But what are the actions and policies that would be most effective? How is one to accomplish this complex task? Clearly, city leaders require knowledge and expert assistance if they are to be successful. In this chapter and the next, we will examine two questions that are essential to effective strategic–economic planning. I have included a more extensive discussion of these two topics in a recently published co-authored book: *The Urban Response to Internationalization*.[1] The content of the present chapter will not reiterate what was written there but will be predominantly new material. First, in this chapter we will review the literature on economic competitiveness, especially at the urban regional level and we will also examine approaches to strategic planning. Second, in the next chapter we ask the question: what can economic or economic geographic research and analysis tell us about the determinants of urban economic competitiveness, the alternatives that face city leaders and the best options from the stand-point of a specific city with its individual assets, experiences, institutions, and aspirations. Ultimately what the city leader seeks to do is to ensure the enhanced competitiveness of his/her city in relation to other more-or-less competing cities.

Paul Krugman gained notoriety by stating that countries, and by extension regions, do not compete with each other, only firms do. Places do not compete, according to Krugman because they cannot go out of business.[2] Roberto Camagni responded that they certainly do the equivalent, in that they can suffer long-term out-migration, stagnant investment, falling per capita incomes, and rising unemployment.[3] At the level of journalism, we remember that Toronto and Atlanta both 'competed' for the site of the 1996 Summer Olympics – Toronto lost and Atlanta won. More recently, New York, London, Madrid, Paris and Moscow were engaged in a similar exercise – and London was selected by the 2012 Summer Olympics selection committee. Chicago,

Dallas and Denver all sought the headquarters of Boeing Aircraft – Chicago won and the others lost. So clearly there is something going on among cities that one can only call competition. To win these 'competitions,' each city must struggle to enhance its 'competitiveness,' that is, its ability to compete against comparable other cities, in ways that are specific to the prize at hand – a site selection, a niche in the bio-technology industry, an airline hub, and so forth. As the authors of one study on urban competitiveness wrote: 'The efforts of virtually all countries to open their economies to international trade and investment are diminishing the economic influence of nations and increasing the importance of MAs (metropolitan areas) as centers of international economic transactions.'[4]

One supporter of the Krugman view is Mario Polèse who argues that 'the fundamental socioeconomic processes that explain long-term economic growth primarily operate at the national/societal level, and not at the city level. The reason for this . . . is that cities (agglomerations) do not constitute distinct institutional environments.'[5] What he finds deficient is the notion that mere agglomeration, 'steering the location of industry,' and clusters can be used to jump start an urban economy or give support to Jane Jacobs' city as 'engine of growth' hypothesis. The counter to his position is that he fails to consider the richer array of policy options that are available to local authorities. As we will see when we consider the strategic–economic planning actions of the ten EU cities in this study city leaders can take, and in some instances have taken, very effective actions to mobilize and to organize local resources, and to put in place educational and cultural assets and a wide range of urban amenities that attract and retain both desirable firms and a highly educated and skilled labor force. These actions have demonstrable impacts on the competitiveness of an urban region. Chapters 4, 5 and 6 will be devoted to making this case. Furthermore, a study done for the government of Ontario, and which we will examine later in this chapter, concludes that 'it is vital that we regard (Ontario's and Canada's largest city-regions) as the prime assets responsible for our provincial and national economic competitiveness.'[6]

APPROACHES TO URBAN ECONOMIC COMPETITIVENESS

Until very recently, the Krugman-Polèse notion that concept of competitiveness was attached only to the firm and the nation was most widely held. Subnational entities, such as provinces were ignored, perhaps with good reason since they are usually torn in their economic policy between the conflicting interests, and voting power, of both urban and rural interests. Hence they are usually thought to be entities that are, in reality, required to respond to such a wide array of objectives that no consistent approach to competitiveness is possible. In Europe, cities such as Amsterdam, Barcelona and Copenhagen argued that the economic well-being of the entire 'nation' was dependent upon the economic vitality of the principal city. But until very recently, cities were simply ignored without much thought being given to it. Urban economies were seen to be primarily collections of firms responding to market forces over which no one had much if any control and, after all, it was the nation that set the tax rates, managed the trade barriers, gave the subsidies, and regulated the transportation and communication infrastructures which are, it had been asserted, the actions that set the context in which the competitive firm functions. Today, the caveat regarding sub-national entities and competitiveness continues to be true, but one must also have reservations about the nation.

At the most general level of analysis an individual nation is made up of regions and although a nation, such as is the case with the United States, may be top-ranked by the annual World Economic Forum that gathers annually at Davos, Switzerland, in any year one or several of its regional economies may be in serious decline. This was certainly true for the US industrial heartland in the 1980s following the OPEC oil price hikes and for California and Connecticut in the 1990s when there were cutbacks in federal spending on defense. Today, nations are weakened in their policies for competitiveness by the forces of globalization that were discussed in the previous chapter and by their collective desire to cut both taxes and, albeit less successfully, expenditures. Some firms, such as Toyota, have closed operations in the US and moved to Canada in part because of the availability of a tax-supported national health care system – the US system in which the employer pays much of the health care cost of its employees has become too costly for competitive production. However, Toyota also indicated that its choice of Ontario was in part due to the fact that low-tax Alabama had developed an educational system which was so ineffective that workers had to be trained to do tasks on the production line through use of pictographs rather than a text. The low-cost approach to economic competitiveness, at whatever level of government, is not a strategy that can be effective in the long run, especially in a relatively high income, industrialized economy.[7] The economy of the 21st century needs skilled workers for whom the firm will play a premium, rather than low-wage illiterate workers who can be found everywhere.

At the simplest level of understanding, we must remember that the objective of economic policy must ultimately be that of some positive impact on the humans in whatever economy is being considered. Urban competitiveness should never be seen to be little more than a horse race. People are citizens of nations, but they reside and work in specific places; that is, in neighborhoods that are in cities that are in urban economies and urban regions. The positive or negative events that occur in the national economy can be only very indirectly related to theirs; however developments in other regions with which they may be in direct competition are usually far more significant. Hence, it must be recognized, *pace* Polèse, that if we are to have positive impacts on the economic futures of the residents of a nation, the most efficient and effective way to do that is to have the urban region as the focus of policy. Certainly monetary and fiscal policy, trade policy, and a variety of regulatory policies have their impact on the general environment in which the urban region is situated. But, as will be demonstrated below, for national policy to be effective it relies on the appropriate decision being made at the local level, whether in the public or the private sector. In the words of Christian Wichmann Matthiessen: 'with the fading of the role of nation states a new condition of international competition will be focused on the large cities.'[8] Strategic–economic planning, the subject of this study, must be rooted in the local space if it is to have any effect at all.

Nonetheless the nation has maintained its central role in many analyses, even though it is clear that this is no longer a valid approach. I remember that a decade ago I approached a major US foundation that was advertising itself as one of the primary supporters of research on competitiveness. When I raised the subject of urban competitiveness I was told by the director of that program that competitiveness was a phenomenon that was relevant only to the nation and the firm and that cities had absolutely nothing to do with it. How times have changed! Much analysis is still being done on national competitiveness in Europe, if for no reason other than because the data that are required for a statistical analysis of competitiveness are not available at the level of the urban region. As Alexis Jacquemin and Lucio Pench wrote: 'the majority of reports concentrate on variables at the level of the nation, because these indicators are well known and are often more easy to obtain.'[9] In addition, many organizations have been established to respond to the needs and aspirations of subnational regional governments such as provinces, *länder*, autonomous communities, and so forth. One thinks of the EU Council of Regions, The Assembly of European Regions, the Association of European Border Regions, the Working Communities of the Adriatic Alps, of the Western Alps, of the Danube Countries, of the Pyrenees, of the Alps, of Galice-Nort Portugal, and of Lower and Middle Adriatic and the Jura Working Community, as well as the Associations of European Wine Growing Regions and of Fruit and Vegetable Growing and Horticultural Regions, and the Association of European Regions with Industrial Technology. However we cannot allow our approach to the study of competitiveness to be dominated by the issues of the political clout or the availability of data for nations, regions and urban economies and its methodological implications; it would be far more productive to focus on the contribution that each level of government can make toward improvements of the economic situation of firms and the well-being, as they define it, of the residents of the individual national economies. Clearly the policies adopted by national and sub-national governments do have their impacts, as will be made clear as we review the experiences of the ten cities of this study, but it is equally clear that the primary actor must be the local actors of the individual urban region. Of course, the firm remains a central element both in all approaches to the study of competitiveness and in the design of policy by the city; however, we should consider the firm to be the demander of sets of urban assets which are supplied competitively by individual urban economies.

Challenges in the Study of Urban Competitiveness

While a strong argument can be made that the study of competitiveness must be focused primarily on actors and policy initiatives that are taken at the level of the urban economy, there are several difficulties that arise due to issues of definition, data and methodology. The first thing that confronts researchers is the concept of urban competitiveness itself. Some writers have accepted the argument of Michael Porter and of Paul Krugman that if competitiveness is anything it is productivity.[10] This is based on the notion that the objective of competitiveness is that of increasing the standard of living of the nation, over time. Productivity is, of course, a major part of urban competitiveness but by itself it does not get us very far. For example, there are problems of measurement: Does one use labor productivity or total factor productivity?[11] How does one measure productivity in private and government services sectors? What determines whatever notion of productivity one accepts? How does this lead to a program for city leaders who want to enhance their city's competitiveness? Some of these issues will be examined in greater detail in the next chapter, where we will also consider industrial districts, clusters and agglomeration, structures which are seen by many as being central to the competitiveness, and productivity, of an urban region.

A somewhat expanded approach was offered by Donald McFetridge in 1995 who argued that there are two alternatives: 'The first is to emphasize real per capita income or productivity growth. The second is to emphasize trade performance.'[12] However, recent experience would suggest the weakness of trade performance as a component of a definition of competitiveness. The United States is annually declared by the World Economic Forum to be the most or second most competitive national economy but, while its productivity is envied by almost all industrialized economies, it is experiencing a string of balance of trade deficits that has been continuous since 1971 and which has currently ballooned to what is arguably an unsustainable level. Furthermore, as has often been observed, the balance of trade surpluses of the EU are the consequence not of a competitive economy but of the macro-economic stagnation which has dampened EU imports for over a decade.

While McFetridge has an idea as to how one can define competitiveness, he sees it as applicable only to the firm, and for the firm it boils down to simply 'the sustained ability . . . to operate profitably in open markets.'[13] At the level of the industry he uses Michael Porter's concept of revealed comparative advantage, which measures the export strength of that industry. But for the nation, and presumably other geographic regions, the concept of competitiveness is 'not particularly useful . . . Nations are not firms.' So we are back with Paul Krugman. In Britain, the Office of the Deputy Prime Minister, in a major work on urban competitiveness, adopts Michael Storpor's definition which takes regional competitiveness to be: 'the ability of an economy to attract and maintain firms with stable or rising market shares in an activity, while maintaining stable or increasing standards of living for those who participate in it.'[14] They continue to argue that while competition can be a zero-sum game, competitiveness creates situations in which all regions can derive positive benefits.

Michael Porter argues that the industry is the central entity in his approach and that competitiveness, or competitive advantage, consists of an interaction between the nation and the firm: 'nations succeed in particular industries because their home environment is the most dynamic and the most challenging, and stimulates and prods firms to upgrade and widen their advantages over time.'[15] His approach to the location of firms refers to '(n)ation- or location-based advantages' implying that firms consider only the advantages of the nation in siting their facilities.[16] However, in his diamond of determinants,[17] while 'demand conditions' can be taken to be the responsibility of the national government and 'firm strategy, structure and rivalry' is up to the firm or its industry, the remaining two – 'factor conditions' and 'related and supporting industries' – are powerfully affected by policies implemented by local authorities.

The Competitiveness Institute states that competitiveness is virtually synonymous with the concept of the cluster and that the primary, if not sole, policy that can be implemented in the interest of enhancing the competitiveness of a nation or region is the promotion of clusters of firms in the same industry or closely related industries.[18] In the next chapter several serious reservations with regard to the importance of clusters in competitiveness will be offered. Essentially, it will be argued that in certain instances certain types of clusters may be valuable components in a project to improve competitiveness, but that they cannot be relied upon as the sole or even primary policy initiative and that their promotion should be done with considerable care.

The final definition that will be included here is that of the Urban Competitiveness Project: 'Urban competitiveness refers to the degree to which a city, or urban region, in comparison with other competing cities, is able to provide the jobs, income, cultural and recreational amenities, degree of social cohesion, governance and urban environment to which its current and targeted new residents aspire.'[19] This is uniquely broad and 'bottom-up' in its conceptualization. It is not specifically directed in its policy recommendations and considers far more than productivity or per capita income as the policy objective. It recognizes, for example, that some societies, such as the US and Japan, prefer to work almost 2000 hours per year while much of the EU opts to work 1600 hours per year – at the extreme, Norwegians work about 1450 hours per year. Various societies have similarly differing preferences for the income distribution, tolerance for social exclusion, and work-leisure trade-offs. It implicitly asserts that not all societies will take the same approach to urban or regional competitiveness.

Since there is no single variable for urban competitiveness, researchers have had to fashion their own indicators, or benchmarks, of the competitiveness of a city. This, of course, begs the question of the availability of the data that are required for such a statistical analysis. Many researchers in various parts of the world find it virtually impossible to get comparable data for a large number of cities in one or more countries. For example, when Richard Florida did his study of the importance of the 'creative class' for the economic vitality of an economy, he was able to use US Census data and data from other sources for over 100 US cities; when he applied his approach to Europe he was forced to examine most of the then 15 member states of the European Union plus the United States.[20] Comparable data for European cities or urban regions are not yet available, even for individual countries which have a large number of large cities, such as Germany where the sub-national entities, the *länder*, often generate different data series using different definitions. So studies of national economic competitiveness live on, especially in Europe, even if only out of necessity.

The common practice of benchmarking is justified by this inadequacy of available data as researchers seek to gain an understanding of the relative position of one or more cities through a process of ranking cities using data that is both available and asserted to be linked somehow to urban competitiveness. However, benchmarking has been criticized as being 'policy by imitation of best practices.' Seeking to be at the top of a list of cities or urban regions with regard to some of the standard economic or social variables on the assumption that this is the best path to a competitive urban economy misses the fact that, as Ron Boschma puts it, 'imitation of a subset of factors that contributed to success in one region may be detrimental for another region because of the mismatch between the new subset and the existing structures and routines.'[21] Simple benchmarking misses the 'territorial dimension,' the 'historical trajectory,' and institutional particularities of the successful region that Boschma finds to be so important.

In some studies patents granted is used as an indicator of competitiveness without really examining what the data tell us. Is the patent applied for in the city in which the research is done or in the headquarters city of the large firm of which the research unit is just one part? Are all patents of equal economic importance or do we see a flurry of patents all protecting some niche of the one single advance that is of any significance? All researchers who have tried to indicate urban competitiveness quantitatively will recognize the temptation to use data simply, or at least primarily because it is available, and how difficult it is to reject this temptation. The same can be said of another frequently used variable – scientific citations – specifically how is this linked to the competitiveness of the host urban region? If the scientific advances are published then they are made available to firms in all cities and no special advantage accrues to the city in which the research is done. Perhaps concurrent with this mass of published research one could assume there is an equally impressive amount of tacit knowledge being generated, but while this is possible it cannot be assured. Or one could assume that with so much research being done there would be a large population of highly educated students who could be important for local firms – but then why not just use a variable for the number of students, perhaps in certain fields of study. In both instances, it would not be unreasonable to assume there might be some connection between patents or scientific citations and urban competitiveness but some empirical verification of the specific linkage involved in that assumption remains to be provided.

In China, Mexico and the United States it has been possible to conduct research that utilizes a methodology that takes advantage of data for scores or hundreds of series of economic and social data, for scores or hundreds of cities or metropolitan areas so that insightful statistical work on urban competitiveness is possible and generates research that can be of use to city leaders everywhere.[22] The greater number of statistical series that are available in these countries and the fact that their value as indicators or determinants of urban competitiveness can be empirically verified, avoids reliance on the need to make assumptions with regard to the value of data being used. The challenge for researchers in Europe and elsewhere is to find a methodology of similar validity that is suited to the data at hand.

In Britain, the Office of the Deputy Prime Minister (ODPM) has issued several reports having to do with competitiveness of cities in the United Kingdom. The 'technical paper' on competitiveness and its measurement written by Mary Hutchins, as a part of this effort, highlights the difficulties encountered when working on urban competitiveness in Europe, as well as in most other countries. For this reason, it is worth examining in some detail. Hutchins notes 'the lack of robust city level data that is comparable on a trans-national basis' and that 'many studies of competitiveness rely on regional data, in some cases modeling regional data to provide city figures.'[23] As a consequence of this lack of data, the indicators of competitiveness are usually whatever happens to be available, at the NUTS I, II or III level (regions with populations of 3–7 million, 800 000–3 million and 150 000–800 000 respectively). A review of the methodology of several of the major examinations of urban competitiveness (Innovative Functional Urban Areas in North West Europe, Robert Huggins, Barclays Competing with the World, and Business Strategies Limited) generates a long list of variables with regard to employment, productivity, research and development, levels of education, characteristics of the labor force, demographics, patents, GDP, and so forth. As is usually the case, there is little evidence of a defensible methodology for selecting which variables legitimately can be utilized in the evaluation of a city's competitiveness.

The use of patent data and of scientific citations has been given a skeptical look above, but much the same can be said about many other variables. For example, employment, growth in employment and unemployment are often used as indicators, with high rates for the former two and a low rate for the latter presumably being considered to be positive with regard to urban competitiveness. But if a city is 'competitive' it may be growing rapidly and attracting migrants, many with low or inappropriate skill levels. It may also be restructuring out of older declining activities and into new high tech activities. This will release workers with unneeded skills from the declining industries. In both instances, a city which is competitive and is moving into favored rising sectors would have high levels of unemployment, and total employment and growth in employment might be unchanged. In unintended support of this, Gardiner, Martin and Tyler demonstrate that the EU is composed of two sets of regional economies: those in which productivity gains are accompanied by increasing employment and those in which employment falls.[24] These variables would therefore inaccurately capture what is actually happening in the city.

In the ODPM and most other studies when employment or demographic data are used, it is often the percentage of the total work force or population in some category or activity that is used. However, it may well be the actual number of individuals in that characteristic that is related to competitiveness. For example a smaller city may have double the percentage of individuals that a much larger city has, but the much larger mass of individuals in the larger city is the important thing. Furthermore, using the total or percentage figure fails to capture the effectiveness with which these individuals are brought together in productive interaction. This integrative function is one of the key contributions that can be made by city leaders and is one of the primary differentiating factors between successful and unsuccessful urban economies. Two thousand researchers at a university are most certainly more likely to engage in innovative activity than would be the same two thousand in a city with no university. The university is just one example of a structure that promotes innovative, interactive, and therefore ultimately productive activity. There are many such subtleties that are missed when data are trawled for using a large and undiscriminating net.

This, as has been noted above, is one of the dangers of the recently popular benchmarking approach to evaluation of a city's competitiveness. Many of these studies use data such as total population, total employment, total air passengers, and the percentage of the population above a certain age or between two ages (for example, between 16 and 55) with some level of educational attainment to position a city in relation to a handful or larger number of similar cities. The ODPM study uses as indicators for 'innovation' data for tertiary education, employment in certain sectors, R&D expenditures, and high-tech patents. As with most benchmarking efforts, what is lacking is some method for determining just which of the possible variables actually are of demonstrable importance for the competitiveness of the urban region.

One must recognize, of course, that most of these efforts are rather heroic efforts to do something meaningful in a situation in which the obstacles to the effort are enormous. Given this understanding of some of the difficulties or challenges that confront researchers of urban competitiveness, and those who seek to design and implement policies to encourage its enhancement, we can now examine the major efforts to assess it.

Some Approaches to Assessing Urban Competitiveness

There is no single, best way to assess urban competitiveness. Some of the studies of it use a statistical methodology while others rely on benchmarking, with the choice principally determined by the quantity and quality of the data that are available. Some begin from the premise that the competitive urban economy must develop its comparative strength in high technology activity or must enhance its creativity or must be successful as a learning region while others assert that the end that is sought must be productivity or per capita income. In contrast to these more narrowly focused approaches to the desired end, some studies take the much broader approach that some locally generated definition of communal wellbeing should be the ultimate objective. Some emphasize the transition from manufacturing to services to knowledge-based activity and see it as an inexorable one-way path, while others see the possibility of competitive urban regions based on niche manufacturing, logistics, administration or culture and recreation. Some of the approaches that are more narrowly focused are done out of ideological or theoretical conviction, but others may have been conducted after an extended process of examination of local experiences, capacities, and so forth that suggests the efficacy of a narrowly targeted process of policy implementation. Given this rich array of approaches to urban competitiveness one cannot do full justice to them all, and the content of this

section of the chapter will be an examination of their variety and the consequences of the adoption of one or the other of them.

The approaches that will be examined here can be separated into three categories: 1) those that begin with the assumption that the successful urban region
must concentrate its efforts on some specific characteristic or attribute such as
creativity or high technology or knowledge-based activity, 2) those that are
more general in their focus, and 3) those that are based on a statistical methodology. The work reviewed here will be from articles and reports that I did not
examine in *The Urban Response to Internationalization*. Only brief references
will be made to those latter works in the three sections which follow.

Specific focus approaches

Since so much of current thinking about survival and success in the economy
that we face at the outset of the 21st century is dominated by the rapidly
advancing state of technology in production, transportation and communication, it is entirely understandable that researchers would fashion an approach
to urban competitiveness that would be centered on some aspect of technology. This approach is one that tends to be advocated by the consulting community rather than by academic researchers. Interviews with city leaders in the
ten cities confirm the understanding one has that once convinced of the need
to be part of the technology-intensive future, consultants develop an approach
focused on this and then take it to several dissimilar urban economies and
recommend that approach without giving attention to the factors that make
that particular urban economy different from the others. This difference in
history, assets, aspirations, location and economic structure calls for a nuanced
approach to strategic–economic plan design. The planning community is
inspired from time to time by new concepts, such as clusters, the Triple Helix,
policentrality, networking, learning region, the creative city, and so forth.
Unfortunately, the latest concept is often applied indiscriminately and therefore inappropriately.

All of these concepts, as well as technology itself, are of great importance
for regional development, but each urban region has its own characteristics
and potential. Some urban regions can do quite well, in terms of satisfying
employment, income growth and welfare maximization as port-logistics,
culture, recreation, manufacturing, service, bridge or port of access, research,
or headquarters cities, or some combination thereof. Not all of them can
succeed as a center of one or more clusters in bio-pharmaceutical or information-communication technology, nanotechnology, and so forth.

General focus approaches

These works do not specify that a successful city or urban region ought to try
to fashion its economic activity toward one of the specific foci that many

researchers and policy advisors argue are necessary for the economy of the future. Rather, they either assert that, among others, creativity or being a learning region are most important or they suggest that the general health of the urban economy is what should be pursued. For example, Ann Markusen classified cities as hub-and-spoke districts, satellite industrial platforms or state-anchored industrial districts; Jane Pollard and Michael Storper saw them as intellectual capital, innovation-based or variety-based industries; and Cynthia Negry and Mary Beth Zickel presented a set of metropolitan economies that were marked by the various pairings of changes in manufacturing employment and in population.[25] Each then discussed the consequences of each category for long term competitiveness.

An approach that tries to be very current is that offered by Meric Gertler, Richard Florida, Gary Gates and Tarta Vinodrai for the Ontario (Canada) Government. They assert boldly that: 'To be successful in this emerging creative age, regions must develop attract and retain talented and creative people who generate innovations, develop technology-intensive industries and power economic growth.'[26] This is an application to Ontario's and Canada's metropolitan regions of Florida's work on the 'creative class.' They use data for four indices – talent, Bohemian, mosaic and tech-pole – to establish rankings of Canadian and US cities for four population sizes for metropolitan regions of one million or more to less than 250 000. The Canadian cities are represented throughout the ranking and the authors conclude that 'Ontario city-regions have a solid foundation in these areas to compete against US city-regions.' Of more interest is their emphasis on the importance for urban competitiveness of higher education, immigration, and the arts and creativity. While creativity is the specific focus in this report, in its application creativity can be applied to any sort of economic activity, from bio-pharmaceutical research to logistics to culture and recreation.

A different tack is taken by Dennis Rondinelli, James Johnson and John Kasarda who stress the capacity of a metropolitan area 'to adjust to the complex international social, political, and economic changes that are intensifying business competition,' and assert that in 'the emerging global economy, international trade and investment will be key drivers of urban and regional growth and crucial sources of local jobs and wealth.'[27] Their policy suggestion is a rich and varied list of many initiatives that will facilitate the city's successful penetration of foreign markets. Growth in exports should be a primary indicator of competitiveness in this model, but in their ranking of metropolitan areas by growth of exports during the brief period 1993–1995, Detroit is ranked number two and Austin is sandwiched between Newark and Milwaukee. It is difficult to imagine a ranking of metropolitan regions by competitiveness that would generate such a listing.

The notion of a learning region has been most fully developed by Peter

Maskell and Gunnar Törnquist with reference to the Öresund region, which comprises Copenhagen and the province in which it is located, Sjaelland, and the southernmost province in Sweden, Skåne, and its major cities, Malmö and Lund. They argue that: 'the gist of industrial competitiveness in high-cost areas shifts step-by-step from static price competition towards dynamic improvement, benefiting firms that can create and apply new knowledge more swiftly than their competitors . . . Learning regions are, therefore, a contemporary consequence of the way in which firms react to the global opening of markets.'[28] They state that history and the existing economic structure create congenial situations for interactive learning and that these two elements provide the soundest basis for development into the future. Hence, it is explicit that no specific activity, such as bio-pharmaceutical or information-communication technology, has to be privileged for an urban region to be successful. The institutional structure of such a learning region will consist of universities, technical schools and business schools, as well as science parks and a variety of targeted research activities, rooted in the past and present but providing the base for the economy of the future through a network of knowledge spillovers, industrial clusters, exchange of tacit knowledge and scale economies in the creation of knowledge.[29]

The importance of the knowledge base to the competitiveness of an urban region was stressed by Bill Lever, who also cautions us that the city in which the knowledge is based and/or generated has no assurance that it will be able to capture the economic benefits from that activity.[30] Research may be done in one facility of a large firm, while the job creation may occur at another location. Furthermore, he suggests that with regard to what he considers to be the most important elements of the knowledge base urban region, such things as educational, transportation and communication infrastructure, R&D activity, papers published and so forth, may be elements over which local authorities may have little or no control. Hence policy formation and implementation may be a risky venture for them.

These examples suggest how a metropolitan region can become successful and competitive without focusing its strategic–economic planning activities on a specific currently favored activity. Both the specific and general focus approaches are essentially conceptual in their methodology, having recourse to data only as needed to examine an individual point that is to be made. In the next section we will examine approaches that are more systematic in their use of data.

Statistical methodology approaches

The objective of the statistical methodology approach is that of gaining a realistic understanding of the competitiveness of a metropolitan economy. This method also generates a set of variables that can be used in the development of a strategic–economic plan for that city. The most prevalent methodology in the statistically-based studies is to use a small number of independent variables as indicators of urban competitiveness. Appropriate weights are given to each of the indicators, data are obtained for each of the indicators for each of the cities. This value is used for the ranking of the urban economies from most to least competitive. Then a regression/correlation analysis is done using large numbers of dependent variables that theory and the literature suggest might have power as determinants of urban competitiveness. The product of this exercise is a set of variables that have been demonstrated to have significant explanatory value for an urban region's relative competitiveness. These variables can then be used in a benchmarking effort in which there is statistical verification of each of the benchmarks that are being used – a clear contrast with the studies that were discussed in the 'Challenges in the Study of Urban Competitiveness' section of this chapter. As was noted earlier, China, Mexico and the United States are the three national economies for which sufficient data for a large number of metropolitan areas or cities is available for statistically-based research on urban competitiveness, and such research has been conducted in each of the three. A small group of economists has applied this methodology to competitiveness evaluations of cities in each of these countries.

In China Ni Pengfei wrote a Ph.D. dissertation entitled *China Urban Competitiveness: Theoretical Hypothesis and Empirical Test* in 2001 that was published by Nankai University. Included is an abstract and English text of 88 pages in which both his methodology and results are given. In essence, Ni ranked 24 Chinese cities using a variable composed of measures of income and urban assets – income growth, urban assets and income generated per unit of cost. He then explained the ranking using 'hard' and 'soft' variables.[31] His hard variables include factors of production, infrastructure and economic structure, and the soft variables include variables relating to culture, social structures, and city administration. From this Ni draws 15 conclusions and offers a set of fairly conventional policy recommendations for enhancement of a city's competitiveness: investment in infrastructure, openness to foreign investment, market and administrative reforms and increasing research and development. He is rather critical of the state of city planning for economic development or competitiveness enhancement, finding that planners often are not aware of the true comparative strengths of their city and adopt strategies that are willed rather than reasoned, and that at the national level there is a significant regional imbalance between coastal and interior cities that is not being addressed.[32]

Most impressively, Ni has followed up his initial study with a series of three annual reports on the competitiveness of Chinese cities in which he doubles the number of cities included in his analysis.[33] Unfortunately for scholars who are not functional in Mandarin, these studies are published only in Chinese text, although I understand the next one will have an abbreviated text in English.

The second work on Chinese cities, that is available in English, was carried out by Shen Jianfa and So Man-shan in which they examined the competitiveness of 215 cities according to a set of 55 variables that represent the city's performance and other indicators.[34] Their approach is similar to that of Ni in that they see urban competitiveness as being composed of three distinct components: economic, social, and environmental competitiveness. Economic competitiveness is in turn composed of three sub-groups: growth of urban economic capacity, economic performance and economic structures; there are five sub-groups for social competitiveness and two for environmental competitiveness. The third level of their competitiveness structure consists of 55 indicators each of which is linked to one of the ten subgroups. They conclude that the strength of the most competitive of China's cities is due to investment, skilled labor and foreign direct investment, as well as social stability, quality of life and the quality and quantity of infrastructure and services.

In Mexico Jaime Sobrino did an initial study of 'industrial competitiveness' of 24 Mexican cities using six 'static' and five 'dynamic' explanatory variables.[35] The static variables include those that relate to the capital–labor ratio, indicators of urbanization, economic structure and infrastructure; the dynamic variables include exports, productivity, the importance of science parks and the increase in industrial concentration, and are roughly similar to the hard and soft variables used by Ni. His approach is somewhat narrow in that industrial competitiveness would exclude from the analysis cities that are competitive in areas such as logistics, culture and recreation, research and development and services. However, he later expanded his scope to include 39 cities and defined urban competitiveness to include industrial, commercial and service competitiveness.[36] Sobrino did his second study for two time periods, 1988 and 1998, and was thereby able to highlight the differing experiences of Mexican cities over time. His results for the ranking of the cities for each of the three aspects of urban competitiveness vary dramatically, highlighting the importance of the definition of urban competitiveness that is used. It also indicates clearly that different cities have dramatically different roles in the national complex of urban economies. Finally, it suggests the value of choosing a measure or indicator of urban competitiveness that is general enough to encompass the variety of paths to providing satisfying economic lives for a city's residents. His most important conclusion with regard to change over time is that there was a great deal of movement of cities up and down the competitiveness ranking, suggesting that purposeful action on the part of city leaders could have very positive longer term impacts on the economic future of individual Mexican cities.

Finally, I will note briefly the work done by Peter Karl Kresl and Balwant Singh in two papers on the competitiveness of cities in the United States.[37] The methodology that was discussed at the beginning of this section was applied in a straightforward way: metropolitan areas were ranked using a composite variable of three indicators: manufacturing value-added, retail sales and some measure of professional services. This ranking was then 'explained' through a regression-correlation analysis which generated a set of variables that were all statistically significant determinants of urban competitiveness. Metropolitan areas were then ranked for each of the determinants, which could then be used as statistically significant benchmarks by city leaders in the design of their strategic–economic planning. The two Kresl and Singh papers presented rankings for the periods 1977–1982 and 1987–1992 and they captured the significant rise and fall in competitiveness of cities in the Industrial Triangle (Pittsburgh–St. Louis–Milwaukee), the south and west, and the North East. Pittsburgh, Houston, Denver and Detroit all rose by at least ten positions between 1977–1987 and 1987–1992, while New York, Atlanta, Los Angeles, San Diego and Philadelphia all fell by at least ten positions. Between the two periods, cities in the Industrial Triangle and the Center (Minneapolis–St. Paul–Phoenix) gained in competitiveness, while those in the South, North East, and Pacific Coast declined. Not only could city leaders understand that their city was in a region that was suffering a deterioration in competitiveness, they could also ascertain the specific aspects in which they were weakest and strongest as they design a strategy to turn their situation from negative to positive.

The results of these studies done in China, Mexico and the United States are not striking or unexpected in their conclusions, but they are supported by a quantitative methodology that gives them added credibility. Each is also similar enough to the conclusions of researchers in the other places to give strong support to the notion that in the homogenizing world economy of today cities everywhere are finding themselves to be in similar situations. The policies that are effective in one urban region should have general applicability in most other urban regions; similarly, the findings of researchers in each of these places should have similar relevance to researchers everywhere.

APPROACHES TO STRATEGIC PLANNING

Once we have a solid understanding of the determinants of urban competitiveness, we can use this information in designing a plan to enhance the urban competitiveness of an individual urban region. At the outset, it is important that we differentiate clearly between normal strategic planning and what I will refer to as strategic–economic planning (SEP). For many decades cities have done much planning, but little of it is directly relevant to the enhancement of competitiveness.[38] This usual planning has to do with land use, social housing, transportation infrastructure, accommodation of the needs of whatever economic interest presents a demand, cleaning up of industrial sites, water front development, urban renewal, and so forth. A Google search will uncover hundreds of sites related to these types of strategic planning. In all countries these activities have captured a great deal of the time and attention of local authorities. Some of this is remedial work to make up for past inattention or the negative consequences of past economic activities. Some of it is to build on the assets a city already has in order to make it even more congenial to visitors and residents alike. All of these actions make the city more attractive and viable than it would be without them. Furthermore, good housing, efficient transportation, urban amenities and attractive urban spaces are all aspects of a competitive urban economy, but in themselves they do not address the specific economic competitiveness needs of that city. Hence, it is worthwhile to present a focused discussion of urban strategic planning for competitiveness enhancement – that is, SEP.

The general strategic planning process is quite complex, nonetheless there is less controversy over its basic nature; hence, a discussion of it need not be as long and detailed as was the case with urban competitiveness. Strategic planning requires that several issues be dealt with effectively. The list of these issues is indeed a long one, and here I will list just ten of the principle ones:

1. How can the strategy of the planning exercise be set? (It should be noted parenthetically here, that while the word 'strategy' is used throughout this chapter, the strategy chosen may be multi-faceted so that strategies might in some cases seem to be more appropriate.)
2. How can planners determine the best means of achieving the strategy of the plan?
3. Which entities can assist the effort, and which can hinder the planning process?
4. What can local governments control or affect or realistically hope to accomplish?
5. What do state and national governments control or affect?
6. How can local actors be most effectively mobilized?
7. How can costs be contained?
8. How can local government be made most effective?
9. What criteria should be used to assess success? How long should the evaluation period be?
10. What links to external entities, such as other similar cities, are useful?

These are general questions that are relevant to all strategic planning exercises, whether for rational land use or for competitiveness enhancement. It is not necessary to develop each of these ten planning issues; needless to say, this is an intricate, involved and time consuming process. With regard to SEP for competitiveness, the research that forms the basis of the content of Chapters 4–6 has, as we shall see, made it clear that while some cities have made the effort to do this effectively, others have failed to do so, and some have not bothered with it at all.

Perhaps the most common approach to strategic planning is that which focuses on four distinct aspects of the entity for which the planning is being conducted. These are reducible to two pairs of positive-negative elements: accurate, realistic assessment of the entity's relative strengths and weaknesses *vis-à-vis* other competing entities; and an equally realistic assessment of the potential for achievement of that entity, that is, the opportunities that confront it, and of the threats posed to it by those same competing entities. Of equal importance are: 1) the four elements, strengths-weaknesses-opportunities-threats (SWOT in the terminology of the planning community), 2) the need for accurate and realistic assessment of them and 3) the comparative or relative grounding of the initiative.

Strategic planning for land use, urban housing, traffic management, and so forth are all targeted rather narrowly toward the achievement of one specific objective. The objective is clear from the outset, there is little need to make a comparison with other cities, the actors are clearly identified as are their tasks, and the evaluation of performance is rather straightforward and can be done within the existing structures. Land use and other planning have obvious impacts on the area's economic competitiveness and future but this is generally not the primary objective behind the initiative(s). SEP is distinctive in that its aim is the optimal use of the available human and other resources toward achievement of some objective that is determined through a deliberative process, with actors engaged as their need becomes apparent during elaboration of the plan, and it is all done in relation to the future design of the local economy. Effective SEP is a rigorous exercise which can be seen as having five distinct components:

1. an objective examination of the urban region's strengths and weaknesses in relation to other competing regions,
2. involvement of the general public and of all major entities in the region in an exercise that will make explicit the actual aspirations and concerns of local residents and entities,
3. design of a strategic economic plan that realizes the realistic aspirations and concerns that have just been identified,
4. mobilization of local human resources in the context of clear responsibilities

and lines of authority and with an understanding of who or which agency is in charge of the process, and

5. regular monitoring and evaluation of progress and performance.

These steps are little more than common sense, but each is crucial for a successful experience with SEP. Douglas Webster and Larissa Muller have elaborated this procedure, in a paper presented as a World Bank course, into a series of eleven steps that achieve essentially the same thing.[39] However many steps there are in the procedure, the crucial element is realistic appraisals of the assets of the urban region, of how those assets compare with those of its competitors, of the strategic options that are available to the city leaders, and of the performance of individuals or entities with regard to specific tasks. The dangers of self-deception, favoritism and ignorance that are inherent in making these appraisals are clearly evident and no elaboration of them should be necessary. A review of the planning processes of many cities, metropolitan areas or urban regions will reveal that it is often the case that not all steps are followed. When this is the case, the results of the exercise are usually not very successful.

With regard to the design of the plan itself, I have offered an approach that I believe accomplishes what is required for effective SEP. Since it has been published already I will not present it in its full detail,[40] but will limit this discussion to the principles behind its design and to how it can be used. In essence, the model asserts that the city leaders must make a choice between two basic goals that are intended to achieve the ultimate objective of the exercise – 'economic vitality in an increasingly internationalized environment.' On the one hand, the goal could be 'quantitative expansion,' in which the urban region does better what it has been doing in recent decades; on the other hand, the goal could be 'qualitative restructuring,' which entails breaking the links with the old economy and charting a new course of economic activity. In order to do either successfully, the city leaders must choose a strategy or combination of strategies that will be most realistically realizable. For an expansion, the strategies could be export promotion or serving as a bridge city or serving as a regional center; for restructuring, the strategies could include developing niches, becoming a research and development center or serving as an international headquarters city. For each of the strategies to be realized, the urban region must have a certain set of required assets; these could include transportation and/or communication infrastructure, urban amenities, a dynamic community of small- and medium-sized firms, specialized business services, linkages or alliances with other domestic or international cities, a labor force with certain skills, and so forth. It is most important that the city leaders gain an accurate understanding of their economy's comparative strengths and weaknesses in regard to these urban assets. This can be achieved through use of the methodology of the quantitative approach to urban competitiveness or, less accurately, through a benchmarking project.

The result of this exercise will be a strategic–economic plan that is realistic, in accordance with the aspirations of the residents of the urban region, and clear in all of its aspects with regard to action and responsibility.

SUMMARY

In this chapter the objective has been that of demonstrating the relationship between analysis of urban competitiveness and its crucial role in the process of urban strategic–economic planning. The section on SEP was rather brief as the basic idea of strategic–economic planning is not controversial and is agreed to by those who practice it. It is basically an effort to use most effectively the assets of an urban region toward the achievement of a generally agreed upon set of objectives. The essential point here is that the process of developing the SEP must be open to all sectors in the community, the objectives chosen be the product of extensive study and consultation, that responsibilities be clearly assigned, and that the implementation of the plan should be subject to regular monitoring with regard to the performance of all of the actors.

The study of urban competitiveness is open to much more diversity of approach and for that reason it receives the bulk of the discussion of this chapter. Here there are different methodologies in use, largely due to the availability of a large number and variety of statistical series for a large number of cities. The specific and general focus approaches are most common in Europe, but are also used by many researchers in North America and elsewhere. In these approaches theory and empirical results of studies on some aspects of competitiveness or of urban and regional development are used to give insights that are more or less closely related to urban competitiveness. However, in three countries, China, Mexico and the United States, researchers are able to gain access to enough relevant data so that they are able to do studies which generate statistically significant results that are directly focused on the competitiveness of urban regions or metropolitan statistical areas. These latter studies are of especial interest to city leaders as they give realistic and accurate appraisals of the strengths and weaknesses of any urban economy, and these appraisals can then be used in the critique of past planning or in the design of a strategic–economic plan. In this way, analysis of urban competitiveness and strategic–economic planning can be closely and beneficially linked.

NOTES

1. For complementary and more extensive treatment of urban competitiveness and strategic planning see Peter Karl Kresl and Earl Fry, *The Urban Response to Internationalization*, Cheltenham, UK and Northampton, MA, USA: Edward Elgar, 2005, Chs. 2 and 7.
2. Paul Krugman 'Competitiveness: A Dangerous Obsession,' *Foreign Affairs*, Vol. 73, 1994, p. 34.
3. Roberto Camagni, 'On the Concept of Territorial Competitiveness: Sound or Misleading?,' *Urban Studies*, Vol. 39, 2002, pp. 2395–411.
4. Dennis A. Rondinelli, James H. Johnson, Jr. and John D. Kasarda, 'The Changing Forces of Urban Economic Development: Globalization and City Competitiveness in the 21st Century,' *Cityscape: A Journal of Policy Development and Research*, Vol. 3, No. 3, 1998, p. 100.
5. Mario Polèse, 'Cities and National Economic Growth: A Reappraisal,' *Urban Studies*, Vol. 42, No. 8, July 2005, p. 1446. See also: Mila Vreire and Mario Polèse, *Connecting Cities with Macroeconomic Concerns: The Missing Link*, Washington: The World Bank, 2003, pp. 8–11.
6. Meric S. Gertler, Richard Florida, Gary Gates and Tara Vinodrai, *Competing on Creativity: Placing Ontario's Cities in North American Context*, Toronto: Ontario Ministry of Enterprise, Opportunity and Innovation, and the Institute for Competitiveness and Prosperity, November 2002, p. 25.
7. Edward J. Malecki, 'Jockeying for Position: What It Means and Why It Matters to Regional Development Policy When Places Compete,' *Regional Studies*, Vol. 38, No. 9, December 2004, pp. 1104–8.
8. Christian Wichmann Matthiessen, 'Vesteuropa 1990,' *Geografisk Tidsskrift*, Vol. 90, 1990, p. 46.
9. Alexis Jacquemin and Lucio R. Pench (eds), *Pour une Compétitivitée Européenne*, Brussels : De Boeck and Larcier, 1997, p. 29.
10. Krugman, 'Competitiveness: a Dangerous Obsession,' *Foreign Affairs*, March–April 1994, pp. 28–44; and Michael E. Porter, *The Competitive Advantage of Nations*, New York: The Free Press, 1990.
11. This issue is raised in Michael Kitson, Ron Martin and Peter Tyler, 'Regional Competitiveness: An Elusive yet Key Concept?,' *Regional Studies*, Vol. 38, No. 9, December 2004, p. 993.
12. Donald G. McFetridge, *Competitiveness: Concepts and Measures*, Ottawa: Industry Canada, 1995, p. 24.
13. McFetridge, p. 33.
14. Michael Parkinson, Mary Hutchins, James Simmie, Greg Clark and Hans Verdonk, *Competitive European Cities: Where do the Core Cities Stand*, London: Office of the Deputy Prime Minister, 2004, p. 28.
15. Porter, pp. 71–3.
16. Porter, p. 60.
17. Porter, Ch. 3.
18. See the web-site: www.competitiveness.org/
19. The Urban Competitiveness Project was formed in Ottawa, April 2005, and consists of representatives from China, Canada, the US, Mexico and the EU. Its web-site is not yet on-line.
20. Richard Florida, *The Rise of the Creative Class*, New York: Basic Books, 2002; and Richard Florida and Irene Tinagli, *Europe in the Creative Age*, London: Demos, 2004.
21. Ron A. Boschma, 'Competitiveness of Regions from an Evolutionary Perspective,' *Regional Studies*, Vol. 38, No. 9, December 2004, p. 1011.
22. For examples of the research that is being done in these countries see: Peter Karl Kresl and Balwant Singh, 'The Competitiveness of Cities: The United States,' *Cities and the New Global Economy*, Melbourne: The Organization for Economic Cooperation and Development and The Australian Government, 1995; and Kresl and Singh,

'Competitiveness and the Urban Economy: 24 Large U.S. Metropolitan Areas,' *Urban Studies*, May 1999, pp. 1017–27; Luis Sobrino, *Competitividad de las Ciudades en México*, Mexico City: El Colegio de México, 2003; and Ni Pengfei, *Blue Book of City Competitiveness*, Nos. 1, 2 and 3, Beijing: Social Sciences Documentation Publishing House, 2003, 2004 and 2005.

23. Mary Hutchins, 'Appendix 1: The meaning and measurement of Urban Competitiveness – Technical paper,' in Parkinson, Hutchins, Simmie, Clark and Verdonk, p. 83.

24. Ben Gardiner, Ron Martin and Peter Tyler, 'Competitiveness, Productivity and Economic Growth across the European Regions,' *Regional Studies*, Vol. 38, No. 9, December 2004, p. 1064.

25. Ann Markusen, 'Sticky Places in Slippery Space: A Typology of Industrial Districts,' *Economic Geography*, Vol. 72, No. 3, July 1996, pp. 294–310; Jane Pollard and Michael Storper, 'A Tale of Twelve Cities: Metropolitan Employment Change in Dynamic Industries in the 1980s,' *Economic Geography*, Vol. 72, No. 1, January 1996, pp. 1–22; and Cynthia Negry and Mary Beth Zickel, 'Industrial Shifts and Uneven Development,' *Urban Affairs Quarterly*, Vol. 30, No. 1, September 1994, pp. 27–47.

26. Gertler, Florida, Gates and Vinodrai, p. ii.

27. Rondinelli, Johnson and Kasarda, pp. 100 and 72.

28. Peter Maskell and Gunnar Törnquist, *Building a Cross-Border Learning Region*, Copenhagen: Copenhagen Business School Press, 2001, pp. 43 and 11.

29. Maskell and Törnquist, p. 47.

30. Lever, William F., 'The Knowledge Base and the Competitive City,' in Iain Begg, *Urban Competitiveness: Policies for Dynamic Cities*, Bristol: The Policy Press, 2002, pp. 11–31.

31. Ni, Pengfei, 'China Urban Competitiveness: Theoretical Hypothesis and Empirical Test' (English text), Beijing: Chinese Academy of Social Sciences, 2003.

32. Ni, p. 262.

33. Ni, Pengfei, *Blue Book on City Competitiveness*, Nos. 1, 2 and 3, Beijing: Social Science Publishing House, 2003, 2004 and 2005.

34. Shen, Jinafa and So Man-shan, 'Measuring Urban competitiveness in China,' *Asian Geographer*, Vol. 19, Nos. 1–2, 2004, pp. 71–91. In the bibliography to this paper the authors include several other publications, in Chinese, on the competitiveness of Chinese cities.

35. Jaime Sobrino, 'Competitividad y Ventajas Competitivas: Revisión Teórica y Ejercicio de Aplicación a 30 Ciudades de México,' *Estudios Demográficos y Urbanos*, Vol. 17, No. 2, 2002, pp. 311–61.

36. Jaime Sobrino, 'Competitividad territorial: ámbitos e indicadores de análisis,' Mexico City: Centro de Estudios Demográficos y de Desarrollo Urbano de El Colegio de México, unpublished paper.

37. Kresl and Singh (1995) and Kresl and Singh (1999).

38. I have presented much of this material in this section at meetings of L'Associazione Italiana Incontri e Studi sullo Sviluppo Locale, in Barletta, Italy, 27 October 2005; and Le Centre d'Études du Développement International et des Mouvements Economiques et Sociaux, Turin, Italy, 18–20 May, 2005.

39. Douglas Webster and Larissa Muller, *Urban Competitiveness Assessment in Developing Country Urban Regions: The Road Forward*, Washington: The World Bank, July 17, 2000, pp. 9–13.

40. Kresl and Fry, Ch. 7.

3. The economic and geographic analysis of urban competitiveness

Geographers for decades have been analysing issues that are of central interest to city leaders who are endeavoring to direct the economic development of their urban economy. While their contributions have been invaluable and recognized as such in many parts of the world, in others, most prominently the United States, their voice has been a relatively silent one. The publication of books by two non-geographers did much to bring the concerns and models of geographers to the fore throughout the world, especially in the United States. The first was Michael Porter's 1990 book, *The Competitive Advantage of Nations*.[1] Coming from a Harvard Business School professor who used a methodology that was less central to what social science researchers used, this was not at all confrontational to geographers. Porter's famous 'diamond' highlighted aggregate macro-economic and market demand conditions, factors of production, firm strategy, and local support activities and infrastructure, and was broad enough in its focus to allow everyone to make some attachment to it. The other seminal work, Paul Krugman's *Geography and Trade*, was published in 1993.[2] Geographers complained that there was little in this book they didn't already know and hadn't discussed for years, but the fact that a highly regarded mainstream economist from MIT gave a rigorous economic analysis of geographic concepts and models certainly elevated this literature in the minds of many researchers and city leaders. In spite of the initial reaction many geographers had to an economist intruding in their area of research, this book has become a pervasive item in the footnotes and bibliography of scores or hundreds of papers and books in the years since its publication. Between the two of them, Krugman and Porter also paid homage to the standard fare of geographers: agglomeration, clusters, and spatial relationships in general. City leaders and their policy advisors as well as much of the urban planning consulting industry found these analyses to be sufficiently powerful that almost all either wanted to use them or to design an approach or a model incorporating these insights that had certain perceived advantages for them.

In retrospect it is clear that this stimulus to rigorous city economic development planning occurred at a propitious moment at which the need for it, as a set of responses to the challenges that were noted in the previous chapter and which will be discussed in Chapter 5, was most clearly perceived. Market deregulation, the emergence of manufacturing in Asia as a challenge to that of the established industrial countries, the devolution from nation to city of considerable power and responsibility for economic affairs, demographic changes, and advances in technologies of production, transportation and communication all made it clear that city leaders had to respond creatively or move to the side-lines. In this chapter we will examine what economic geography has to offer in the context of these challenges. We will begin with a summary review of the widely discussed contributions of the two works that provided much of the impetus for what followed, and will then move through the concepts and analytical tools themselves. We will then see what is relevant to this topic in the literature on the role of clusters, agglomeration, networks and industrial districts. The issue of convergence or divergence of per capita income among the diverse regions of the EU is of great interest and importance to the economic futures of urban economies located in the center and the periphery so we will examine recent developments in this subject. Finally, we will give summary treatment to two areas of research which have always been a central element in the study of urban competitiveness and strategy and as a consequence have been widely discussed: first, the role of infrastructure, in its communications, transportation, cultural and urban amenities and educational aspects, and of the quality and quantity of factors of production; and second, the impacts of technological advance on the economies of urban regions. These latter two sections will be kept rather brief since they have been so widely discussed and because it is not an objective of this work to add to that knowledge. Nonetheless, they are both of importance to the design of an SEP and we will review those aspects that are of use to city leaders.

THE IMPACT OF *GEOGRAPHY AND TRADE* AND *THE COMPETITIVE ADVANTAGE OF NATIONS*

It is fair to say that neither of these books added much to the understanding that specialists in urban development had about their subject, but both pulled together or packaged existing knowledge and presented it in a way that resulted in a sudden, dramatic awareness of the issues involved and in the subject itself throughout communities in which economic geography had previously been given little recognition. It is also fair to say that Krugman's *Geography and Trade* was targeted at the academic research community, while Porter's *The Competitive Advantage of Nations* had its primary impact on city leaders and municipal policy makers. While economists appreciated Krugman's effort to bring added attention to economic geography, in conversations with geographers one usually encounters a substantial negative reaction. The latter is somewhat understandable given that Krugman states he is going to bring economic geography under the economics tent and that, in the US, since geography has not for many decades had the status among academic disciplines that it enjoys in Europe, Canada and most other places, this will make it a more serious area of study.[3] The response of geographers was generally to show that in much of what he discussed he had been preceded by some geographer years or decades earlier. Krugman actually recognizes this but puts economic geography in a framework that includes the most recent contributions to the theoretical base of industrial organization and of international trade and argues that this brings rigor and understanding that had eluded these geographers. At one point he writes: 'thanks to the efforts of industrial organization and trade theorists over the past twenty years, it is now possible to do geography as rigorously as you like' – implicitly arguing that such rigor had previously been lacking under the umbrella of geography. While this may be true, giving voice to this reality struck many geographers as rather arrogant and dismissive.

Krugman states that geographers have tended to treat the location of economic activities as an exercise in finding some optimal or at least rational size-structure and placement of towns and cities in a geographic space – Christaller's central place theory is one such approach.[4] *Geography and Trade* consists of three chapters on Center and Periphery, Localization, and Nations and Regions, and in each one Krugman approaches these traditional issues in economic geography using the theoretical concepts of imperfect competition, increasing returns, multiple equilibria, and externalities. When firms or regional economies function in an environment of imperfect competition and increasing returns the choice of location of economic activities is partly dependent upon the actions of decision-makers in the firm or region. Essentially, if all entities are in the same situation with regard to cost of production, resources, factors, transportation costs, and so forth, the first one to act to expand activity will become the preferred location for that activity. One of Krugman's conclusions is that when this is the case, the much maligned local boosterism may very well be a reasonable strategy, which will generate the crucial added demand and production that will give that firm or region the edge over its competitors.[5]

The possibility of multiple equilibria is of direct importance to the subject of this book. If there are X urban regions and all have established their position in the urban hierarchy or the structure of specialization, this is only one position from which there is no tendency to move, that is, one situation of equilibrium. If any one of the underlying elements were different from what it happens to be, such as population distribution, fixed costs, transportation costs, and so forth, then there would be a separate equilibrium for each constellation of those elements. The actual equilibrium distribution of economic activity is predicated not only on the values of the underlying elements but also on what Krugman refers to as accident and history. So rather than being rigidly determined or deterministic, his approach to the location of economic activity is one that allows for almost infinite solutions and for the solution to be significantly affected by the actions of local authorities and actors. This provides an enormous opening for urban strategic–economic planning aimed at enhancement of an urban region's competitiveness and at direction of the local economy toward a structure of activity that is perceived to provide local residents with the economic future that will best take advantage of the potential of the region.

While Krugman's approach does not lead him to specific conclusions with regard to some of the major policy issues that confront Europeans – Europe being where the lectures from which the text is taken were given – such as convergence or divergence of per capita incomes and the consequences of monetary integration, his general approach does give insights into the economic basis for, among other things, regional economies, center and periphery relationships, and the evolution of urban regions.

In contrast to Krugman's explicit focus on regions, Michael Porter continues in the grand tradition of Adam Smith (*An Inquiry into the Nature and Causes of the Wealth of Nations*) and Friedrich List (*The National System of Political Economy*) when he poses the question to be dealt with in his book as being not 'Why do some nations succeed and others fail in international competition?' but rather '(W)hy does a nation become the home base for successful international competitors in an industry?'[6] He then, on the next page, seeks 'a convincing explanation of the influence of the nation,' and 'the national attributes that foster competitive advantage in an industry.' Over 540 pages later the book concludes with three chapters in which he examines the consequences of his analysis for: Company Strategy, Government Policy, and National Agendas. The paradox of what follows is that it is actually at the level of the urban region that his clusters-based approach has been most warmly welcomed and has had its most powerful impact. In his 'diamond,' which represents the 'Determinants of National Advantage,' the national government is responsible for demand conditions; however the remaining three – factors of production, firm strategy, and local support activities and infrastructure – are largely the responsibilities of firms and local, rather than national, government. Given this, it is difficult to assign a dominating influence on the competitiveness of a local industrial cluster to the policies of the national government. However, in his discussion of the role of government Porter focuses solely on 'Governments' real role in national competitive advantage'[7] and makes no reference to city or sub-national governments or to competitive advantage at the sub-national level. After developing his approach to cluster development, Porter writes: 'The theory can and must be applied at two levels, the industry and the nation.'[8] Urban economies have no place in his system.

The notion of the cluster is directly linked to Alfred Marshall's discussion of the 'industrial district,' which is based on a shared labor market, external economies, economies of agglomeration, and transmission of knowledge. However, Porter puts this into a dynamic context of cluster rise and decline; a dynamic that will be of interest to those who have responsibility for the development and continued health of urban regional economies. The rise of clusters is not predicated on a single path of development; rather, each cluster will be dominated by local, or in Porter's framework national, assets, circumstances, and history. The crucial factor is the continued ability to innovate in an appropriate manner. Technology must be effectively imported as well as being developed locally. The shift from expansion to decline is primarily due to a reduced ability to incorporate into the functioning of the firms of the cluster new technologies and innovations. Once this reversal has set in, Porter writes, he has 'found few examples where an industry regained its former strength.' The industrial cluster becomes dominated by 'arrogance, lack of rivalry, and an unwillingness to upset the status quo.'[9] The cluster becomes insular, inward looking, and isolated from regenerative forces from without. While the tendency of most things is to go through periods of expansion and decline, making this a central part of his analysis should put local authorities on notice that it will take continued effort on their part to avoid or at least plan a response to the period of decline.

In the penultimate chapter of *The Competitive Advantage of Nations*, Porter does note that 'successful industries and industry clusters frequently concentrate in a city or region, and the bases for advantage are often intensely local.'[10] He also notes that in addition to the usual array of urban assets – education, infrastructure, and so forth – in some instances the policies of provincial or urban governments were more influential on regional competitiveness than were policies enacted by the national government.[11] In spite of this, the focus throughout his analysis is on national governments and national competitive advantage.

In summary, it must be said that in spite of the negative reaction on the part of some groups of individuals who study urban and regional economic development, and in spite of Porter's apparent lack of interest in urban policy, these two books have had powerful impacts on the way in which these policy analysts have come to view urban economies. Krugman has tried to bridge the gap between economics and geography and has generated something of a tug-of-war between the two disciplines for economic geography; Porter has aimed his analysis on policy makers in national governments, although his primary impact seems to have been on decision-makers in urban economies. Both presented their analyses in 1990, and it must be said, even by their critics, that the study of urban economic development and policy was never the same again.

THE ROLE OF AGGLOMERATION, INDUSTRIAL DISTRICTS, CLUSTERS, AND NETWORKS

The subject of the various ways in which one can structure economic space, apart from political boundaries and jurisdictions, has been given a great deal of attention during the past century. Alfred Marshall wrote about it at the end of the 19th century and Christaller did so in the first part of the 20th century, but it was in the second half of the 20th century that interest and research about these alternative conceptualizations of structure took off. This is not the place to review this extensive literature; rather, we will treat only the aspects of the current state of research that relate to the strategic–economic planning of cities. The first step will be that of defining each of the four terms that have emerged and then of ascertaining the potential for each to be of use to city leaders. This will enable us to examine the recent literature in this area and to be more explicit with regard to what they suggest might be confronted by city leaders in cities of various sizes, location and economic structure.

Perhaps the most general term of the four is that of the *agglomeration*. Economists mean by this term that there are certain economies, or cost savings, that are available when city-size increases. These economies are usually considered to be public rather than private goods, in that it is difficult to charge for their use or for access to them and they are essentially free to all users, without regard to the extent to which they are used. One example is airports. In a small town the airport may have only half a dozen flights each day to one or two regional hubs. As the city grows in size, it makes economic sense for the size of the airport and both the number of flights and the number of cities to which one can fly to increase. At the other extreme we have major international hubs such as New York, London, Tokyo, Frankfurt, Amsterdam, Chicago and Los Angeles from which one has several options for non-stop flights to dozens of similar cities throughout the world. Small firms with limited markets may be satisfied with limited air service, but when Boeing moved its headquarters from Seattle to Chicago, one of the criteria used in the selection of the new headquarters city was that it should have a major hub airport with direct connections to cities throughout Europe, Asia and Latin America. The financial charge to both the small firm and the world-class multinational for use of the local airport is probably the same, as it would be if the small firm was also located in Chicago. Airports are only one example of economies of agglomeration; cultural and educational assets are another, as are the rest of the transportation infrastructure and that of communication.

One way to look at agglomeration is to note that one feature of it is a density of population and of employment that is lacking in smaller cities. The larger the city, the more vertically it is constructed. Since the price of land is relatively high, housing, industry and service activities must respond accordingly. In this dense environment there are maximum opportunities for firms to capture externalities from each other and to benefit from non-traded inputs that are subject to increasing returns. In the former, each firm is distinct and isolated from the others, while with the non-traded inputs approach firms overlap each other in their activities. Ciccone reports on the significance of these agglomeration effects – a doubling of employment density results in a five per cent increase in labor productivity.[12] He finds that since externalities are stronger in some industries than in others, and because increasing returns and transportation costs differ in their impacts in various industries, the gains in production efficiency are in part due to the resulting changes in industrial structure. Those industries most affected expand in relation to others. This beneficial restructuring may be a feature to be found primarily in large agglomerations.

Alfred Marshall wrote about *industrial districts* a century ago and this concept has received a lot of attention during the past couple of decades as researchers began to observe them in actuality and to analyse their economic benefits. For Marshall, industrial districts were collections of firms which had very close interrelationships amongst themselves. They tend to be firms that begin as start-ups, benefiting from contact with other firms in close proximity, and as they grow they remain in this location. They share things that are positive in their economic impact, such as a common pool of labor with specific skills, experience in production of certain goods that is not easily conveyed to distant producers, regional branding which conveys a certain image or quality to all who produce there (as in wine districts), and face-to-face or informal contact among workers and managers in which tacit knowledge (as opposed to knowledge that can be written down and published and made available to all) is routinely passed along among firms in the district. Thus, the industrial district consists of a collection of firms in close proximity, but what distinguishes it from other structures is this frequent and often intense positive interaction among those firms and their employees. Examples of this would be certain areas where furniture is made or a soft-ware district such as Silicon Valley in California or the Third Italy with its areas specializing in eye glass frames or leather goods or shoes. Rantisi shows us how the evolution over a century or more of one such industrial district, New York fashion and apparel, has broken with path-dependency and periodically transformed itself to meet the changing realities of the market, other producers, and its own production activities. In this evolution she highlights the role of agency and of 'individual actors and groups of actors' in determining the course and pace of that evolution.[13]

Closely related to the industrial district is the *cluster*. This too is a proximate collection of firms in similar lines of economic activity, but while an industrial district is dominated by its firms, a cluster of, for example, bio-engineering or electronic instrumentation firms can exist in the midst of a very large urban area that may have several sectors in which it has some competitive advantage, or set of attributes that is attractive to firms in these sectors of the economy. One of the rationales given for the establishment of clusters is that distance makes the transfer of knowledge difficult and costly; this is negated by the clustering of firms closely in geographic space. As a consequence of this proximity, in the cluster there is transmission of tacit knowledge from worker to worker through the face-to-face contact which occurs most effectively in clusters, and there is less 'distance-decay' of knowledge than in non-clustered situations.[14] In summarizing the arguments for clusters, Malmberg states what firms in a cluster share: 1) transactions links with both customers and suppliers, 2) competition in product and labor markets, 3) spill-over of technical knowledge, firm-to-firm, and 4) cooperation and joint projects in research and development.[15] Porter's well-known 'diamond' is the inspiration for Malmberg's approach and of much of the recent thinking about clusters.[16] The publicity that Porter's work gained has given the cluster approach to urban economic development considerable prominence in the field. In fact, there is even a Competitiveness Institute, which takes the position that there is little to urban competitiveness other than the development of clusters.[17] They argue that there are four distinct types of clusters: the industrial cluster (essentially Porter's diamond), the regional cluster (based on proximity alone), the industrial district, and the business network. However, this approach glosses over very important aspects of structure that should be given greater attention.

Malmberg is among several economists who have expressed reservations about the value of clusters on the basis that the cluster approach focuses too much on local relationships, whereas research indicates that firms are most innovative, have the best access to technology and knowledge transfers, and can have the most effective research and development effort when they go beyond the local region to establish contacts with other firms, universities, research laboratories, and so forth, throughout the world. That is, they must be international rather than simply develop local cluster relationships.[18] Britton has found the same to be true for electronics firms in Toronto, and Bunnell and Coe take the argument further by emphasizing the need to go beyond the regional 'scale' and 'to explore interconnections and interrelations between and across scales.'[19] In addition, there may in fact be little or no contact among local firms. Such contact may be illegal due to considerations of anti-trust policy and the fear that the firms will act collusively or will create an oligopolistic market relationship, as is the case with the US automobile industry in Detroit, or it may be that all of the local firms are subsidiaries of large firms headquartered elsewhere and communication is limited to vertical contacts between parent and subsidiary.

David Wolfe and Meric Gertler have demonstrated that there is little evidence that 'direct, non-market interaction and knowledge sharing between local firms in the same industry is rampant.' Furthermore, they find that 'a large component of the knowledge inputs to local production – at least in certain sectors – is drawn from well outside the region.'[20] A similar point is made by James Simmie who shows that, for firms in the United Kingdom, while non-innovative firms concentrate on local and regional markets for 54 per cent of their sales, innovative firms rely on these markets for only 22.4 per cent of sales and national and international markets for 66.8 per cent of their sales. This runs counter to another argument about clusters – that 'local clustering allows rapid perception of new buyer needs.'[21] In many instances, most or all of the firms in the cluster will be subsidiaries of multinational firms located in other countries or on other continents and all of the contact of the firm in the cluster will be vertical with the parent rather than horizontal to other firms in the cluster. What then of the transmission of tacit knowledge (transmitted face-to-face rather than in publications) and the knowledge and technology spill-overs that are part of the rationale for clusters? Simmie argues that these useful contacts for the transmission of tacit knowledge may occur within a large firm or at conferences and other professional gatherings, and need have no basis in the local environment. Thus, it would be advisable to maintain the distinction between an industrial district, with its intense firm-to-firm contacts, and a cluster which is often just a collection of firms in a similar industry. The agglomeration remains distinct from both.

Finally, there is the fourth of the structures we are examining, the *network*. Networks differ from the other three in that they are private structures established by specific firms which have the capability of excluding all other firms. They can charge each other for the services provided by the network, for the maintenance of the network, and can develop whatever type or extent of communication and joint effort they choose collectively or individually to develop. They are often described as clubs.[22] There is no advantage to network participants in geographic proximity, since telecommunications and the occasional, focused conferences are all they require, so networks are essentially different from the other three structures. Each participant may, of course be located in an agglomeration and each may be part of a local cluster but finds its only, or most valuable, contacts are with firms that are quite distant from it; participants that are isolated from other firms in their industry are able with a network to achieve many of the advantages of being in a cluster or an industrial district. This will be of obvious importance to cities, and their firms, located on the periphery of an economic space.

These structures are of *economic significance* to the vitality and future of the cities in this study. All of the cities are large enough to capture economies of agglomeration. It may, however, be difficult or impossible for two large agglomerations in close proximity, such as Turin and Milan or Lyon and

Geneva, each to have a major international hub airport. This will also be true of other transportation assets, such as TGV connections and major highways when the two are in the same country. But even the smallest of our cities, Dresden and Seville, are large enough to enjoy many of the advantages of agglomeration. Industrial districts tend to be located in areas of smaller cities although, as is the case with Silicon Valley, large cities may be near by. With regard to the other structures, what interests us here is the impact they have on the ability of cities and their firms in various situations to compete success-fully for sales, plant locations, jobs and good incomes for their workers, and the many other things that are vital for the economic health of an urban econ-omy. Perhaps the crucial element here is the ability of a city and its firms to participate in the creation of knowledge and technology and to gain access to their transfer. Clearly this happens in industrial districts and in clusters in which interaction occurs. But if distance means that a city is spatially out of the loop, so to speak, and if the transmission of knowledge and technology is constrained by the cost of distance, then urban economies on the periphery will be at a disadvantage in the very important process of gaining access to advances in knowledge and technology. Clearly, for firms in many desirable technology-intense industries these peripheral cities would not be attractive locations for their activities.

We will discuss the implications of this in the penultimate section of this chapter, but for now a couple of things can be noted briefly. First, Johansson and Quigley conclude 'that networks of actors dispersed over space may substitute for agglomerations of actors at a single point'[23]; and this same point can be made with reference to geographically concentrated clusters and indus-trial districts. Advances in technologies of communication and transportation have reduced the cost disadvantage of being on the periphery, or in an isolated location. Second, with regard to innovation, Oerlemans, Meeus and Boekema argue that 'firms engage in innovative networks only if there is a strong inter-nal need to do so. In our view these findings are important because they give a counterbalance against that part of the literature that stresses the generic importance of networks and clusters.'[24] They see a need to focus on the specific mechanism that leads to formation of networks, and this too makes firm-to-firm proximity only one of several factors in innovation and technol-ogy and knowledge transfer.

As a final comment it should be noted that the very existence of these struc-tures has been called into question. In commenting on the notion of such struc-tures as we have just examined, Smith rejects the value of these fixed or limited spatial entities, of scales and boundaries. Quoting Thrift, he states that: 'World cities must not be seen as a succession of bounded states' but should be seen as 'always interactive and constantly in process;' and argues for 'a new urbanism based around globalization and an ontology of movement, networks, flows, fluids, folds, mobilities, nonhumans, practices and complexity.' This new urbanism 'bypasses vertical thinking by refusing to ossify or freeze the flow of the world into unities.'[25] The rise and fall, establishment and restructuring of patterns of interaction during the past 25 years confirm the validity of this argument for even a short period of time. Nonetheless, it must be admitted that many structures do have lasting value to the participants and agglomeration, industrial district, cluster and network are of both practical and analytical value. However, we must always investigate their actual importance in any given, individual situation.

CONVERGENCE AND DIVERGENCE, AND WHAT IT MEANS FOR URBAN ECONOMIES

Since six of the ten cities in this study are located in what is designated the periphery, the question of whether the economic space of the EU has been experiencing a process of convergence of income and economic capacity or of divergence is of great interest. This subject has received a great deal of attention by researchers, especially since the adoption of the SEA. One of the primary objectives of the SEA and of other initiatives of the integration process in Europe, such as the Treaty on European Union (TEU), or the Maastricht Treaty, and the establishment of the Council of Regions, has been the stimulation of economic development in relatively underdeveloped and low income areas – that is, the promotion of convergence. More recently the EU adopted the 'Lisbon growth strategy' which is intended to close the gap in competitiveness with the US and make the EU economy the most dynamic new technologies economy in the world by 2010. A secondary objective of this growth initiative is stimulation of per capita income growth in lagging regions. In Europe, in contrast to the United States, inequality and exclusion are considered to be detrimental and the best way to eradicate or at least reduce them is by making the lagging regions grow faster than the high income regions. In the United States the approach taken tends to be that of letting the unemployed move from a declining region to one of expansion, even at the cost of de-population of large expanses of the national territory. Progress on the Lisbon agenda has been disappointing and at mid-point (2005) the European Commission issued a release in which it was noted that: 'The reform package consists of 28 main objectives and 120 sub-objectives, with 117 different indicators. The reporting system for 25 Member States adds up to no fewer than 300 annual reports. Nobody reads all of them.' It then finished with the plea, 'The European Union cannot boost productivity and employment if Member States do not do their part.'[26] This situation in 2006 seems if anything to be less conductive to achieving the objectives of Lisbon.

The general consensus in the literature is that while there has indeed been convergence of per capita income among member nations, at the level of the regions there has actually been divergence. While low income peripheral countries such as Portugal and Ireland have gained relative to France and Germany, low income regions in almost all countries have slipped relative to high income regions. This is a concern not only because of the frustration and discontent it may generate in low income regions, but also because of the resulting pressure for greater fiscal transfers from high income regions and for increases in the levels of taxation throughout the EU. Hence, the reasons for this divergence at the regional level are very relevant to this study.

The standard theory of economics is divided on the question of regional convergence. The neo-classical model stresses diminishing returns on investment of capital. As capital is invested, with no increase in labor, the capital-labor ratio rises and the economic return to additional investment, its marginal product, falls. Thus, the initial advantage for investors of the high income center location is gradually reduced until it becomes relatively profitable to invest in the lagging region. This suggests that, over the long run, investment will work to equalize the capital-labor ratios in both the center and the periphery and since each worker then will have the same amount of capital with which to work, labor productivity will become equalized, and with it incomes. This works in hand with international/interregional trade theory (the Stolper-Samuelson Theorem) which tells us that as labor intensive goods are produced in and exported from the low wage region, the demand for labor will increase there and wages will rise until they are equalized throughout the trading space. While more a part of the real world than of the theoretical, labor mobility, to the extent it exists, will also work toward income equalization. Countering this view is that of Joseph Schumpeter and the endogenous growth theory. Here the focus is not so much on the capital stock as on technology. With technology being a function of the resources devoted to research and development, technological advance becomes something that is generated within the region, that is, it is endogenous. This allows for increasing returns on capital invested, rather than diminishing as in the neo-classical approach, and for those regions that have no capacity to devote resources to research and development to grow more rapidly than do those with a lower capacity. The high growth, high technology region is attractive to firms and they tend to cluster there rather than move to low wage regions. This results in divergence among regions, between center and periphery or between those that have access to capital and those that do not.

Since divergence among regions has been the recent experience it would seem that the endogenous growth approach would be supported. However, in actuality the situation is somewhat more complex. The factor that causes this complexity is one we discussed earlier, technology transfers or spill-over.

When we introduce technology transfers, it becomes clear that the access to technology is no longer a simple function of the resources devoted to research and development. So the question then becomes one of determining in which situations technology transfers take place and at what speed. Angel de la Fuente reminds us that 'regions (and probably countries) may be far more different from each other than we suspected up to now'[27]; not all regions can be put in two categories – high technology and low technology. Within these two categories there are important sub-categories. Some low technology, and presumably most peripheral, regions are overwhelmingly dominated by traditional activities such as agriculture and artisanal production of goods, while others have small sectors of their economy that use rather modern industrial technology. Giannetti states that if knowledge and technology spillover affects only high tech sectors of the economy then convergence will occur among these regions but will result in greater disparities among regions within individual countries.[28] Furthermore, he concludes that in regions with small technology sectors, knowledge spillover may make expansion of that sector welfare-reducing (the benefit gained being less then the expense of gaining it), whereas starting a technology-related sector in a traditional regional economy may be beneficial as, he notes, was the case with Wales.

In his study of Spanish regions, Fuente finds that where technology diffusion occurs it causes income levels to converge at a rate of 12 per cent per year. Convergence among Spanish regions occurred during the period of his study, 1991–1995, but because of differences in regional productivity rather than absolute convergence (to the same income level) regions converge to their 'steady state' relative incomes and persistent regional income differences remained, and will continue in the long run. Regions in the advanced or high income/high technology 'club' may converge to the same income level, but less advanced regions will continue to be less advanced and 'there would be no reason to expect a significant decrease in regional inequality in the future.'[29] Of the convergence that does take place, Fuente finds that education accounts for 20–25 per cent of it, technological diffusion for roughly one third, and changes in the capital/labor ratio the remaining 40 per cent, with the latter being accomplished by movements of labor from low- to high-income regions rather than from capital flows from the latter to the former.[30] Andrés Rodríques-Pose would add that the reason why technological transfer is not able to bring about absolute convergence is the 'relatively weak economic structure of these regions' and he identifies these weaknesses as being: the absence of networks, the predominance of small firms, lack of competition, and a lack of entrepreneurship.[31]

So what has actually been happening in the EU – convergence or divergence? Both Cappelin, Castellaci, Fagerberg and Verspagen, and Michele Boldrin and Favio Canova agree that convergence occurred up to the end of the 1980s but that there has been little change in national per capita relations since then.[32] The exception to this is the convergence between the EU nine and the three low income entrants, Greece, Portugal and Spain. However, they differ on the impact of EU regional policies, the Structural Funds, on income inequality. Boldrin and Canova conclude that 'there is no evidence that Structural Funds have had a positive impact upon the growth rates of either labor or total factor productivity in the poorer regions,' and that convergence is unlikely to occur during the next two or three decades. Their conclusion is that the convergence of the first decades following the Treaty of Rome occurred the way it did between the US North and South – through labor migration rather than because of regional policy.[33] Since, in their opinion, '(n)o model can predict convergence in levels without migration of labor and capital,' the most important policy initiative that could be adopted by the EU would be measures to facilitate increased labor mobility.

Cappelen et al. criticize the Boldrin and Canova study because it does not take into account either the impacts of growth-affecting factors other than EU Structural Funds or the reform of the regional support program of 1988. When they take these factors into account Cappelen et al. find 'that EU regional supporting through the structural funds has a significant and positive impact on the growth performance on European regions and, hence, contributes to greater equality in productivity and income in Europe.'[34] However, at the level of the region rather than the nation they find that EU regional policy has a greater impact on the more developed regions, that poorer regions are characterized by weak infrastructure and R&D capabilities, and that the support 'is least efficient where it is most needed.' Thus, they argue that Structural Fund expenditures must be packaged with policies that will transform the economic structures and research capacities of poorer regions.

The conclusion one must draw with regard to the convergence or divergence debate is that convergence at the level of the regions will be long in coming and that transfers of funds from rich to poor regions must be accompanied by a variety of measures that will address a broad array of disadvantages that hinder the transformation of the poorer regions.

THE IMPORTANCE OF INFRASTRUCTURE, AND THE QUANTITY AND QUALITY OF FACTORS OF PRODUCTION

Standard international trade theory tells us that the quality and quantity of factors of production and the infrastructure with which they work are central to the determination of comparative or competitive advantage and, as a consequence, they occupy a key position in any discussion of urban competitiveness. The traditional focus has always been on the transportation and communication infrastructures. Lack of a decent highway system in Mexico has meant that manufacturers of electronic equipment prefer to ship their products thousands of miles by air from Asia rather than have them damaged in a truck ride of a few hundred miles from a site in Mexico. The impact of high-speed TGV rail travel on the location of economic activity and the choice of residence and work of individuals in the EU has been very significant.[35] The improvements in inter-modal transportation, that is, truck to ship to train, and logistics in general have reduced the time and cost of shipping products inter-continentally to such an extent that this has transformed the allocation of economic activities throughout the global economy. Several of the ten cities in this study are prime examples of cities for which high-speed rail lines, continued viability of the local airport and limited access autoroutes are central elements in their SEP. As we shall see, reduction in funding for infrastructure from the EU or the national government, company strategies or the acquisition of the primary airline by one with a primary hub in another city or country can have a devastating impact on the economy of that urban region. Efficient, fast, low cost transportation can contribute to reducing the disadvantage of location on the periphery for a city with an otherwise competitive economy.

More recently the cultural infrastructure has been recognized as being important for a city's competitiveness. Research results confirm that urban amenities (specifically cultural assets), some characteristics of the labor force, infrastructure, and educational and research assets are among the most powerful determinants of urban competitiveness.[36] In the last chapter we showed how these research results can be of great benefit to city leaders when they design an SEP. In the highly competitive and continually evolving environment that now exists for urban economies, city leaders cannot simply let these determinants develop according to their own logic. They must be proactive and work to put in place the constellation of factors of production and of infrastructure that will make it possible for their specific, desired economic future to be realized. In later chapters we will see how cultural assets have been central to the economic development strategies of, among others, Lyon and Munich. There is now intense competition among EU cities to be designated the European City of Culture, in recognition of the status this brings to a city and the impact this has on its business environment and tourist industry. It has also been argued that enhancing the city's cultural assets is often the first step toward the regeneration of an urban economy that has gone into decline.[37] In the United States we have seen the relationship between art museums, symphonies, dance and theater, as well as popular culture and the economic success of cities as diverse as Chicago, Baltimore, Los Angeles and Atlanta. In Europe, outstanding architecture has had the same impact on cities such as

Barcelona, Seville, Malmö and Helsinki. Every city now seems to feel a need for a building by Gehry or Calatrava or Piano. However, Hans Mommaas makes explicit the need to avoid a rather simple place-promoting focus on cultural activity with its focus on tourism, status among cultural centers and urban development 'hype' toward an integration of cultural activity into the economic and social life of the city.[38]

Finally, in the era of the 'new economy' the knowledge infrastructure of universities, research laboratories and the model of the 'triple helix' is capturing the attention of city leaders. This is to a significant degree the partner of the cultural infrastructure, as both involve individuals who are creative, imaginative and, perhaps, non-conventional in their personal aspirations and values. Richard Florida's focus on this 'creative class' has been incorporated into the planning of many cities, but as it has been discussed widely there is no need to develop his analysis here.[39] The link to the city is given by P. W Daniels and J. R. Bryson who stress the city as a pool of educated workers who with universities and science parks create the knowledge-based urban economy. They also stress optimistically the linkage between this knowledge-base and the potential for revival of traditional manufacturing in older cities that have not been transformed into service centers.[40] Jan Lambooy ties these place-related qualities to the attraction of additional knowledge workers who in turn contribute to making the city an urban innovation system.[41] Hence, over the longer run often maligned local boosterism, when it supports expansion of the city's cultural assets, can have the concrete impact of making establishment of a knowledge-based economy more likely.

The triple helix model promotes the effective cooperation of three distinct entities: universities, firms and government. Having first rate educational institutions and research laboratories, and cutting-edge firms may not be enough to assure the economic future of the urban region; some policy action on the part of government may be required. Close, symbiotic cooperation on the part of the three entities will be necessary to realize the city's full potential. The triple helix approach would bring the three partners together and would facilitate the effective integration of the various assets of the urban region into a mutually supporting team of specialized knowledge economy entities. We shall see how effective this model has worked when we examine the experience of Copenhagen.

THE ROLE OF TECHNOLOGICAL CHANGE IN URBAN COMPETITIVENESS PLANNING

Rapid technological advance during the past twenty-five years has brought with it a complex mix of benefits, challenges and costs, with most of them having their incidence in, and implications for, urban regions. Technological advance seems to be at the heart of almost all SEPs, whether or not this makes sense in the local situation, and is central to almost all cluster initiatives. Since the consequences of technological change have been discussed by economists and geographers for most of that time period, it will be sufficient here merely to give a summary listing of them.[42]

Positive consequences of technological change for urban regions:

- It promotes the rise of new industries.
- Technological advances penetrate into other industrial sectors such as health care, education, entertainment and finance bringing higher productivity.
- It generates new products that enhance wellbeing.
- Cities are seen as the primary location of choice for entities involved with high technology.
- Demands are generated for an 'attractive' component of the labor force – educated, skilled, highly paid.
- In some circumstances, the disadvantage of peripherality may be overcome.

Negative consequences of technological change for urban regions:

- Local entities lose control over major aspects of the local economy.
- The adjustment costs, in terms of up-trading labor skills and infrastructure, entailed in the transition from the old to the new may present an excessive burden on the local fiscal resources and institutions.
- Streams of immigrants and changes in the demands for factors of production may cause social and cultural disturbance and conflict leading to increased exclusion and poverty among certain sectors of the population.
- Local decision-making and governance structures may be over-taxed by the need to respond creatively to change.
- The intellectual capital of local developers, economic geographers, consultants and officials may be found to have become outmoded and in need of rethinking and redevelopment.

There is certainly enough on these lists to demand the attention of any city leader who is looking to the future. Some of these consequences are rather general in their impact and incidence, some provide cautionary notes to already competitive cities, while others carry some hope and opportunity for cities that need imperatively to improve their situation. The fact that cities are preferred locations for the location of concentrations of higher technology activities gives encouragement to all cities. However, new industries and new products are rather normal consequences of change, but consequences that will not be captured by many cities merely in the course of time. Effective government will be seen in later chapters to be one of the key elements in successful SEP and from the above it is suggested that either local governance structures or the thinking of local actors may be made ineffective by technological change.

Two of these consequences are likely to be of primary interest to city leaders. First, the need for certain components of the labor force and the draw of a successful city will generate flows of migrants that may tax the absorptive capacity of local housing, schooling, health, infrastructure and governance structures. This is most likely to be the case for cities in the EU which require these migrants for their productive systems, as well as to provide tax payers who will support the rapidly growing retirement and health financial obligations of the rapidly aging society. This is most likely to pose the severest test of local authorities in the majority of large cities in the EU as it both expands its membership and works to implement the 'four freedoms,' the freedom of movement of capital, goods, services and people. Second, technological change lowers the economic cost of distance and for many economic interactions reduces the advantage of proximity. This has the potential to reduce the economic disadvantage of peripherality for cities that see this potential and are able to respond effectively to its exigencies. This can be one of the most transformative aspects of change, technological or other, that can make it available to a city that is located on the periphery. Stephen Graham is most enthusiastic in this regard when he concludes that information communication technology 'can empower historically isolated individuals and groups ... and has the potential to provide low-income, urban residents with: the requisite skills to participate in the informational economy; new opportunities to facilitate the communication and networking among individuals necessary for community building; the means to more effectively participate in public discourse; and data and information to understand and attack the problems they face.'[43] While nothing is guaranteed, this is certainly a call to city leaders in peripheral cities and in cities with problems with excluded classes and groups to consider the potential that technology has for easing some of their primary problems.

As is the case with most of the changes or turbulences noted throughout this book, these always present to city leaders a set of challenges, threats and opportunities. It is clear that the consequences of advances in technology can be factors that lead to the deterioration, expansion or even salvation of the individual urban economy.

FINAL COMMENTS

It should have been made clear, to any doubters, that the insights of economists and geographers have much to offer to city leaders in carrying out their SEP. At the same time, it should be clear that most of the concepts, such as clusters, are nested in their own controversies and alternative interpretations, so that there is little that should be applied indiscriminately without careful examination of the local circumstances. The section on convergence and divergence in the EU is important as it sets the scene in which local actors must plan their actions and activities. The disadvantages of peripherality can be exacerbated if fundamental elements such as factors of production or infrastructure are inappropriate or neglected, but can be overcome if technological change is managed effectively. In this chapter we have discussed some of the tools or instruments that are available to city leaders in their strategic–economic planning. In the next three chapters we will examine how the leadership of the ten cities responded to the events with which they were confronted.

NOTES

1.   Michael Porter, *The Competitive Advantage of Nations*, New York: The Free Press, 1990.
2.   Paul Krugman, *Geography and Trade*, Cambridge, MA, USA: MIT Press, 1993.
3.   Krugman, especially pp. 1–11 and 98–100.
4.   For a brief discussion of this, see: Paul N. Balchin, David Isaac and Jean Chen, *Urban Economics: A Global Perspective*, New York: Palgrave, 2000, pp. 48–53.
5.   Krugman, p. 33.
6.   Porter, p. 1.
7.   Porter, p. 127.
8.   Porter, p. 175.
9.   Porter, pp. 170–71.
10.   Porter, p. 522.
11.   Five years later Porter does devote his attention to the situation of urban economies in: Michael Porter, 'The Competitive Advantage of the Inner City,' *Harvard Business Review*, May/June 1995, pp. 55–72.
12.   Antonio Ciccone, 'Agglomeration Effects in Europe,' *European Economic Review*, Vol. 46, 2002, p. 315.
13.   Norma M. Rantisi, 'The Ascendance of New York Fashion,' *International Journal of Urban and Regional Research*, Vol. 28, No. 1, 2004, p. 104.
14.   Jeremy R.L. Howells, 'Tacit Knowledge, Innovation and Economic Geography,' *Urban Studies*, Vol. 39, Nos. 5–6, 2002, p. 880.
15.   Anders Malmberg, *Kluster dynamic och regional näringslivsutveckling*, Östersund, Sweden: Institutet för tillväxtpolitiska studier, 2002, p. 10.
16.   Michael Porter, *The Competitive Advantage of Nations*, New York: The Free Press, 1990.
17.   See the web page for The Competitiveness Institute, www.competitiveness.org.
18.   Malmberg, p. 22.
19.   John N.H. Britton, 'Network Structure of an Industrial Cluster: Electronics in Toronto,' *Environment and Planning A*, Vol. 35, 2003, pp. 983–1006; and Timothy G. Bunnell and Neil M. Coe, 'Spaces and Scales of Innovation,' *Progress in Human Geography*, Vol. 25, No. 4, 2001, p. 583.

20. David A. Wolfe and Meric S. Gertler, 'Clusters from the Inside and Out: Local Dynamics and Global Linkages,' *Urban Studies*, Vol. 41. Nos. 5–6. May 2004, pp. 1071–93.
21. James Simmie, 'Innovation and Clustering in the Globalised International Economy,' *Urban Studies*, Vol. 41, Nos. 5–6, May 2004, pp. 1105–107.
22. See, for example, Börje Johansson and John M. Quigley, 'Agglomeration and Networks in Spatial Economies,' *Papers in Regional Science*, Vol. 83, 2004, p. 166.
23. Johansson and Quigley, p. 166.
24. Leon A.G. Oerlemans, Marius T.H. Meeus and Frans W. M. Boekema, 'Firm Clustering and Innovation: Determinants and Effects,' *Papers in Regional Science*, Vol. 80, 2001, p. 353.
25. Richard G. Smith, 'World City Topologies,' *Progress in Human Geography*, Vol. 25, No. 5, 2003, pp. 561–82.
26. http://europa.eu.int/growthandjobs/index_en.htm
27. Angel de la Fuente, 'On the Sources of Convergence: A Close Look at the Spanish Regions,' *European Economic Review*, Vol. 46, 2002, pp. 569–99.
28. Mariassunta Giannetti, 'The Effects of Integration on Regional Disparities: Convergence, Divergence or Both?,' *European Economic Review*, Vol. 46, 2002, p. 560.
29. Fuente, p. 577.
30. Fuente, p. 595.
31. Andrés Rodríguez-Pose, 'Is R&D Investment in Lagging Areas of Europe Worthwhile: Theory and Empirical Evidence,' *Papers in Regional Science*, Vol. 80, 2001, p. 292.
32. Aadne Cappelen, Fulvio Castellacci, Jan Fagerberg and Bart Verspagen, 'The Impact of EU Regional Support on Growth and Convergence in the European Union,' *Journal of Common Market Studies*, Vol. 41, No. 4, 2003, pp. 621–44; Michele Boldrin and Favio Canova, 'Inequality and Convergence in Europe's Regions: Reconsidering European regional Policies,' *Economic Policy*, Vol. 32, April, 2001, pp. 207–53.
33. Boldrin and Canova, p. 244.
34. Cappelen, Castellacci, Fagerberg and Verspagen, p. 640.
35. R.W. Vickerman, 'High Speed Rail in Europe – Experience and Issues for Future Development,' *Annals of Regional Science*, Vol. 31, 1997, pp. 21–38.
36. Peter Karl Kresl and Balwant Singh, 'The Competitiveness of Cities: the United States,' *Cities and the New Global Economy*, Melbourne: The Organization for Economic Cooperation and Development and The Australian Government, 1995; and Kresl and Singh, 'Competitiveness and the Urban Economy: 24 Large U.S. Metropolitan Areas,' *Urban Studies*, Vol. 36, Nos. 5–6, May 1999, pp. 1017–27.
37. Graeme Evans, 'Measure for Measure: Evaluating the Evidence of Culture's Contribution to Regeneration,' *Urban Studies*, Vol. 42, Nos. 5–6, May 2005, pp. 959–83.
38. Hans Mommaas, 'Cultural Clusters and the Post-industrial City: Towards the Remapping of Urban Cultural Policy,' *Urban Studies*, Vol. 41, No. 3, March, 2004, pp. 507–32.
39. Richard Florida, *The Rise of the Creative Class*, New York: Basic Books, 2002.
40. P.W Daniels and J.R. Bryson, 'Manufacturing Services and Servicing Manufacturing: Knowledge-based Cities and Changing Forms of Production,' *Urban Studies*, Vol. 39, Nos. 5–6, 2002, pp. 977–91.
41. Jan G. Lambooy, 'Knowledge and Urban Economic Development: An Evolutionary Perspective,' *Urban Studies*, Vol. 39, Nos. 5–6, 2002, pp. 1019–35.
42. For a more extensive treatment of the impact of technological change on urban economies, see Peter Karl Kresl and Earl Fry, *The Urban Response to Internationalization*, Cheltenham, UK and Northampton, MA, USA: Edward Elgar, 2005, Ch. 4.
43. Stephen Graham, 'Information Technologies and Reconfigurations of Urban Space,' *International Journal of Urban and Regional Research*, Vol. 24, No. 2, 2001. pp. 405–26.

4. The ten cities and their planning at the outset of the 1990s

In 1987, the context in which the ten European cities included in this study were situated was significantly restructured with the adoption of the Single European Act (SEA), also referred to as the process of 'completion of the internal market.' The popular conceptualization of this was that the member countries of the European Community (EC) would establish a set of markets for goods, services and factors that was as seamless and as tightly integrated as were those of the United States. Specifically, this entailed adoption of almost 300 individual measures that would lead to the realization of the 'four freedoms' – the freedom of movement of goods, services, capital and labor. So much has been written about the SEA and its consequences that it is not necessary to reiterate the details of this dramatic initiative, save to note that the expectation was that per capita incomes in the member countries would increase, over a period of five or six years, by between 4.5 and 6.0 per cent over what they would otherwise have been.[1]

Given the focus of this book, our interest in the SEA is the impact its implementation had on the economic situation of cities in the member countries. Realization of the four freedoms meant that what was being given up was the deep and pervasive structure of intervention in economic transactions on the part of national governments. While market economists would all argue that these interventions were inefficient and that they lowered incomes and increased unemployment for residents of member countries, their supporters would counter that the interventions provided stability, equity and shelter in a world of increasingly impersonal and uncontrollable shocks and economic restructuring. Critics of what was seen as the Anglo-Saxon model of *le capitalisme sauvage* stated with passion that Europeans had different arguments and weights in their collective welfare functions than did Americans and Britons. These arguments may be considered to be accurately descriptive or just hyperbole, but they were offered often and loudly, by journalists, politicians and academics, all of whom could speak with some conviction and knowledge of the European situation.

What is important in this is that the process which was being undertaken removed to some degree the national government from the structure of support that had been given to economic activities that had formed the basis of economic activity that sustained urban economies throughout the member countries of the EC. To a considerable degree the locus of decision-making about the economic and social matters that concern city dwellers had shifted upwards in the hierarchy to Brussels and the institutions of the EC. Henceforth, the policies with regard to regional development, transportation infrastructure, city-center redevelopment, financial and other market regulation, social policy, education, culture, and so forth would be increasingly determined and funded by the European Commission and its Directorates General. Concomitantly, the responsibility for the strategy of development for an urban economy and the initiative for designing projects and formulation of proposals for funding, have shifted downward to the governments of the cities. Therefore, the SEA opened a new avenue of communication between the individual cities and Brussels. Henceforth, cities would have to be more proactive in competing against each other for the attention of funding agencies in the EC.

Nonetheless two other features of the new situation of EC cities have developed. One is the increased value in cities finding areas in which they can cooperate, such as making joint proposals for, among other things, high-speed rail lines that would serve several of them, or general appeals for increased funding of renovation of decaying central districts of cities in economic difficulty.[2] The second is the fact that the national governments still have a powerful role to play, either through their unique role in the European Council or their role as an entity that can facilitate or hinder approval of any specific city initiative. There is evidence that city initiatives that involve their national government as participants, or at least as co-proponents, are more successful than are those in which the city circumvents the national level and appeals directly to Brussels.

The ten cities that are included in this study differ in many ways. With the exception of Copenhagen, which was included because of its very interesting Oresund project with southern Sweden, none of the cities is a national capital. Capitals have economies that are often artificially supported or at least directed because of their status; this status also limited the degrees of freedom they have to reconstitute themselves in response to new opportunities. Some of the cities, but not all, are important transportation centers, or facing the loss of major industries, or important service centers. Some are important cultural and recreational sites, while others can fulfill a point-of-access or a bridge city function.[3] Since much of the discussion in this book includes considerations of economic space and gives priority to concepts such as clustering and networking perhaps differentiating the cities by geography is the most appropriate.

There is more than one way to conceptualize the geographic structure of the cities of the EU. One could imagine a vertical structure according to economic weight or role in the global hierarchy or size, and so forth. Or one could consider a structure of differentiated specialization among many cities of roughly the same stature, however defined. Cities could be clustered or ranked according to some geophysical characteristic, such as northern or coastal cities, or some economic characteristic, such as industrial production or high technology importance. The possibilities are, while certainly not endless, at least numerous. Each is suited to the specific question(s) being asked. Given the issues that are expected to arise in this study the ten cities will be classified as either core or periphery, more or less along the lines of the well-known DATAR analysis which produced what became known as the 'blue banana.'[4] Core cities have a dense structure of economic activities of a wide variety and they are generally in close proximity to other such cities so that networks are easily formed and significant interaction is a strong potential, albeit one that is not always realized. Peripheral cities are distant from the band of dense economic activity that runs from south-east England, down the Rhine River valley to Piedmont and Lombardy in northern Italy. They may be important regional centers of activity but they lack the easy contact with other similar cities. Hence, the response of these two types of cities will, or should be expected to be, rather different. The veracity of this assertion will be tested as a consequence of the work that will be done on each of the cities. There is, it must be noted, no expectation that cities in the core will inevitably have a more positive and prosperous economic experience than will any individual city in the periphery. This is where the astuteness and willingness and ability to act on the part of local leaders comes in and is one of the primary foci of this entire study.

The core cities we will examine are: Amsterdam, Lyon, Milan and Turin; those on the periphery are: Barcelona, Copenhagen, Dresden, Hamburg, Munich, and Seville. In this section we will detail the strategic plans that each of these cities adopted, or at least the dominant thinking in each city around 1990–1992. In the chapter which follows we will examine the extent to which these plans were actually realized.

CITIES IN THE CORE

The four cities in this group all lie in the crescent that is centered on the Rhine River Valley and its imaginary continuation southward through Switzerland into north-western Italy and north-westward to south-eastern England. As the previous chapter has suggested, this central location should confer some advantages to them in comparison to cities that are relatively isolated from this core of European economic activity and in most cases isolated also from other major urban centers. Networking should be easier, as should a more finely articulated specialization in certain specific activities in which the city has some advantage. These cities should not be found to be in a condition of decline, unless they are narrowly focused on one type of activity and that activity is being negatively affected by the factors that will be detailed in the next chapter.

It should be noted that the very idea of a core-periphery structure has come into question in recent years. The EU, in the form of its Committee on Spatial Development, has in recent years promoted the notion of 'polycentrism.' While, as Francesca Governa and Carlo Salone tell us, 'the precise meaning of polycentricity has remained elusive,'[5] it must be taken as a conceptualization of the EU economic space which is an alternative to that of core-periphery. This new conceptualization captures the increasing importance of urban economies that are more widely dispersed than was the case a couple of decades ago. Places on the periphery such as Hamburg, Barcelona, Munich and Manchester are more important than they have been in a very long time. So there is some truth to the idea that mapping of key centers throughout Europe has developed to the advantage of some non-core areas. But economic dominance or importance is not the only aspect of urban economics that is of interest. In this study we are also interested in the ways in which cities that have proximity to the concentrated mass of consumer demand, institutional and structural density, thick transportation networks and so forth of what is referred to as the core do their strategic–economic planning, imagine their future and relate to other urban centers differently than cities that are deprived of these advantages. We will be interested in discovering the extent to which central or peripheral location does in fact matter for Amsterdam and Copenhagen or for Lyon and Barcelona. For this reason, the core-periphery structure will be retained for this and the following two chapters in which we examine the experiences of the ten cities.

Amsterdam
Amsterdam is unique among the ten cities in this study in that planning was a normal activity. The topographical characteristics of the Netherlands, of course, make this a necessity. The first requirement of living both below sea level, and with a high population density, is that constant attention be paid to land use planning. The efficient use of land must be based on the activities that are going to be undertaken on it. Hence, land use planning is integrally related to economic activity planning, both by the national government and at the level of the city. It is also the case that policy coordination among levels of government must have a much higher priority here than in the rest of the EU. Since the planning of economic activity is the primary interest in this research we will begin there, and to understand the specifics of Amsterdam's economic planning we should begin with a review of the thinking of city leaders and their concerns at the time, about 1990.

Leaders in Amsterdam had a certain anxiety when looking to the next decade or so with regards to the economic health of the city. In the most general sense they were concerned about competition for some of the central activities of the city economy. Unlike most of the cities located in the periphery, those we will examine in the following section of this chapter, Amsterdam was in close proximity to large cities that could challenge it directly. Both Brussels and Frankfurt were powerful competitors in the financial sector. Antwerp, Bremen and Hamburg posed challenges to Dutch sea-to-land intermodal transportation, and while the Amsterdam port was only one-tenth as important as that of Rotterdam there were significant positive spin-offs for the city. Brussels and Cologne were targeted to get the links to the TGV connection between the Continent and England. So the picture for the financial and other services sectors of the Amsterdam economy was not without serious concern.

While we are focused on Amsterdam, it must be remembered the planners consider the city to be part of a 'polynuclear metropolis' referred to as the Randstad, which consists of the urban regions of Amsterdam, the Hague and Rotterdam.[6] Nonetheless, as each city has its own distinctive economic character: Rotterdam – logistics, the Hague – administration, and Amsterdam – finance and services, it does make sense to discuss the Amsterdam economy as a separate entity, understanding the limits to doing so.

The primary assets of Amsterdam at this time were the region's major international airport at Schiphol, the strength of the major financial firms, its location in the center of a large and significant economic space, the efficiency and user-friendly nature of its bureaucracy and its responsiveness to English as a second language for almost the entire population. These latter two factors made those in Amsterdam feel that the competition from France would not be a major factor, especially when trying to attract regional headquarters and production facilities of Asian firms.

In the city itself, there were some transportation problems to deal with, but the primary physical concern was that of suitable housing and office space. Amsterdam was in the curious position of having spent many years building 'social housing' for low-income residents, and of finding itself without enough housing that was suitable for the high-income, highly-skilled work force it was seeking to attract to its finance and services sectors. It was also noted that there was a similar shortage of high level office space. As a consequence the city was losing out to locations in its periphery and elsewhere in the Randstad area.

The central theme of the plan for Amsterdam's next decade was that of continuing with the strengths of the city's economy and of doing what had to be done to ensure that Amsterdam was able to assert itself as a major actor in the post-SEA period and the new technology economy that were to come. This meant in part that the Randstad region must be strong for the city to be able to realize the potential gains from its position as economic and administrative center, but Amsterdam also argued that the principal city had to be strong for the region to be successful. This had obvious implications for national governmental expenditures on transportation and communication infrastructures and on education, for the vitality of Amsterdam's city center, and so forth. One conceptualization that was put forth was that of Amsterdam's 'Three Ports': air, sea and telecommunications, with the latter being the innovation for this planning period. A consultant's report suggested that Amsterdam invest in a teleport and intelligent buildings, and that it become an 'intelligent city.'[7]

What differentiates this approach from that of some of the other cities is that the city and other levels of government did not try to subsidize or otherwise direct the actions of actors in the private sector or to use state enterprises to shape the economy of the future, but rather they devoted their efforts to making the Amsterdam environment as supportive and congenial to activities that were only generally specified. So there was no great effort to develop information technologies or bio-engineering; university research efforts were encouraged, science parks were supported, as were all aspects of the infrastructure – housing, communication, transportation, education and culture. Technological advances were to be applied not only to production of goods but were also to be applied pervasively to such mundane things as waste disposal, a major problem in a country with so little space for dump sites. Proper disposal could also generate significant quantities of increasingly scarce industrial raw materials. What was hoped for as a set of results from this planning exercise was an enhancement of the position of Amsterdam among the principal cities of the EC, enhancement of the competitiveness of the city's financial and other service sectors, some developments in technology-related activities, a general assurance that Amsterdam would continue to be an outstanding place for domestic and international firms to do business and use the city as a base for operations throughout the EC, and that it would be an attractive place for skilled and educated workers to live. No dramatic transformation was anticipated; just efforts to make the best of what Amsterdam already had.

Lyon

Lyon's future was, as is the case with so many European cities, tied directly to its past. For centuries the city had served as a bridge between the Mediterranean world and that of northern Europe. The Rhône River was the natural linkage for commerce and human movement, and when the Mediterranean world was economically strong Lyon's function was all the more valuable and the city thrived; the reverse was, of course, also true. It became a primary center for the silk trade and for making silk fabric and goods. Lyon was also very much the 'second city' to Paris, much as Chicago was to New York, and was seen as a rather quiet provincial town backed up against the formidable barrier to east-west transportation – the Alps. Unlike other countries such as Germany, Italy, Canada and the United States, both the economic and political centers of France were located in one city. Therefore, corporate headquarters, decision-making of all sorts, the primary transportation hub, the center of learning and culture, and so many other things were to be found in Paris. The implementation of the SEA was a wake-up call for Lyon, as it was for so many other 'second cities' in Europe – Birmingham, Barcelona, Turin, Rotterdam, among others. These cities formed the core of the Eurocities movement, countering the notion of a Europe of regions with Europe as a network of cities. Lyon put itself at the center of this movement and used both the opportunities for city action and development in the post-SEA world and the power-base and information-sharing network of Eurocities to transform itself from the sleepy provincial city on the periphery of the French hexagon into one of the principal urban centers of Europe.

In spite of its 'second city' status in France, Lyon had considerable assets at its disposal. First, it was the country's second major transportation center, with well developed rail, road and air infrastructures. Second, with its educational institutions, some research laboratories, and a few large firms in bio-pharmaceuticals, industrial machinery and electronics there was a strong potential for Lyon in combination with high technology centers in Grenoble and St. Étienne to make the province, Rhône-Alpes, become one of Europe's principal technology centers. Rhône-Poulenc Agrochemie, Mérieux, and science and research parks such as Technoparc Gerland are three examples. Third, the financial sector was well developed, with Crédit Lyonnaise at the center of a complex of local banks plus the offices of sixteen international banks. Fourth, the international presence in Lyon was enhanced by over 100 foreign firms, of which one-third were American and two were Japanese, and also by the international headquarters of INTERPOL. Finally, Lyon had impressive cultural assets in its Opera, orchestra, Renaissance historic district, several museums including the Musée des Beaux Arts, probably the best art museum in France outside Paris, and, of course, its famous culinary delights. The challenge was, of course, to take actions which would enable the city to realize the potential gains from these assets.

Transportation was an immediate concern, and the primary initiative was to upgrade the airport at Satolas (now St. Exupery) to status as an international airport with on-site connections to TGV rail lines planned for Barcelona and Turin in addition to the south of France, Paris and elsewhere. Discussions were planned with North American airlines that were to lead to them establishing non-stop flights. Another effort was made to enhance the city's cultural assets and international recognition by renovating the Opera and putting a dance theater on the top floor for the Danse Biennial that had been held for several years. The Renaissance historic district was given attention with new hotels, shops and restaurants.

City leaders in Lyon saw international city-to-city relationships to be, at the margin, more likely to be of benefit than were the traditional vertical nation-to-city connections. In the DATAR cartography, Lyon was considered to be at the 'north of the souths.' That is, a twist was put on the city's historic role as north-south bridge but identifying the south not as Mediterranean France but rather Turin and the Italian peninsula, on the one hand, and, on the other, Barcelona and Iberia. This structure was to be made real with TGV lines and a dense network of relationships, exchanges and cooperative ventures knitting these three cities together. It must be said that much of the business community was indifferent to schemes that were not solely based on profit, but it was thought that these linkages would be very useful in getting small- and medium-sized firms to think and to act beyond the boundaries of the Lyon region or of Rhône-Alpes.

This focus on small- and medium-sized firms became another central point in the strategic thinking of leaders in Lyon. Clearly, Lyon could not challenge other EC cities such as London, Paris, Frankfurt, Milan and Brussels in the primary financial activities, but it was thought that there was a niche in the financial sector for a city to specialize in the needs of smaller firms for financial advice, capital and other financial services. Crédit Lyonnaise began to develop special facilities for this type of firm and the Lyon stock exchange began to move into this area as well. This was combined with efforts of the Chamber of Commerce to make small firms more aware of the possibilities of export markets and more capable of trying to penetrate them.

In summary, Lyon's approach was to internationalize itself in all manners, to enhance its international reputation and attractiveness as a place to do business and to visit, to strengthen its capabilities in certain areas of technology-related economic activity, and to assert itself on the European urban scene through an active role in organizations such as Eurocities. Lyon aggressively moved away from the nation-state dominated pre-SEA environment into that of Europe as a network of active cities and sought to position itself so that it could be successful in this strategic design.

Milan

City leaders in Milan felt they had reason to feel satisfied with the economic performance of their city. After all, Milan was the economic powerhouse of Italy; it ranked first in research and development activities and in finance and was arguably one of the primary financial centers in Europe. Milan was also not a one industry city, to the extent that its neighbor Turin was, as it had roughly equal strengths in rubber and plastic, metal products production, machines and mechanical tools, and furniture. It was also one of the world's leading centers of fashion. In the cities rankings Milan usually came out just behind London and Paris if the economy provided the criteria, and behind some of the capital cities, including Rome, Brussels and Madrid if the criteria were broadened. So in general things looked rather good for Milan.

However, there were some changes that were affecting most of the world's industrialized cities and Milan was not immune from their effects. The long-term shift of population from rural areas to large cities was slowing so population growth in Milan was down considerably; the service sector was expanding and the OPEC price hikes of a decade or more ago were having their impact on manufacturing output and employment; the global and European economic integration processes were continuing to work their effects on production location, structure of output, and international trade; and, finally, most large cities were experiencing a shift of population and economic activity from the center of the city to rings of surrounding suburbs. So behind the good news was a dark cloud of uncertain proportions.

In spite of its general strengths, Milan did have some problems that city leaders realized needed attention. Most of them were based on the weak linkages between Milan enterprises and the rest of Europe and the world. Research and development is one of the areas in which this inward looking was problematic. At the first instance, there was a lack of interaction between firms engaged in research and those in manufacturing and the advanced services (taken to be computer software). This suggests that Milan functioned as an agglomeration but not as an industrial district or even as a cluster. The lack of strong and active relations with similar firms outside Italy meant that access to knowledge about recent developments elsewhere was lacking and the very important function of technology transfer was underdeveloped, to say the least. The software sector was well represented in Milan, but the industry was composed of many small firms that were undercapitalized and isolated. As a result the technological standards of this sector were considered to be well below those of similar/competing urban regions elsewhere in Europe and exports were negligible. Throughout manufacturing, research tended to be done in-house rather than transferred from advanced centers in the rest of the world. Public research was far below what it should have been, given Milan's rather dominant position in the Italian economy.

A somewhat similar story is to be found in the financial sector. True, this is one of Milan's strong points, but the Italian policy toward its banking sector did not work to Milan's benefit in the long run. The policy was that of maintaining many local banks – presumably on the understanding that no one in Siena would ever be able to get a loan from a bank based in Turin. So Italy remained a country with many small banks and in which the large banks were still small by international standards, and in which these banks had underdeveloped relations with the banking world outside Italy. City and Italian leaders understood that Milan had the potential to become one of the premier financial centers in Europe, but they seemed to be unaware that certain actions had to be taken to realize this potential.

So what was the strategic thinking of Milan's leadership at this time? Using as a base the observations that have just been made in this section, the plan was presented in the Milan Project report which was issued in 1987.[8] There were three elements that were central to the project: 1) a cooperative structure of governance that would combine the sub-national state of Lombardy, the province of Milan, the commune of Milan and the surrounding communes; 2) the five local universities would provide the necessary population of scientists and researchers; and 3) the Milan business and financial world whose active engagement would provide the necessary financial resources. There were eleven sub-projects in which analysis was done on topics such as new technologies and the social structure, the Milan financial sector, urban stresses and conflicts, the labor market, and so forth. Four specialized conferences were held in which the results of this analysis were presented, with a very useful discussion of 'vicious' and 'virtuous' circles and longer term consequences of actions or the lack thereof.

The result was a set of eight areas of interest for which analysis of the current and recent situation was examined and some suggestions as to what ought to be done to develop the potential for, for example, decision-making or headquarters functions, the financial services sector, research and technology, the place of Milan in the European urban network or hierarchy, regional governance, and effective coordination of actions and policies among the municipalities of the greater Milan region. This was the 'big' strategic planning effort of Milan prior to the current one. It was a very substantial undertaking; unfortunately, the 'tangentopoli' political corruption scandal, to be discussed in the next chapter, made it impossible to realize the objectives of the Milan Project.

Turin

In the post-SEA years Turin officials appeared to be rather content with their situation and confident that what had sustained the local economy to that moment in time could be relied upon to do so in the years to come. Italian industrialization had begun in Turin, thanks to factors such as cheap hydro-electricity from the nearby Alps. Access to cheap energy fueled the development of the automobile, textile machinery and consumer electronics industries. Large firms such as FIAT and Olivetti had come to dominate the economy; they were already globally-focused companies so the adjustment to the completion of the internal market should pose no problems for them. True, the rest of the economy consisted of small firms whose managers did not think much beyond their own province, Piedmont. But FIAT and Olivetti could be trusted to carry Turin through the adjustments to the SEA and whatever else was in store in the future. At this time there was no agency in the urban region that was dedicated to encouraging inward investment by foreign companies. Turin was already an internationally focused city and the issue of adjustment problems was thought to be more relevant for those cities whose economies were focused primarily on the Italian market.

Housing was not perceived to be a problem for the city as there was a movement of people to the suburbs and it was anticipated that a proposed subway would solve any transportation problems by the end of the 1990s. There was no need to seek out foreign investment since FIAT and Olivetti were well-established multi-national companies. The education system was geared to engineering and the first-class program at the Politecnic was already linked to similar programs at Brighton, Graz, Grenoble, and Stuttgart. The Agnelli Foundation had just sponsored the Technocity initiative which, among other things, supported research and the training of labor, with Turin's strong industries, electronics and mechanics, being the primary foci. The financial sector was growing nicely and was second in Italy only to Milan, and the banks were working with smaller companies to get them prepared for the increased competition that was promised by the SEA. Finally, the airport was third after Rome and Milan for cargo.

With this solid base, Turin leaders thought their economy was poised to assert itself on a broader stage. One conceptualization being promoted was that of the 'Four Motors,' Catalonia, Rhône-Alpes, Baden-Württemburg, and Piedmont, a concept about which regional administrations were enthusiastic but which fell on deaf ears when presented to the business community where decisions were made on the basis of profit rather than on that of grand designs.

The city government itself had no mandate for economic development; this was given to the Chamber of Commerce, in this instance both the Chamber of Commerce for Turin and the Federation of Piedmont Chambers of Commerce. The chambers had been working collaboratively with the province of Piedmont on regional economic development. It provided legal, other business services, and training for over 400 smaller firms, circulated materials to 15 000 companies, and gave seminars to 1000 individuals per year. With the city and the regional government out of the picture with regard to economic development planning, the chambers and the provincial government had this responsibility; a curious structural arrangement indeed.

A clear focus, and one that was very much in the spirit of the times in the heady days of 'A Europe of Regions,' was provided by a study done by the Institut du Future in Paris.[9] Turin was placed in the high technology Euro-region of Lyon-Grenoble-Turin, which was seen to have the potential of becoming one of the EC's centers of industry, technology, and science in the post-SEA economic space. Turin was seen as being part of this trans-Alpine region, indeed even as its capital, rather than as a part of the rest of Italy; its vocation was clearly to be on a grander scale than that of the nation. The collective assets of Lyon-Grenoble-Turin were indeed considerable and in the competition to succeed in this area this region was, at this time, thought to have a good chance. Turin itself was seen to be a 'super laboratory' with the potential to be a 'European city of science, of experimentation, and of discovery.'[10]

In spite of this, Turin in 1990 seemed to have been rather complacent; secure in the knowledge that FIAT and Olivetti had taken the economy rather far and could be expected to experience continued success in the years to come. As a consequence, there was little if any strategic thinking being done in the relevant agencies at this time. Partly this was due to the fact that manufacturing had taken the city's economy rather far during the previous century, much, rather ominously, like the manufacturing economies of Detroit, Pittsburgh and Buffalo in the United States, but it may also have been due to the weak position of the city government in planning its own economic development. The province is often torn between demand of competing urban centers and between urban and rural needs; the Chamber of Commerce represents one constituency in the community, and perhaps not the one that finds significant change very congenial. This was clearly a city that was going to face a severe test in the 1990s.

CITIES ON THE PERIPHERY

In contrast with the cities located in the core, these six cities do operate under certain disadvantages. Each of them is more or less isolated from other major economic centers. As a consequence they are likely to be the dominant or principal city in their economic region. Cooperative ventures with equals is difficult, there is often the tension between this principal city and smaller cities not willing to be directed by it, and there is also usually a competition within the sub-national governments for financial support between this urban center and rural and primarily agricultural interests. Both Barcelona and Copenhagen explicitly argued that the superior levels of government must redirect their support from rural areas to the needs of the principal city on the grounds that if the principal city were strong and vital positive spread effects would work to the benefit of the entire region; if that city should not be able to gain support for its housing, education, and other infrastructure needs the entire region would be dragged down. Agriculture was not a growing sector for the future and would not be capable of carrying the 'nation,' be it Catalonia or Denmark. Thus, the strategic challenges of these cites are generally more of a life or death nature than is to be found in the core.

Being on the periphery is not all disadvantage, however. Core cities can become complacent, while those not in the core often are a bit brasher with something to prove about themselves. In the United States, Chicago has made its 'second city' status the foundation of its assertiveness and desire to prove itself in relation to the core city, New York.[11] Within national economies on the periphery the internal disparities in regional incomes are greater relative to those in the core so that national governments may face greater pressure to tax incomes of city dwellers so as to be able to make transfers to disadvantaged rural or agricultural regions; in peripheral countries only the large urban economies can establish beneficial linkages with the richer and more dynamic core of the EU.

Thus, it is not geographical location that makes core and periphery of interest, but also the array of policy options, feasible aspirations, and a host of similar issues.

Barcelona

Of the cities in this study, Barcelona seems to have been the one with the clearest focus and most fully articulated strategic plan for the development of its economy. It would be a diversion to present fully the details of the plan or the process of developing and implementing it. But it should be noted that there was a well worked out structure of participation in decision-making and clear lines of responsibility. The plan was headed by the Executive Committee, which consisted of the City Council, the Chamber of Commerce, the Economists' and Entrepreneurs' Association, two labor unions, the Development Agency, the Trade Fair, the Employers Association, the Port, and the University of Barcelona. This was organizationally superior to the General Council which consisted of 163 economic, cultural, civic and other institutions. This approach is radically different from the rather closed and limited participation approaches taken in some other cities.[12]

Before examining the strategic objectives of the Barcelona Plan 2000, it would be useful to review what city leaders thought the situation of the city was in 1990. From this we will gain an understanding of why they set the specific objectives they did. First, it must be remembered that this was just before Barcelona was to host the Summer Olympics in 1992. On two previous occasions when Barcelona hosted such events, the two world fairs in 1888 and in 1929, the following years were marked by sharp economic declines; officials were determined to avoid this experience after 1992. Barcelona had never been a favorite of General Franco, due to its position in the Civil War of the late 1930s, and following the fall of his government the economy of Barcelona had continued to be rather weak, with unemployment being close to 20 per cent as late as the early 1980s. Weak investment, the concentration on a declining textile industry, and a lack of large firms suggested that, even though unemployment had fallen to 8 per cent, the economy needed some help. The

Olympics was the event that was to serve as the focal point for restructuring the city's economy. It is generally understood that Barcelona was able to get the support of the Spanish government only because Seville was to host the World's Fair and Madrid was the EC City of Culture, all in 1992. Since each of the principle cities had something, the gates were opened for all.

Second, this was a period in which European cities were beginning to find themselves and to become more proactive. Barcelona was an enthusiastic participant in the Eurocities movement, along with cities such as Lyon, Birmingham, Rotterdam, Milan, Frankfurt and about 25 others. Barcelona also saw itself as the principle city in an extended Euro-region that encompassed Valencia, Palma de Mallorca, and Saragossa, as well as Toulouse and Montpellier in France. This was consistent with the conceptualization of 'Europe as a network of cities,' in which national and sub-national borders were gradually becoming less significant. In the post-SEA years, cities were to become the important actors on the economic scene.

Third, there was also recognition that while the economy of the future would, to some degree, be one of advanced technology in new industries, 40 per cent of Barcelona's work force was in manufacturing. Textiles had formed the basis of the Barcelona economy during the 19th century and in the 20th this gave way to mechanical and electrical manufacturing. In the 1970s expansion of automobile and electrical and mechanical appliance manufacturing also brought the direct investment of foreign multi-national corporations. Therefore, it seemed preferable to promote advanced technology in existing manufacturing activities than to scrap this vital sector and move totally into information-communications technology, bio-engineering, and so forth. One could argue that Barcelona was, therefore, more like Chicago or Montreal than like Toronto or Boston.

Fourth, whatever direction Barcelona chose for its economy there were several general weaknesses that had to be overcome: the transportation infrastructure lacked intra-metropolitan beltways and expressways, business and financial services were underdeveloped, there was some deterioration of urban areas, the telecommunications infrastructure was in need of up-grading, there was a lack of headquarters and decision-making functions, and more facilities for training of professionals were needed. Offsetting these weaknesses were: strong traditions in manufacturing and in entrepreneurial activity, a history of effective planning, European in its orientation (perhaps because of the relationship between Catalonia and Spain), advanced health treatment and medical research, a diversified labor market, design second only to Milan, and an excellent location. This was all apparent in the assessment of Barcelona's assets and liabilities city leaders had done prior to designing Plan 2000.

More could be written about Barcelona's situation, as seen by its city leaders, but this is sufficient to give us an appreciation of why Plan 2000 included the objectives that it did. The operational structure of Plan 2000 consisted of: General Objective; Strategic Lines; Line Objectives; Tools, Measures, and Actions; Harmonization Strategies; and Strategic Plan. The heart of the process was the Strategic Lines, of which there were six: 1) reduction of social imbalances, 2) training and human resources, 3) provision of advanced services to business, 4) development of Barcelona as a cultural, trade and tourist center, 5) improvement of public services and infrastructures, and 6) industrial development. Each Strategic Line had its Ad Hoc Commission, of between 42 and 102 members representing 20–35 institutions, and a schedule for its work. This was all subsumed under three specific general strategies. The first was that of making Barcelona one of the primary centers of the Mediterranean Macro-region. The goals for this first strategy were primarily up-grading Barcelona's presence in the global urban community, including taking a leading role in Eurocities, giving Barcelonans a stronger sense of the identity and character of their city as a major urban region, and improving all aspects of the transportation infrastructure. The second strategy was improvement of the quality of life for Barcelonans and enhancing their capacities to develop their individual potential. Paramount here were improving water quality and waste treatment and reducing pollution and noise levels, developing all levels of education, research and professional skill development, improving the housing stock especially for the lower income residents, and giving a higher priority to improvement of cultural assets and infrastructures. The third and final strategy was development of the industrial and advanced business service sectors. This entailed new structures for trade fairs and distribution centers, and for bringing companies, research laboratories and universities into closer and more productive contact. This latter initiative was targeted at facilitating the inward transfer, diffusion and development of new technologies. Finally, the third strategy would seek to enhance the competitiveness and access to advanced technology for the sectors in which Barcelona already had strength: design, medical services and research, finance, urban tourism, and software in flexible manufacturing. All in all, this was a rather comprehensive and specific strategic plan.

A decade or so later, what would one expect to see as the consequence of this effort? Basically a Barcelona that is more integrated into European- and world-wide urban structures, a city with an enhanced quality of life for its residents and an enhanced attractiveness to foreign firms and professionals as a place in which to do business and live, and an economy that has retained its strength in manufacturing but with this sector being more aggressive about introducing new ways to produce its goods and new products to its output line.

Copenhagen
This city has the reputation of being a congenial and easy-going place without

a care in the world. But in 1990 Copenhagen found itself a high-income and highly-educated city in a country with the same characteristics, but with an underlying fear of being marginalized. The central issues that were discussed were focused on the tax system. Rates were among the highest in Europe, with the personal income tax base at 68 per cent and with a corporate income tax rate of 40 per cent. In addition, the value added tax, at 22 per cent, was far above that of the rest of the EC. With entry in the EC and with adoption of the SEA, tax harmonization was looming in the future; how could the expensive education and social welfare system be maintained if taxes were to be cut to EC levels? Were the attributes of Copenhagen that had made it attractive sustainable without the existing level of revenues for the central government? Denmark's, and Copenhagen's, impressive economic situation were the consequence of a very rapid development during the post-WWII period. It was not until 1940 that industrial output exceeded that of agriculture, and industrial exports rose above agricultural exports only in 1964. So to older Danes, the economic good life was a fairly recent thing, and there was some anxiety about its being maintained in the changing world of the SEA and the modern developments that were challenging national and urban economies everywhere. The Industry Council doubted that Danish firms were prepared to meet the sharper competition of the post-SEA European economy.[13] Some analysts argued that, in part because of the generous payments from the Common Agricultural Policy, the mainland of Denmark would benefit from the SEA, but that Copenhagen and the rest of the island, Zealand, would be the losers.[14] Should this be the case, given that the country lacked adequate east-west bridge connections, the country could be pulled apart. In short, there was a wide array of concerns in Copenhagen at the beginning of the 1990s.

A strategic response to this situation was made difficult in Copenhagen by two political factors. First, the Copenhagen Council had been dismantled because, according to sources in the city, the minister with responsibilities over urban matters was from a small town and had little sympathy for the capital city and the Prime Minister wanted to simplify structures. Other cities such as Barcelona and London have experienced similar decisions to disband metropolitan governing or planning councils. Second, it was argued that it is exceedingly difficult to gain acceptance of plans, since they disturb existing situations and alter property rights, in a country that is as super-democratic as Denmark. Nonetheless, two bold initiatives were undertaken in Copenhagen that were intended to put the city's economy on a more secure footing.

The first of them was establishment of the 'Principal City (Hovedstad)' initiative. It was here that the case was made, more explicitly and publicly than in any of the other ten cities, that the national government should redirect its expenditures from the needs of rural areas and agriculture to the needs of the region's and the nation's principal urban center. Only if this center was strong and generating positive spread effects would the rest of the country be economically strong. The Hovedstad initiative was to some degree designed to do what the Copenhagen Council would have done but with a more specific mandate, that of developing a strategy for economic development that would be a joint city and national government project, that would treat both Copenhagen and the rest of this economic region, that would focus on job creation, and that would examine existing regulations and identify any unwarranted hindrances to economic development. Attention was also paid to the city and its research, medical, service, culture, and tourism and congress assets. As is inevitably the case, considerable attention was also paid to the regional air and road transportation infrastructure. Unlike their counterparts in many of the other cities in this study, Copenhagen officials did not express concerns about inadequate housing, traffic congestion, crime, and the other social pathologies that seem to be rather pervasive in urban centers.

The second initiative was that of taking advantage of Copenhagen's disadvantageous geographic location. Far to the north and west of the crescent core of economic activity (DATAR's 'blue banana') Copenhagen was clearly a peripheral city, but one that was so peripheral that it could serve as a bridge to other 'cores,' those of Scandinavia and the Baltic region. Copenhagen held a conference in 1991 on 'The Top of Europe' and had offered programs such as 'Baltic Managers in International Marketing' to reach out to this latter area. However the project that was to capture the most interest and funding during the decade of the 1990s was that of constructing a bridge-tunnel link between Copenhagen and Malmö and the rest of southern Sweden. The Øresund project was intended to provide a transportation and mental link between the EC and the Scandinavian peninsula, with Copenhagen as its center, and perhaps its chief beneficiary.

The notion that Copenhagen could become the 'metropole of the North,' so to speak, was exhilarating to many but clearly there were challenges that stood in the way of its realization. With regard to the Baltic, Stockholm had at least as good a claim to be the future dominant city in this region. As we will see, Hamburg had its own visions of becoming the 'metropole of the North.' In spite of the assertions of many in Copenhagen, there really was very little reason for Swedish and Norwegian businessmen and firms to set up their EC operations in culturally congenial Copenhagen when it made good business sense to push right on to Amsterdam, or Munich, or Paris, for example. There was also the intention to make Copenhagen a 'point of access' city for firms from Asia or North America and their base for their European operations. The airport, at Kastrup, and the extensive connections of SAS were thought to give Copenhagen some hope for success. The competition was not only the established 'point of access' cities, London, Paris and Frankfurt, but also other aspirant cities such as Amsterdam.

In the early 1990s an outside consultant, Ernst and Young, was engaged to suggest a future orientation for Copenhagen's economy. In addition to high-lighting the city's potential as a 'hub of the North,' three industrial sectors were identified as being worth developing: life sciences and bio-pharmaceutical, information-communication technology and environmental technology. The assets required for each were already in place and all that was required was an extended focus on facilitating and promoting development of these industrial sectors.

Copenhagen's strategic planning response to its perceived dilemma at the end of the 1980s was imaginative and took good advantage of its advantages. But the decade of the 1990s was going to provide a difficult test.

Dresden

Of the three German cities included in this study, Dresden is the only one that was obligated to make the transition from being a city in the German Democratic Republic to that of being a member of the Federal Republic. This involved a dramatic change in the functioning of social, political and economic institutions and processes. As we shall see not all of the consequences of this are negative. But certainly there was a complete change in mentality, from one in which personal initiative, risk-taking, and uncertainty were transformed from a close to zero valuation to one in which they comprised the norm of the day. Economic survival of individuals and entities was made dependent upon the degree to which this transition could be made. What one would have expected *a priori* turned out in fact to be the case: political entities such as the city government (Landes Hauptstadt Dresden) made the transition fairly quickly but the business/economic bodies such as the Chamber of Commerce had more difficulty in coming to some accommodation with, and an understanding of, the new world of corporate business activities and relations.

The problems confronting decision-makers in Dresden were substantial. In 1991 these problems were enumerated as being: a shortage of local purchasing power, underdeveloped credit and banking services, difficulty in selling East German products in the West, out-migration of skilled workers, difficulties with regard to high rents and occupancy termination for business places, and lack of clear property ownership.[15] A decade later, all but the first two on the list have been ameliorated. In the first years after the fall of the Berlin wall and the unification of the two Germanys, over 70 000 industrial jobs were lost, 20 461 in 1991 alone. Dresden was ranked 34th among German economic centers (now that figure is 14th). The city was usually seen in comparison with its close neighbor in Saxony, Leipzig. The latter was seen as the center for heavy industrial production and Dresden was considered to be more of an administrative and governmental center. Local officials argued this was a simplistic and false notion. Certainly Dresden had its *Kulture und Kunst* (Culture and Art) but there was also a significant concentration of light manu-facturing in industries such as optics, machinery, food processing and electro-technology which had their origins as far back as the 19th century.[16] These industries came to serve as the heart of Dresden's development of high tech-nology activity – research and development, design, and production.

In the early 1990s, following both the SEA and unification, Dresden had an economic strategy that focused on three key elements: light industry, services, and a bridge function between the EU and Central Europe, principally with Poland and the Czech Republic. As is clear from the previous paragraph, this strategy did not take a great deal of thought or innovation since light industry and services were historic strengths of Dresden, and both geography and recent history made this bridge function a natural.

With regard to light industry, it should be noted that Dresden's labor force was roughly 30 per cent university and technical high school (the equivalent of university which is narrowly focused on science or commerce or music, for example) educated, 60 per cent trade-skilled, and 10 per cent unskilled. In fact, in 1992 there were 60 000 employed in technology-related firms. However the lack of large firms was a handicap in the growing need to compete in a rela-tively market-based EC economy. Only 4.2 per cent of firms had more than 50 employees and in leather, textile and clothing only 2.5 per cent employed more than 10. During the 1990s the pressures exerted by the forces of globalization and the emergence of competition from low-wage countries posed severe chal-lenges to much of Dresden's economy that was not technology related. In the technology sectors Dresden joined many other cities in attempting to interest large companies such as Siemens and IBM to establish the large facilities with global connections and access to the latest technological advances that were so clearly needed.

It was certainly not assured that Dresden would be able to insinuate itself as a regional services center since its service sector had been largely govern-ment services and other services that had been supplied in the context of a centrally planned economy. Financial services were very underdeveloped and there was little or no experience in providing the sort of business services, such as consultancies, accounting, insurance, soft-ware, and so forth, that would be needed in the 'new' economy of the EC. These business services could be expanded only if the local economy was able to attract or develop the larger sized firms that would require them. It was anticipated that health services would be competitive and that education would be strengthened through an up-grading of the university and technical high schools as well as close linkages with entities such as the Wirtschaftshochschule (School of Economics and Business) in Bayreuth. Given its location it was thought that Dresden could develop its air services, in passengers and freight, for not only the immediate Dresden region, but also for contiguous areas of Poland and the Czech Republic.

The bridge function between East and West is the strategic element that is most worthy of discussion. Here Dresden's four decades in Central European structures such as COMECON had a residual positive effect. Many individuals in Dresden had studied the Russian language and/or at universities in Central Europe. The mentality of Central Europe was not at all well suited for interaction with the West, but among individuals and institutions in Dresden and Poland and the Czech Republic there were personal relationships, a common mentality and many inter-institutional linkages that neither of the other German cities in this study, Munich or Hamburg, could share. It was not clear at the outset what could be made of this, but there were great hopes that Dresden could be in a unique position to serve as a bridge. It was felt that at least for the first few years into the 1990s both Berlin and Munich, Dresden's natural competition in this regard, would be hampered by their historic relationship of domination over the cities of western Poland and the Czech Republic. Vienna was also thought to be burdened in this way from the Hapsburg period, but in addition Austria was a country of small firms that would be incapable of extending their reach into Central Europe.

The strategic thinking of Dresden leaders was a natural outflow of history and geography. This did not assure success but it did mean that there was minimal risk of the sort that attaches to going forth into uncharted waters.

Hamburg

To a greater extent than is the case with the other cities in this study, Hamburg's economic situation is dominated by its location. It is on the sea, in the periphery, in the north and toward the east. Each of these geographic characteristics will have its impact on Hamburg's development in the post-SEA period. Historically, of course, Hamburg was a Hanseatic city, that is an important sea port in the Baltic region, it was far removed from the dynamic areas of the Rhine valley, and it was situated at the mouth of the Elbe River, which gave it access to much of Central Europe as far as Prague.[17] The economy that was built on this base was largely focused on commerce, ship-building, and industries that benefited from cheap water transportation. As of 1990, Hamburg was still planning to build upon this historically strong base – but there were problems that were clearly developing. In the economy that was emerging, bulky commodities were losing their share of total shipping as international trade expanded and lightweight goods such as machinery, consumer electronics and clothing gained importance. For these latter goods, inter-modal logistics with larger ships loaded with containers sought ports which had access to highway and rail systems and which were close to consumer markets. This altered the competitive advantage of Hamburg's port. Production of low-cost ships in emerging countries, such as Brazil and South Korea, caused a crisis in ship-building in all industrialized countries, and Hamburg was no exception. In short, the city's economy was under stress in 1990.

But there were bright spots in Hamburg's geographic position. The unification of the two Germany's gave new life to the Elbe connection as it gave access to a sea port to cities such as Leipzig and Dresden, although Leipzig's growing automotive industry and Dresden's electronic industry were not likely to need to ship their goods on barges. But in a more general sense, Hamburg was in competition with Munich, Hannover and Berlin as a bridge-city between east and west, and as a focal point for efforts to bring the business and economic activities of the former DDR up to West German standards. Similarly, Hamburg sought to become a focal point for the Baltic region and its relationship with the EC. Here Copenhagen was a competitor and, although not at this time a member of the EC, Stockholm had historically had strong political and economic relations with the Baltic States. Finally, Hamburg sought to position itself as a bridge between the EC and the Nordic countries. While Denmark was a member of the EC it was also part of the Nordic Council and this meant that the free circulation of labor and goods between Denmark and the other Nordic countries positioned the customs and immigration clearances at the Danish-German border. This was thought to give Hamburg an advantage over Copenhagen as the 'metropole of the North.' In fact, in Hamburg they liked to think of themselves as the 'southernmost Scandinavian Metropole.'[18] The improvements underway in the transportation infrastructure in Sweden and Denmark, including the Öresund bridge-tunnel connecting Copenhagen and southern Sweden, could actually work to Hamburg's advantage as rail and truck shipments might just go through Copenhagen without stopping and make their northern EC base in Hamburg.

Of all these positioning initiatives on the part of Hamburg, the only one that took any real action on the part of city leaders, other than general encouragement of private sector actors, was the unification of the two Germanys. The Senate in Hamburg adopted an 'Action Program' consisting of measures designed to enhance the city's competitiveness in comparison with Munich, Hannover and Berlin. The first was upgrading or rebuilding the rail lines connecting Hamburg with the major cities in the *neue länder*, the five provinces of the German Democratic Republic. Given the growing importance of trucking and container traffic, highways had to be improved. Major improvements were also needed in the region's communications infrastructure. While these were important for Hamburg, they required funding from the Federal government in Bonn, and all Hamburg could do was to lobby to ensure that these improvements were undertaken.

Two other elements in the Action Program, however, were under Hamburg's control. First, the Chamber of Commerce and other entities could mount programs to facilitate the engagement in expansion of trade on the part of small- and medium-sized firms. They could give assistance in marketing, distribution, financing and export know-how. Second, Hamburg organizations could increase information and communication between itself and the *neue länder*, including supporting trade missions and Economic Commissions between Hamburg and individual cities such as Dresden and Leipzig.

These initiatives were all aimed at making the best of Hamburg's geographic position. There was no understanding at this time that major changes in the composition of Hamburg's economic activities were required. The city remained the major center in Germany for media, and aerospace and the related industries were gaining strength, so city leaders felt the growth in these sectors along with the expansion of goods and services related to the city's enhanced position as a turntable, or *drehscheibe*, between the EC, the Nordic countries, the Baltic region and Central Europe would more than off-set the anticipated declines in ship-building and some other traditional manu-facturing activities. At the outset of the 1990s there was no sense of urgency on the part of Hamburg's city leaders.

Munich

This southernmost of the German cities in this study had had the most positive economy of perhaps any city in Europe. It had not experienced a significant down-turn in decades, if it had problems they were the problems of success, it had had a consistent focus to its strategic thinking since the mid-1970s, and, if anything, it was thought that rapid growth should be reduced somewhat. The strategic plan for Bavaria, and Munich as well, was put in place by provincial Minister of Industry Jaumann in about 1975, was supported by Bavarian premier Franz-Josef Strauß, and is continued today by his successor Edmond Stoibel. This focus was on Munich's and Bavaria's strength in certain areas of technology-related production, such as electronics and transportation equip-ment. In addition Munich had the largest media industry in the EC and its insurance industry was Germany's largest and ranked number two in Europe. So Munich was very comfortable in its economy and had little desire or need to make any significant changes in its strategy for economic development.

The problems that came with this success were those of a lack of industrial sites and a skilled labor shortage, as well as a shortage of suitable housing for the workers that were already there.[19] More rapid growth might not be possi-ble without a rethinking of the economic space of the Munich region and the sense of the time was that Munich had grown large enough and further growth should be managed if not contained. The labor shortage was pervasive and included not only skilled engineers and other specialists for Siemens and other companies producing sophisticated goods, but also low-skill workers for hotels and restaurants.

Entities such as the Chamber of Commerce sought to make Munich firms increasingly competitive, since 45 per cent of output was exported. An effort was being made to make small- and medium-sized firms more successful in the export market with provision of consulting services, foreign trade advisory services, participation in trade fairs, recruiting of both workers and additional firms, and so forth. There was a feeling that Munich's city government had to be continually pressured to be more 'Wirtschaftsfreundlich' (friendly to business).

The space problems were real but had not yet forced Munich's leaders to think much about reaching out beyond the city itself. Therefore, while the province of Bavaria was important for overall strategic thinking and funding for various projects, the county of Oberbayern was quite insignificant from the vantage point of Munich. As expansion continued this relationship to the county would alter dramatically.

Franz-Josef Strauß was known for his interest in South-eastern Europe – Jugoslavia, Albania, Bulgaria, and Romania. Munich has always had certain cultural, dress and culinary affinities with Hungary and Czechoslovakia. Vienna might provide competition to Munich as a bridge to the region, but Austria was not a member of the EC and Vienna was, as was noted above in the discussion of Dresden, a small firm economy without the capacity to extend its reach very far or very significantly. While dramatic extension into South-east Europe was still a potential to be realized in the early 1990s, several things were being done to establish such a bridge. For example, Munich institutions were providing training for Yugoslavian managers, and it was thought that the opening to the East would be far more important for Munich than was unification of the two Germanys.

In 1990 the strategic thinking of the leadership of Munich was concentrated on the continued development of the key sectors, realization of several 'Flagship' projects such as terminal 2 for the airport and several industrial sites, and some issues attaching to globalization – loss of some firms to low-wage countries and slow growth in the German and EC economies.

Reinforcement to Munich's strategic thinking was given by the issuance of the report *München und der Europäische Binnenmarkt*, by the IFO research institute, in 1989.[20] IFO recognized that insurance, media and electronics were Munich's strong sectors and would lead the city into the post-SEA years. Two-thirds of employment was in financial, transportation, trade, government and organization services. While these services were characterized by lower productivity gains than were to be found in manufacturing, the growth of employment was expected to be greater. While the expansion of sales of manufactured goods was expected to be weak in Germany, anticipated cost reductions should lead to turnover growth of more than 5 per cent in the EC and other export markets. The conclusion of the IFO study was that the

Munich economy should expect more opportunities than risks from implementation of the SEA.[21] With regard to the operations of the city itself, IFO had the expected things to say about housing, industrial sites and worker training. However, they did stress language training, which they considered to be especially weak in Munich, concerted efforts at city marketing, and more coordination among the staff of city departments working in related areas, such as economic development, city planning, and so forth.

All in all, in 1990 Munich could, and did, feel rather satisfied with its economic development efforts. Steady focus was given on a few areas of strength. Growth was not in itself a problem but did create some ancillary problems. Some over-all management and marginal tinkering seemed to be all that was needed.

Seville
For Seville, the 1990s was to be a decade of renewal. To understand this, we have to remember that during the industrialization of Spain in the 19th century manufacturing was concentrated in the north, due to proximity to markets, availability of capital, and so forth. Andalusia was primarily an agricultural economy, although it accounted for about one-third of Spain's GDP. After the fall of General Franco, the national government in Madrid continued to be unresponsive to the needs of the south for expenditures on infrastructure. So at the end of the 1980s, Andalusia and Seville remained primarily agricultural in production, and underprovided in infrastructure. Banking in Spain was liberalized only in 1986 and the south continued to lack access to both modern banking and adequate capital. Rich Adalusians tended to invest their funds outside the region. It was felt that scientific and technical education was adequate, however university graduates continued to migrate out of the region due to lack of suitable employment. Rice, citrus crops and other fruits and vegetables are the primary products, with the faint advantage being that products from Andalusia enter the market earlier in the season than do crops from elsewhere. Not much on which to build a modern economy.

The key non-agricultural sectors of the economy, tobacco, coinage, and shipbuilding were all dominated by state monopolies or regulation. There were few if any linkages to local firms and these remained overwhelmingly small, almost all with 6 employees or fewer, although they accounted for two-thirds of local exports. There were a few large, predominantly foreign firms, including a few from Japan, but inward investment in anything but food processing could not be considered a success.

While there was no plan to take advantage of the SEA, 1992 was nonetheless the pivotal year for Seville as this was the year of the World's Fair. City leaders in Seville naturally sought to use this event to refocus the nature of the local economy and to break the resistance to expenditures on infrastructure for which they had been asking Madrid for decades. The national government was split on the idea of the Fair; the Foreign Ministry was attracted to the idea of 1492 plus 500 years and the possibility of an opening to South America, but the Finance Ministry had no funds. As was noted in the discussion of Barcelona, once an event for each of the three primary cities, Madrid, Barcelona and Seville, was in hand, then the coffers were opened. This happened in 1987 and Seville was able thereafter to gain access to a growing stream of pesetas. While some still clung to the notion of Seville becoming a bridge between Europe and South America, others focused more on infrastructure and the hoped-for new economy.

In addition to improvement in local roads, the airport, and so forth, an effort was made to work with Aquitaine in France and Madrid for a TGV line from Seville to the north and the rest of the EU. While some thought education to be adequate, a former professor stated that classes were very large, especially in science and engineering classes, and that while there was sufficient money available for research, teaching the large classes left little or no time in which to do the research. A new university was planned for the middle of the 1990s and it was thought that this would ease the difficulties of an essentially underfunded educational system.

The central element in the post-1992 plan for the Seville economy was unquestionably the plan for the site of the World's Fair itself, Proyecto Cartuja '93. The expectations for this project were most clearly given in a study done for the city by Professor Manuel Castells.[22] The communications and telecommunications infrastructure put in place for the Fair would be the basis for establishment of a technological-scientific complex. This complex would be an incubator for new technology-related firms, the site of applied research activities – food processing was a sector mentioned by several people, and linked closely to researchers from the University of Seville and the government of Andalucia. It would facilitate the diffusion of technology, especially to the smaller firms which characterized the Seville economy. An additional role for Cartuja would be that of serving as a link between the North and the South, that is between the EU and the economies of the developing world.

Local leaders stated that relations among the public and private sectors in Seville and with the government of Andalusia were very good and that there was general agreement as to the direction the economy should take. Much of the budget, however, comes through Madrid and until the Fair was supported there were decades of frustration in Seville and Andalusia with being ignored.

In spite of the general support for infrastructure improvements and the notion of the Fair and Cartuja that would follow it, there did not seem in 1990 to be a real sense of what the post-1992 economy would look like or of the specific direction in which it would evolve. There was a commitment to strategic economic planning in Seville in 1990, but the details were left unsettlingly vague.

COMMENTS IN CONCLUSION

The decade of the 1990s began with the SEA having just been implemented and the collapse of the system of the Soviet Union, two events that had the potential of dramatically altering the context in which the urban regions of Europe functioned. Concurrently, the capacity to intervene and the primary policy mandates were reducing the role of nation states and enhancing that of both the EC and the urban regions themselves. In responding to these and the other changes noted in this chapter cities acted in line with their geographic location, their history, and the challenges and opportunities with which they were presented. While core cities would appear to have an inherent advantage over peripheral cities, the experiences of Munich and Barcelona suggest that this advantage need not be a dominant element. Some of the cities – Amsterdam, Barcelona and Munich – were able to build upon planning traditions of more than a century, while most of the others were new to planning. The familiarity of the former cities with planning has shown clearly in the planning that was undertaken in the early 1990s. The proximity of cities in the core offered the advantages of access to a large market, a dense transportation infrastructure and a variety of possibilities for joint action. However, this proximity also meant that they were confronted with powerful competitors, as is the case with Amsterdam.

The most common approach to strategic–economic planning during the first years of the decade was that of presentation of the city as a key player in a geographic structure. Hamburg looked to the Baltic and the Elbe for its future, Copenhagen began the Öresund project, Dresden sought to provide an east-west bridge, Lyon saw itself as the linkage between northern Europe and the Iberian and Italian peninsulas, and Munich reached out to central Europe and the Balkans. Some of the cities – Barcelona, Copenhagen, Lyon, Munich, and Seville – envisioned a future dominated by high technology and introduced initiatives designed to position themselves well in this new economy. Others failed to focus on this until another decade had passed. A few of the cities, of which Turin and Milan are the prime examples, seem to have thought they could continue focusing on the activities that had been keys to their economies for one or more centuries. One thinks of the frog sitting in a pot of water on a hot stove not realizing how hot it is getting until it is too late. Several of the cities, especially Amsterdam, Barcelona and Lyon, sought to develop multi-city networks and formal network organizations. Copenhagen, Hamburg and Munich failed to do much to insinuate themselves into these inter-city linkages.

The responses of these ten cities to the challenges they confronted in the early 1990s varied from the extremely active to the lethargic. In the next two chapters we will see what the consequences of these different responses were and how the city leaders changed their opinions with regard to the necessity of strategic–economic planning.

NOTES

1. Michael Emerson, Michel Aujean, Michel Catinat, Philippe Goybet and Alexis Jacquemin, *The Economics of 1992*, Oxford: Oxford University Press, 1988, p. 218.
2. I have discussed this in Peter Karl Kresl and Earl Fry, *The Urban Response to Internationalization*, Cheltenham, UK, and Northampton, MA, USA: Edward Elgar, 2005, Ch. 6.
3. For a discussion of these functions see Peter Karl Kresl, 'Gateway Cities: A Comparison of North America with the European Community,' *Ekistics*, Vol. 58, Nos. 350–51, September–October 1991, pp. 351–56.
4. Roger Brunet, *Les Villes 'Européennes'*, Paris: DATAR, May, 1989.
5. Francesca Governa and Carlo Salone, 'Italy and European Spatial Policies: Polycentrism, Urban Networks and Local Innovation Practices,' *European Planning Studies*, Vol. 13, No. 2, March 2005, p. 267.
6. *On the Road to 2015*, Amsterdam, Ministry of Housing, Physical Planning and Environment, 1988, p. 34.
7. *Strategic Assessment: The use of Telecommunication as an Element of Competitive Strategy by the City of Amsterdam*, Amsterdam: Cambridge Systematics Inc., 1989.
8. Pier Giuseppe Torrani and Giuseppe Gario, 'A Metropolitan Process Analysis Experience: The Milan Project,' Milan: Istituto Regionale di Ricerca della Lombardia, 1987.
9. Irnerio S. Seminatore, *Torino 2000*, Paris: Institut du Futur, Université de Paris VIII, undated.
10. Seminatore, p. 22.
11. As this author argued in the paper which got him interested in urban economies: Peter Karl Kresl, 'Variations on a Theme: The Internationalization of "Second Cities": Chicago and Toronto,' in *The New International Cities Era: The Global Activities of North American Municipal Governments*, edited for the New International Cities Era Project by Earl Fry, Lee Radebaugh and Panayotis Soldatos, Provo: Brigham Young University, 1989, pp. 185–98.
12. *Pla Estratègic Econòmic I social Barcelona 2000*, Barcelona: Ajuntament de Barcelona, 1990.
13. Otto Christensen, 'Er vi klar til det europæiske hjemmemarked?,' Copenhagen: Bøsen, March 15, 1988.
14. Jack Burton, 'Denmark: A Bridge to the North: *International Management*, June 1990, p. 70.
15. *Dresdens Wirtschaft in Zahlen*, Dresden: Stadtverwaltung, Amt für Wirtschafsförderung, 1991.
16. Wagner, Herbert, *Rede von Oberbürgermeister Dr. Herbert Wagner beim CDU-Wirtschaftsparteitag*, Dresden: Office of the Mayor, May 22 and 23, 1992.
17. *Hamburger Wirtshaftspolitik im vereinten Deutschland*, Hamburg: Senat, 1990, esp. p. 19.
18. *Hamburg – Ein Wirtschaftszentrum der EG*, Hamburg: Handelskammer Hamburg, 1989, p. 17.
19. *Hat München als Produktionsstandort noch eine Zukunft?*, München: Wirtschaftsamt, December 14, 1989, pp. 4–5.
20. *München und der Europäische Binnenmarkt*, München: IFO-Institut für Wirtschaftsforschung, August 1989.
21. IFO, p. XII.
22. Manuel Castells, *Proyecto Cartuja '93*, Seville: La Sociedad Estatal Expo '92, 1988, p. 55.

5. How these planning initiatives fared during 1992–2005

The plans that were, to varying degrees, adopted in the first years of the 1990s were not implemented in a 'frictionless,' high-certainty economic space in which specific actions could be expected to have predetermined consequences. In reality, this economic space was, as it almost always is, marked by very significant disturbances that made the consequences of a multifaceted SEP quite uncertain. If this was disruptive at the level of the national economy, it was potentially exaggerated at the level of the urban region given that the latter is comparatively more specialized and less diversified in its economic activity. Thus, urban economies that rely heavily on production of goods in industries that are vulnerable to outsourcing or to competition from imports from emerging economies will be particularly hard hit, while those that are specialized in high-skill labor production or high level services will be shielded from competition from abroad and will probably experience positive impacts from liberalization of goods and capital flows.

TURBULENCE

The argument could be made that disruptions caused by one or more of the elements of turbulence will create an environment that is so unpredictable and so volatile that effective strategic–economic planning by local officials will be virtually impossible. The argument could be continued to posit that, since any planning will be inappropriate to the situation that exists when the plan is subsequently implemented, local officials can do little more than react to unpredictable events in hopes of maintaining the viability of local economic actors as best can be done. Hence, the nature and consequence of turbulence must be examined at the outset of a study of urban strategic–economic planning; once this is done turbulence can be introduced into the planning experiences of the ten cities of this study in this and the next chapter. The consequences of turbulence will also be discussed in Chapter 7. So, what are the elements of turbulence from the standpoint of urban economic planning and how important have their consequences been?

The Elements of Turbulence

One of the major elements of turbulence since the SEA has been the EU's *external trade relations*, especially those with the newly opened countries of Central Europe (the Czech Republic, Slovakia, Hungary and Poland) and with the emerging Chinese economy. As is indicated in Figure 5.1 EU exports to and imports from Central Europe have expanded from $25 billion and $28 billion, respectively, in 1992 to $95 billion and $86 billion in 2002, or between three and four times. With regard to trade with China the picture is quite different, as is shown in Figure 5.2. While imports from China have almost duplicated the experience with Central Europe, rising from $32 billion to $88 billion, or by 2.7 times, during the same period, EU exports to China have increased only from $21 billion to $51 billion, by just over 2.4 times. So while trade with both areas has expanded significantly, the story here is the inability

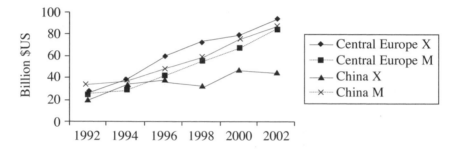

Source: International Monetary Fund, *Direction of Trade Yearbook.*

Figure 5.1   European Union trade with Central Europe and China

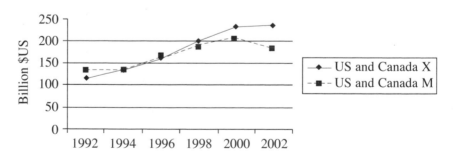

Source: International Monetary Fund, *Direction of Trade Yearbook.*

Figure 5.2   European Union trade with the United States and Canada

of EU firms to succeed in exporting to China. The EU trade balance with Central Europe has improved from a deficit of $3 billion in 1992 to a surplus of $9 billion in 2002, whereas the deficit with China has risen from $11 billion to $37 billion during this period.

While some of the imports from China are of products that were previously manufactured in industrialized countries, such as those of the EU, many of them are merely assembled and consist of components that are produced either in other low-wage economies or in industrialized economies, such as the EU itself. Manufacturing is an activity that is predominantly done in or close to large urban economies. Trade with Poland, Hungary, the Czech Republic and Slovakia is more closely integrated with production in the EU and the expanding demand, albeit slowly, in these economies has had the effect of allowing the EU to maintain its trade surplus with its primary Central European trading partners.

When we turn to EU trade with two established industrialized economies, the US and Canada, the picture is just the reverse of that of trade with China. Here EU exports have more than doubled during the period from $115 billion to $238 billion, while the stagnating EU market has increased its imports by only 40 per cent, from $132 billion to $185 billion; the $17 billion trade deficit of 1992 has been transformed into a surplus of $53 billion a decade later.

The *common currency* for the EU members that chose to participate, the euro, replaced the European Currency Unit which had served as a unit of account but not as a circulating currency on January 1, 1999. At that time the value of the euro was about 1.18 to the US dollar. By the end of 2000 it had fallen to just 0.85, four years later the euro had soared to 1.34 to the dollar, and as this is written in early 2006 the rate had settled to 1.20. The initial decline was about 28 per cent, the subsequent rise from 0.85 to 1.34 was over 57 per cent and the most recent decline was by over 10 per cent. By any yardstick, this is rather extreme currency volatility over a period of just six and a half years.

Behind both the trade performance of the EU and the exchange value of the euro is an important causal factor – the *macro-economic performance* of the Euro zone as an economic region. Table 5.1 presents US economic performance relative to that of the Euro zone, and data for the rate of unemployment. The table begins with 1995 as this is the first year for which the OECD gives data for the Euro zone. During the period 1995–2003 it is clear that US macro-economic performance was superior to that of the Euro zone in the three series given: growth of gross domestic product, manufacturing output and retail sales. The figures for GDP and manufacturing output indicate that the US economy has grown more rapidly than that of the Euro zone, but the difference in growth of retail sales for the two economies explains that the trade surplus the Euro zone has *vis-à-vis* the US is an indication of economic weakness

Table 5.1   Macro-economic performance – United States and the Euro zone

	1995	1997	1999	2001	2003
GDP (1995=100)*	100.0	107.6	104.6	108.0	109.7
Manufacturing output (1995 = 100)*	100.0	107.2	109.8	104.7	105.6
Retail Sales (1995=100)*	100.0	107.9	106.9	117.8	126.3
Unemployment rate – United States	5.6	4.9	4.2	4.7	6.0
Unemployment rate – Euro zone	11.3	11.6	10.9	8.0	8.9

Note: *The index is US performance divided by that of the Euro zone.

Source: OECD, *Main Economic Indicators*, various years.

rather than of strength. This weak macro-economic performance is one of the major negative factors in the future of the ten urban regions that are included in this study.

In addition to these macro-economic and global elements of turbulence that confront the EU's major urban regions, there are some less dramatic but nonetheless powerful *micro-economic developments*. First, there has been the opening of financial markets and the impacts this has had on the domestic banking structures of several of the EU economies. Countries, such as Italy, which have chosen to maintain banking systems that are composed of many small- and medium-sized banks are ill-prepared to meet the challenges of larger banks from Germany, the Netherlands and Spain that are intent on creating EU-wide structures through a policy of acquisition of banks in several countries. Insurance companies are primarily large funds of paid in premiums that need to be placed in financial markets. Governments often feel that if they can exert sufficient control over the operations of insurance companies they can be more certain that those placements will be made in national financial institutions rather than being sent abroad to increase the capital stock elsewhere. These local concerns are often not amenable to the logic of overall efficiency gains. Second, the DG for Competition has in recent years become much more activist in its efforts to promote a true EU economic space. It has been aggressive in applying common, transparent, pro-competition rules of operation with regard to cartels, transportation, energy, mergers and acquisition, with its interventions being aimed at both EU and extra-EU firms. As established ways of doing things, protected markets, long-lasting relationships among firms and status quo-preserving policies of governments have all come under examination and revision, much of the productive activity of the EU has been disrupted. Again, the long term EU-wide benefits are set along side the short term local need for adjustment with the result being resistance to what, in the framework of the Maastricht Treaty on Economic and Monetary Union, must be considered to be 'progress.'

The Consequences of Turbulence

The major elements of turbulence that have had the potential to affect negatively the performance of the ten cities have just been enumerated. The importance of this turbulence for any individual city was largely determined by the economic structure and specialization of that city. Since the German economy has been so sluggish throughout the period of this study, cities such as Dresden and Amsterdam, whose economies sell many of their goods and services to Germany, have been particularly hard hit by macro-economic stagnation. Munich and especially Hamburg are linked to aerospace production and as long as Airbus finds the global market to be receptive they are far less affected by the state of the German or EU economies. But for these latter cities the exchange value of the Euro can pose significant problems if it rises and Airbus consequently loses sales to Boeing. The opening to Central Europe has increased demand of some EU 15 products, but this region has also become an attractive place to relocate some production from cities in the west. Manufacturing centers such as Turin and Barcelona have lost production facilities to locations in Central Europe. While both Hamburg and Dresden were able to develop important logistics and economic relationships especially with Poland and the Czech Republic, Munich was disappointed in the economic impact of the opening to the East due primarily to the weakness of the demand for Munich produced goods there.

Passage of the SEA had very positive impacts on both of the Spanish cities, coming as it did so soon after Spain became a member of the EEC. Barcelona in particular was able to insinuate itself as a key participant into the European urban structure and to use membership and the SEA as vehicles for the transformation of its economy following the isolation of the Franco years.

Increased competition from Asia has had a broad based negative impact on industries such as ship-building, steel, motor vehicles, electronics and consumer goods. Hamburg saw its ship-building industry virtually disappear but both it and Amsterdam became centers for Chinese offices related to logistics and marketing. Munich lost much of the production of Völkl skis to China, but has been able to retain production of the high quality and high price end of the product line as well as the headquarters; this can be seen as a response that is typical of that of many EU urban regions – the low skill activity is lost to Asia but the high end, design and headquarters functions remain in Europe. Cities that have traditionally been centers of the textile industry, such as Barcelona and Dresden, have lost this activity to producers in Asia and other low wage countries.

So macro- and micro-economic and global and regional political turbulence have had their impacts on the ten cities studied, but the specific impacts are dependent upon the economic structure and specialization of that individual urban region. This is, of course, as should be expected. The seriousness of these consequences will be examined in greater specificity as we discuss the experiences of each of the cities.

As a more general proposition, the elements of turbulence could have enormous implications for the process of urban strategic–economic planning. These implications range from local factors such as the stability of economic and political relationships within the urban region, the break-down of whatever common vision existed prior to the turbulence, and the continued validity of the assumptions about the future on which the planning is to be based, as well as such global-contextual factors as the openness of the global economy, the feasibility of a production and distribution system based on movement of inputs and finished goods across national borders, and the integrity of global financial structures. National economies such as Israel, or most of the nations of Africa and of the former Soviet Union, have experienced turbulence of this nature for decades and have adopted responses ranging from relative autarky to structured trading relationships with a limited number of privileged partners. It is, however, a new experience during the post-WWII period for the industrialized and internationally open economies of North America, Europe and Japan. Certainly, the urban economies of the industrialized nations, which have emerged into global relationships during the past two decades prior to 1990, would be confronted with the need to adapt their actions to this environment of turbulence.

In 1986, on the eve of the decade covered in this chapter, an edited book was published with the title *Planning in Turbulence*.[1] The contributors were Canadian and Israeli academics and planners, with the experience of Israel being the central commonality for the authors of the chapters. While the thinking articulated in this work has evolved in the ensuing two decades, some of the basic ideas are still valid and it does give us an understanding of the way in which planners approached the context of turbulence with which they were being confronted at the outset of the period being studied in this chapter. It can be argued that Israel is fraught with specific, local elements of turbulence, but it cannot be denied that this is a prime example of a society living in a context of turbulence. David Morley and Arie Shachar argue that in this state of intense uncertainty certain phenomena are present: 1) 'there exists a high degree of goal conflict at all levels of society, to the extent that clear-cut directions are not easily discernible,' 2) 'the deluge of information to which we are submitted itself blurs the edges of underlying values and goals,' and 3) the turbulence creates 'a pervasive class of problems that was no longer amenable to formal planning at all.'[2]

Given the security dimension of the Israeli case, some of the relevant observations will be more suitable for a discussion of the decade or more in the wake of the spate of terrorist attacks that have followed September 11. One consequence is the fact that a high degree of uncertainty about events in the near future makes it very difficult to do long-run planning and the attention of the political community is drawn to focus on the short-run. When a society is primarily responding to short-run considerations there is a premium to be paid for effective institutional response to relatively complex situations. The greater the complexity and the uncertainty the more it may become necessary to resort to 'improvisation as a planning style.' But improvisation 'has to be accompanied by a capacity to look at counter-conventional ideas – to be able "to think the unthinkable" – and to foresee sophisticated policy shifts as they are emerging.'[3] Planners and their political masters must be willing to accept higher levels of risk taking in their decision-making. If crisis and turbulence become 'routine,' economic planners may find themselves marginalized as considerations that are closer to the viability of the state gain centrality in decision-making.

Decision-makers are overloaded with information, not all of which is consistent with the rest of the observations. Individuals and institutions with their own objectives and perspectives are difficult to meld into one coherent approach or vision, and some see this as an opportunity to assert their particular view to the detriment of the common effort. All of this makes some central problems exceedingly difficult, if not impossible, to resolve. We will return to this topic in the final chapter of the book, but for now it is sufficient to note the difficulties for planning that are inherent in a period of turbulence, crisis and uncertainty.

CITIES IN THE CORE

The basic understanding about cities in the core is that those in the core will be more tightly integrated economically into their close surroundings than are those on the periphery. The latter will have little in the way of a near-by market for their output and will be comparatively more linked with distant markets. Data for exports by metropolitan regions are not available for the EU so it would be difficult to test this assertion. But the essential characteristic of cities in the core is that because of its economic advantages, both cities and people tend to congregate there. Therefore, within a radius of 100 or 500 miles a core city will have access to far more consumers than is the case for peripheral cities. Thus for turbulence such as terrorist attacks that makes travel of people or goods more costly or time consuming or increases the feeling of being under siege – a permanent state of crisis – core cities are likely to find that a larger portion of their economic activity will be negatively affected than will be true for peripheral cities.

Core cities in the EU are also more likely to be negatively affected by economic stagnation in the major member economies since they are relatively more dependent upon aggregate demand of large contiguous nations. Amsterdam is far more dependent upon the German market and Milan is more dependent on the French or German markets than are Seville and Dresden on French market demand.

Most of the other elements of turbulence – the opening to Central Europe, the emergence of China as a competitor, introduction of the Euro, outsourcing, and so forth – should have a generalized impact that is greater for peripheral than for core cities. If the former are indeed more reliant on distant export markets, it stands to reason that a rise in the value of the Euro or slow-down of growth in North American or Asian markets should have more negative impact on them than on core cities.

Amsterdam

The stresses in the Amsterdam economy, which had begun to appear by 1990, developed fully by mid-decade. Ship-building collapsed and became a mere skeleton of the traditional industry, Fokker aircraft was reduced to producing only wings for aircraft assembled elsewhere, and unemployment rose to about one in seven members of the labor force. While finance continued to be an important activity for Amsterdam, with large banks such as ING and AMBRO being important second tier institutions in the EU, the sector was hardly what it was in the 16th century or even in 1900. More than the other cities being studied, Amsterdam was affected negatively by the lack of economic growth in the EU and especially by the stagnation in Germany, the Netherlands' most important trading partner. Nonetheless, during the period 1995–2001, Amsterdam was at the top of the economic growth ranking for large EU cities; clearly some sort of adjustment had been made.

In one sense, Amsterdam continued to function as a key part of the Randstad, along with Rotterdam and the Hague. Logistics was central to the function of the Randstad. The port of Rotterdam was one of the EU's largest, with much of its cargo passing through to Germany; most of the shipments to Amsterdam, however, were destined for a radius of 25–30 kilometers from its port. Thus Amsterdam's port activity was more of an integrated element in a local industrial structure than was the case with Rotterdam. Schipol airport is in a suburb of Amsterdam and it continued to be the other component in the logistics activity of the region. The merger of the Dutch airline, KLM, with Air France could have posed a serious threat to the Amsterdam economy, but Schipol is apparently guaranteed 30 per cent of the joint intercontinental traffic of the merged airline. The two hubs actually have somewhat different functions with Air France serving the *francophone* areas in Africa and Asia and with KLM serving the Americas and Asia, with its link with Northwest Airlines. KLM also has a rich network throughout Europe and serves 21 cities in the UK, whereas British Airways serves only nine. So Schipol has continued to develop its role as a point-of-access city to the EU and as a hub for North American and Asian travelers to Europe.

As the decade continued, Amsterdam continued to have success in attracting direct foreign investment and headquarters offices. There have been roughly 90–100 new foreign offices in the Amsterdam area, with about 55 per cent of them being subsidiaries of US firms. The city also has about two-thirds of the distribution centers in the EU, with many of them being Japanese and Chinese offices of five or fewer employees, as well as 1,650 EU regional corporate headquarters offices. Two factors other than the logistics facilities have helped Amsterdam succeed in this activity: 1) the persistent effort to cut bureaucratic procedures and red tape for foreign firms, and 2) the facility almost all officials and business people have in conducting their business in the English language. These two factors are especially important for representatives of Asian companies, and is a clear advantage for Amsterdam and the rest of northern Europe over France, Spain, Portugal and Italy. Both factors have been developed as results of conscious policy decisions on the part of elected and appointed officials in both Amsterdam and the national government.

Spatial or land use planning has always been important in the Netherlands and Amsterdam has both found itself in a challenging situation and planned imaginatively. While spatial planning has not been developed to any degree in this study, for Amsterdam it has a more direct linkage to strategic–economic planning than is the case elsewhere. As was noted in Chapter 4, Amsterdam has had the unusual problem of having too much social housing (about 75 per cent) and too little housing for the middle and managerial classes. As a consequence, the city, while retaining its charm and vitality, was becoming a residential space for immigrants and low income residents. The absence of suitable housing was forcing other social groups to move to the suburbs or even to other parts of the country. But more crucially, it was making it difficult for Amsterdam to realize its potential as a headquarters and decision-making center in the EU. The solution was to create new places for those who required other than social housing. To the north, across the river, there are some small towns that are attractive residential areas but much of the land is a marsh which is suitable only for wetlands conservation. The middle classes clustered to the west, while higher income housing was concentrated in the south (Vondel Park) and in towns such as Hilversum, to the south-east. The imaginative solution for additional middle class housing was the creation a decade ago of Java Island in the shallow sea immediately to the east of the city center; some apartments for high income residents were built along the water front.

The vitality of the city center has been challenged by some difficulties

Amsterdam has had with assimilation of immigrant groups. The initial recent immigrants, during the 1960s and 1970s, were from Indonesia and Surinam – countries in which Dutch was a major language. These immigrants were absorbed with little difficulty; they found jobs, integrated into the community and, in fact, are now one of the major components of the home owners on Java Island. During the 1980s and 1990s, however, Moroccans have been one of the primary immigrant groups; they do not speak the language, have tended to entrench themselves in their own ethnic community, have had less success gaining employment, and are seen by the rest of the population as being a group that is characterized by the usual set of social pathologies. Unease with this separate community within the greater Amsterdam community was by all accounts one of the factors that induced the Dutch to vote so strongly against the EU 'Constitution' in early June 2005.

In summary, the Amsterdam economy was negatively affected by external factors such as the slow growth of the EU and German economies as well as by internal factors such as an inability to absorb socially and economically its most recent immigrants. But the Netherlands has had a long history of economic planning and Amsterdam has been rather successful in taking actions that have enhanced the metropolitan region's competitiveness and have enabled it to realize its potential as a point-of-access and a headquarters city. In the next chapter, we will examine whether these functions will provide an adequate base for the economy of the next decade(s).

Lyon
To a considerable degree, during the period from 1990 until today, Lyon has continued to be strongly affected by its second city status within France. One indication of this is the strong adherence on the part of city leaders to participation in Eurocities, which began as an organization of 20–30 cities of a similar status. Now Eurocities has expanded to over 100 member cities and this second city identification has been weakened, but leaders in many of the original members such as Turin, Barcelona, Manchester, Rotterdam, and Lyon meet often to share problems and their solutions and to consider projects which they could propose as a group to EU agencies in Brussels. It is agreed that this grouping has little or no attraction to the major firms in these urban regions, but benefit to them has long ceased to be a major concern of Eurocities. A second indication of Lyon's second city status is the frustrating experience the city has had in upgrading its airport to something more than a minor regional facility. The efforts undertaken periodically to establish flights from Lyon to one or more cities in North America, for example New York and Montreal, or in the Middle East or Asia, have never succeeded. The problem here has been the unwillingness of Air France to allow this to happen. Having merged with KLM, Air France is content to have only two European hubs,

Charles de Gaulle (Paris) and Schipol (Amsterdam-Rotterdam). Whenever a US airline began a connection to New York, Air France would establish several similar flights, thus making the Lyon market unattractive financially. The realization has come slowly in Lyon that the city simply does not have the critical mass of traffic to support direct inter-continental flights.

The Four Motors structure (Lyon, Barcelona, Stuttgart and Turin) has been replaced by two others completely opposite in their geography. The first is Lyon-Geneva-Turin, in recognition of the possibilities for successful initiatives in this tighter triangle of relationships in several sectors of activity. The second is the Lyon-Montreal-Beijing-Shanghai sort of structure of periodic meetings of officials, visits of trade delegations, and so forth. This structure is more in accord, than was that of the Four Motors, with the economic realities confronting major economic actors in each urban region. Of French regions, Rhône-Alpes is the most active in the promotion of inter-city and inter-region structures, and Lyon and Lille are the only French cities to participate in Eurocities.

The focus on small- and medium-sized firms was dealt a couple of blows that make significant action here problematic. First, the major banking institution in Lyon, and a major supporter of the smaller firm initiative, Credit Lyonnais, suffered major financial difficulties, the resolution of which transformed the bank into just another French bank headquartered in Paris. Second, the Lyon stock exchange failed and with it the hoped for specialization in the exchange of shares of smaller firms. As we will see in the next chapter, the focus on small firms is still part of Lyon's strategy, but it is less centered on financial aspects.

Given the rather ambitious plans city leaders had for Lyon at the beginning of the 1990s, it should not be surprising that one topic that emerged from the experience of implementation was that of bringing individuals and entities from different sectors together and getting them to work together. The mentalities or cultures of academics, businessmen, officials, entrepreneurs and researchers in laboratories are often dramatically different and they can be welded into effective common action only through local structures that combine a certain respect for these cultures with something that makes it work. Clearly, in the case of Lyon things did work. The major projects, such as the Tony Gerland Science/Technology Park, the completion of the TGV lines (with Lyon-Turin still to be accomplished), and the congress center Cité Internationale, were realized in spite of the cultural contrasts/conflicts of those participating in their planning and implementation. The factor that emerged in the case of Lyon is the personality and status of the individual at the head of the structure. Communauté Urbaine de Lyon is the administrative entity that provided the coordination, and the Mayor of Lyon during much of this period was Raymond Barre, former French Prime Minister. Barre was highly respected by all participants, he had good connections with the government in Paris, and he was a highly effective leader. At other times during this period the then mayor had personal difficulties and things rather fell apart. So Lyon demonstrates that who is in charge is a vital consideration for successful implementation and realization of a strategic plan.

Finally, with regard to the macro- and micro-economic turbulence, during the 1990s this did not seem to be a problem for Lyon. China and India and other developing economies were causing some difficulties for vulnerable industries but the threat was not seen to be pervasive. Markets were being opened but the EU and the governments of member states were creatively foot-dragging so the pace was slower than had been imagined when the processes of the SEA were adopted. The Euro caused some difficulty but it was primarily that of uncertainty. After the dramatic events of the early 1990s, the Euro settled into a slow steady decline in relation to the dollar and other currencies, and this was certainly beneficial to the producers and exporters of Lyon. Local firms were far less aware of the changes in the international economy than were the large multinational firms, and it is these firms that caused difficulty for Lyon. As interest rates, inflation, exchange rates, local labor costs and so forth moved against production in Lyon, large firms relocated their activities accordingly.

All in all, Lyon seems to have emerged from the 1990s with much of its late 1980s economic strategy accomplished although, as has been noted, there were disappointments along the way. A clear strategy, an effective local institutional structure, and someone in charge who has status, clout and the respect of all go a long way toward ensuring success.

Milan

It was clear in Milan that the inward focus of its business, research and financial sectors was not going to be effective in the post-SEA world. Borders were becoming less economically significant, domestic markets were being flooded with imported goods, and competing urban regions in the EU and elsewhere were arousing themselves to the realization that a new way of thinking and acting was required if marginalization was to be avoided. City leaders in Milan were aware of this, but they were constrained in action by several factors that were either local or Italian in nature.

First is the fact that the tradition of planning in Milan had always been essentially limited to territorial initiatives with regard to transportation and communication infrastructures, to land use planning, to the supply and quality of industrial sites and housing, and so forth. There was little if any experience with strategic–economic planning. Certainly the territorial planning was closely linked to the needs of the economy and had its impacts on the economy, but economic considerations were never the primary consideration in the design of the plan or its initiatives. An economist looking at what was done would in all likelihood declare the exercise to have been an inefficient one – that is, not an efficient use of resources or of the potentialities of the planning process.

Second, the structures of governance in Italy made metro-wide planning virtually impossible at this date. This was especially true in the situation in which Milan found itself in the 1990s with many economic activities being transferred from the city of Milan to the outlying rings of suburbs. The city became less dominant in planning and actually had no mandate for planning of the economy – as has been noted earlier the chamber of commerce, the province, and other economic entities had this function but there was no single locus of power that could compel concerted action on the part of independent actors. In contrast to Turin, the Milan territory is a very densely structured and utilized one. This space is divided up into the city proper, and several other major regions. Each of them has its own notion of what is needed and of how to proceed with getting it done. Whatever was accomplished, in a collective sense, had to be the result of voluntary action, and this always means lengthy discussion and compromise – another exercise in inefficiency.

Third, and most importantly, in 1992 the city became embroiled in the *tangentopoli* political corruption scandal that rocked all of Italy with its consequences. Milan was the center of the entire scandal and the effect of this was to immobilize public authorities in any big projects, expenditures or initiatives for the ensuing decade. The well thought-out strategic planning initiative of Milan, the Milan Project, sadly came to naught, and no other vision could be considered or discussed until the aftermath of the scandal had been overcome through time. So, for ten years Milan was dead in the water, so to speak, and the promise of the Milan Project was impossible to realize.

Unfortunately, this period was one of dramatic change and development throughout Europe. Munich kept on its path of expansion, cities such as Lyon became mobilized and accomplished major advances, and the Spanish cities developed substantially now that Spain was a member of the EC and they could gain access to funding from Brussels. They also hosted the Summer Olympics (Barcelona), the World's Fair (Seville) and the European City of Culture (Madrid) in 1992 and had at least the potential of a major economic stimulus and the knowledge that they had 'arrived' on the European scene. During this crucial and exciting decade of change in Europe, Milan was self-absorbed in political recrimination and reform. It was not until the end of the decade that Milan could begin, once again, to focus on its future economic development and to design a plan to realize the resulting objectives.

Turin
The complacency on the part of Turin's economic leaders that was noted in the

previous chapter appears, in retrospect, to have been astonishing. Following the OPEC oil price hikes industry everywhere had experienced a period of difficulty. Manufacturing value added fell in Turin during the 1980s by 3 per cent, but there was some solace in this because the decline for Italy as a whole was 12 per cent.[4] In 1988, a respected, local research office of the regional government of Turin (*La Provincia di Torino*) noted 'the return of the large firms' and stated that 'the driving force remains firmly and completely with the large and medium-sized firms.'[5] Sadly, this driving force was to be a weak one during the next decade and a half – Olivetti has had its difficulties, and FIAT lost market share, shifted some production out of Italy, dramatically reduced its work force in Turin during 1986–1996 from 92 000 to 47 000, and was profitable in only three years during 1992–2001. The profit in those three years was dwarfed by the loss in 1993 alone.[6] Thus, the 1990s were not kind to Turin and this climate of stagnation made realization of some of the objectives of city leaders difficult or impossible. The subway had yet to be built (completion of the first line was expected by the end of 2005), the high-speed rail and road tunnel through the mountains that separate Turin and Lyon is still a dream, and the technology agenda was hampered by cut backs in funding for universities by the government in Rome, in spite of strong evidence that there is a close linkage in the Italian system between publicly funded research in universities and other facilities and innovation in production by firms.[7]

As this difficult decade progressed it became apparent to many observers that one of the key problems for Turin, as well as for most other cities in Italy, was the structure of government and of responsibilities and the capability of the system to make strategic decisions. The lack of an effective system of governance was both cause and effect of: 1) a lack of a sense of a metro-wide sense of community, 2) no shared vision of the future, 3) a resentment and suspicion of the intentions of large Turin on the part of its smaller 'partner' municipalities, and 4) an inability to implement coordinated plans for either economic development or infrastructure initiatives.[8] It was found to be impossible to weld together the economic strategies of a large multi-national enterprise such as FIAT, with its global vocation and its proclivity to subordinate its presence in Turin to its need to generate profits, with the totally locally-oriented vision and aspirations of the local city leaders. The difficulty of coordinating regional, provincial and municipal planning was a problem that was endemic to the Italian structure of governments and not just a problem of Turin.

The general macro-economic stagnation hit Turin hard as the participation of Italy in the exchange rate mechanism resulted in uncertainty about the value of the Lira and then alternating significant benefits or hardships in both the domestic and export markets for Turin manufacturers as the rate fell or rose. This only added to the secular deterioration of Turin's position *vis-à-vis* the rest of Italy: in 1951 output per capita in Turin was 2.3 times that of the national average; by 1961 it had fallen to 1.6 times; today it is only 23 per cent above that average. Between 1980 and 1993, while value added per capita stayed roughly 130–135 of the national average for Bologna and Milan and rose from 106 to 120 for Rome, value added per capita for Turin fell from about 125 to 107 of the national average.[9] Clearly Turin was in economic difficulty, beyond the general malaise that afflicted the EU economies in general and the rest of Italy in particular.

The *tangentopoli* scandal did not affect Turin to the degree that it did Milan, but Turin had had a less dramatic counterpart a decade earlier, when in 1983 the mayor's office was involved in financial corruption. This effect was similar, however, as public projects were halted for most of the next decade. The period 1993–1997 was, however, one in which progress in governance was made. The election of Mayor Castellani brought budgetary reform and an end of a series of deficits in the city's finances. His group of advisors became a *de facto* planning commission and his ideas became a *de facto* economic plan. This included realization of the plans for Technocité, a research district to the north-east of Turin, as well as initiatives that laid the groundwork for what would be accomplished in the next decade. His presence was a counter to the notion that was taking root among the population that, with the difficulties of FIAT and Olivetti, Turin was entering a period of decline.

Turin is an example of a city that was lacking a strategic focus at the beginning of a decade of difficulty, in part because of ineffective governmental structures, and in part because of over confidence in the resurgence of its traditional economic structure in a rapidly evolving economic environment which made that resurgence impossible to realize. In fact, Turin manufacturing was in the midst of a long process of de-industrialization and lost over 40 per cent of its employment in the quarter century between 1971 and 1996. When the crisis developed, the urban region lacked a 'shared vision of the future of the area – a necessary premise for any attempt at strategic planning.'[10] The partial relief that was provided by the expansion of the service sector was not the result of anything done by city leaders, but rather by the effects, felt everywhere in the industrialized world, of such factors as demographic change, higher incomes, women increasingly joining the work force, and technological change.

Much of the imagination of city leaders was given over to the notion of Turin being locked in a Turin-Lyon-Barcelona structure with Lyon being the conduit between northern Europe and the Iberian and Italian peninsulas. This was fine for Lyon, as one could envision a transportation node there with trans-shipment, warehousing, inter-modal connections, value added activities, and so forth. But in this structure would Turin ever be more than a point of transit, through which goods flowed without having any local impact? Would the only benefit be somewhat faster access to markets for Turin products? As has been noted above, this sort of conceptualization of space is enormously appealing to cartographers and city leaders, but is usually noted with only passing curiosity by the people who produce the goods, and distribute and market them.

The strategic planning situation does improve for Turin toward the very end of the decade of the 1990s, but that is a story for the next chapter.

CITIES ON THE PERIPHERY

Cities on the periphery, as was argued above, are relatively more likely to be negatively affected by turbulence such as stagnation in their own national economy or in the global economy since they lack the dense market in close proximity that is enjoyed by core cities. Consider the geographic isolation of Seville, Dresden and Copenhagen in comparison with the position of Amsterdam, Lyon or Milan and the point is inescapable. Most peripheral cities are not nested in the dense transportation network that is typical of core cities, so disruption of rail and major air hubs will impose less of a burden on their economies than is likely for core cities. But for all of our peripheral cities, with the exception of Copenhagen, fluctuations in the value of the Euro will have a disproportionate impact on their economic activity. This latter observation is true to the degree that peripheral urban economies are relatively more reliant on global demand than are core urban economies. Most of the six peripheral cities are in nations that were not early members of the European Community; thus, their integration into the rest of the EU is more recent than is that of the core cities and any disturbance that would reduce the effectiveness of the integration process would bear relatively heavily on them. Most of them are also larger net recipients of transfers from Brussels and a diversion of funds from these transfers to growing requirements for security and anti-terrorism initiatives would slow down if not halt many of the infrastructure and income maintenance initiatives that have been adopted.

Much of the discussion of the comparative burden of elements of turbulence on core and peripheral cities and urban regions is speculative, in part because of the lack of data on the relevant economic activities, for example trade flows, for these entities. Nonetheless, it can be suggested with some confidence, as was done earlier in this chapter, that these two categories of cities will not be subjected to the same impacts as a consequence of economic and political turbulence.

Barcelona
More than any of the other cities in this study, with the possible exception of

Lyon, the SEA had a very positive impact on the economy of Barcelona. Furthermore, the SEA compounded the positive effects of Spain's membership in the EC. Barcelona's positive experience is largely the result of the city's assertion of itself, due, in part, to its position as a left-wing political entity in a right-wing province, the cultural relationship between Catalan Barcelona and Catalonia, and Castilian Spain and, in part, to the opportunities offered to an assertive city by the burgeoning Eurocities Movement, of which Barcelona was a charter member. Not only was access to the relatively enormous EU market significantly improved, but there was also participation in EC projects, one of which was the Airbus initiative which was centered in nearby Toulouse, just across the border in France. After an initial period of adjustment to changes that began with the OPEC price increases in the 1970s, productivity began to rise, unemployment declined and investment increased. On the negative side, the opening up to Central Europe meant a considerable delocalization of production to that area from Barcelona. Thus, while manufacturing was initially the heart of the Barcelona economy, the OPEC price hikes and then the shifting of production to the east combined to force a restructuring of economic activity in Barcelona out of traditional manufacturing, and the SEA and EC membership offered new markets and opened new possibilities in the services sector and higher value added manufacturing. These events have generated a 'forced restructuring' of the city's production out of its past reliance on manufacturing so that by 2005, 80 per cent of employment in Barcelona was in the service and knowledge sectors of the local economy.

The two primary elements in strategic thinking in Barcelona in 1990 were capturing the potential benefits from the Summer Olympics of 1992, and linkages with other Eurocities cities. The Olympics helped in the transformation of the waterfront from an unattractive dock and trucking area into one that has emphasized the residential and recreational potential of the beach and shoreline areas. There were also some residual of sporting structures and hotels, but perhaps the most lasting impact has been a very positive one on tourism. Any visitor to the Zona Gottica and the Ramblas, almost any day of the year, can attest to the touristic attractiveness of Barcelona. The city's distinctive architecture and its theaters and museums confirm that city leaders value highly cultural assets as a key element in an urban strategic–economic plan. This has had an impact of industrial activity as fashion and design have assumed an important position in the economy. For example, Renault and Volvo both have design and new product divisions in Barcelona. Thus, we can conclude that some of the major elements in the Olympic planning have been achieved.

Participation in Eurocities and other inter-urban networks has an extraordinary importance in Barcelona. The city is now the headquarters of United Cities and Local Governments, the successor to the International Union of Local Authorities, participates in Metropolis, and is a key player in CIDEU, an organization with membership of about 80 cities primarily throughout Central and South America. Through this latter organization, Barcelona has been able to position itself among Spanish ex-colonies in the New World in a way that is far more effective than the nostalgia-based approach of Seville, which we noted in the previous chapter. The fascination with Quebec, as a minority culture and language community in a larger nation state, continues but, as is the case with South America, economic linkages and transactions are insignificant on both sides of the Atlantic.

Since 1992, there has been some development of industrial clusters in Barcelona. Multi-lingual audio-visual, agro-industry, media, electronics and aerospace are the primary ones, although there is also a wish to develop the city's potential to become an actor but not a major player in bio-chemistry. City planners recognize the benefits of clusters but expressed the concern that they are often too inward-looking and may not be as open to developments in the rest of the world as would be hoped. Nonetheless, there are some ICT firms at the industrial park Marenostrum, with IBM as the key firm, logistics activities have been expanded around the linkage with France, and an industrial district '22@' has been the most important industrial site renewal initiative. 22@ is located in the eastern part of Barcelona, close to the redeveloped shoreline beach area and is intended as a place in which there will be an integration of residence and work in knowledge-intensive activities. This integration of work and residence is one of several initiatives designed to reduce reliance on the automobile by making long commuting less necessary and to expand use of public transportation. Two new lines for the Metro will also be part of this effort.

Barcelona would appear to have achieved the major objectives of its strategic thinking in the early 1990s. First, the Olympics had a positive impact on tourism, transportation infrastructure initiatives were largely accomplished. Second, the city was able to insert itself in major international inter-urban networks such as Eurocities, Metropolis and CIDEU. Finally, the transition from an economy based on traditional manufacturing to one of services and higher technology manufacturing has largely been accomplished. Barcelona became one of the 'hot' cities in the EU toward the end of the 1990s, and the challenge in this situation is always that of sustaining the forward motion and avoiding the tendency to rest on one's laurels. Thus, the experience of Barcelona during the next decade will be as fascinating as have been the previous 12 to 15 years.

Copenhagen

At the outset of the 1990s, Copenhagen's economy was in considerable difficulty. Unemployment was double digit, growth was slow, and the city was in danger of being marginalized. The complacency of the late 1980s proved to be ill-considered, and something more than the geographically based concepts of a conceptual bridge between north and south or point of access for Asian and North American firms was required. In 1994, in an attempt to improve its image and to attract more foreign firm regional head offices, the municipalities of Copenhagen and Frederiksberg and the counties of Copenhagen, Frederiksborg and Roskilde established Copenhagen Capacity. This organization has been quite successful in marketing the region and in providing input in strategic–economic thinking. Its analysis is based on three different models of decision-making: the benchmark model, the cost/benefit estimate model and the logistic model presenting to a company that is interested in building a facility in the greater Copenhagen metropolitan region some understanding of how the region compares with alternatives, an understanding of the potential net benefits of such an investment, and some sense of the strategic locational advantages of the region. This analysis is not in itself a strategic–economic planning exercise, but is fully nested in the plans of the metropolitan and regional authorities. For the past decade, the Copenhagen region has been dominated by the potential and then the actual consequences of the strategic initiative to link the Copenhagen area with its contiguous areas across the Øresund in Sweden.

The Øresund bridge-tunnel linking northern Sealand in Denmark with Skåne in southern Sweden proved to be just what was needed. The project was actually pressed for by the economic authorities in Skåne in response to an economic slowdown that was even more severe than was that in Copenhagen. Both sides of the Sound suffered delocalization of manufacturing. In Copenhagen, much of the delocalization consisted of production moving to lower cost locations to the west of Denmark in Jutland, and this was slowly replaced by higher technology activities in Copenhagen. However, in Malmö and other cities in southern Sweden industries such as shipbuilding moved to South Korea, Brazil and other lower cost countries, but nothing else moved in. In Gothenburg, to the north, the ship-building loss was made up for by increased production by Saab and Volvo in aerospace and marine engineering activities. So for Skåne the Øresund project was a life-saving venture and officials there pressed strongly for its adoption. What makes this project so interesting is that what was being attempted is not just the expansion of the economic reach of Copenhagen into adjacent territory, but the creation of a cross-border urban agglomeration in which two distinct cultures and languages, factors which made the success of the project open to doubt, were expected to blend into one, or at least to accommodate each other with little friction.

First, the legal barriers to the complete range of economic and social activities had to be removed. Each country had its own tax system, rules for settlement and for work, regulations for business activity, and so forth. During the ensuing years, great progress has been made toward creating a seamless economic space throughout the Øresund region, in part through the acceptance of each country of the *acqui communitaire* of the EC as a condition of membership, although it must be assumed that there will always be some residual vestiges of the distinct national systems that obtained prior to the integration process. Progress has not been as rapid as had been originally thought, in large part because of the position of the Swedish government. While wanting to give assistance to economic development in Skåne, this assistance has the effect of also enhancing the competitive position of Copenhagen, a city which is seen to be a threat to the position of Stockholm as a center of the Baltic, of Sweden, and of Scandinavia. At first, the Swedish government threw up considerations of environmental impacts of the bridge-tunnel project, but once this was completed their recalcitrance was shown by unenthusiastic funding of various projects. Seen from a distance, Swedes and Danes appear to be almost identical in all ways. But in actuality, a continuing challenge has been that of integrating two peoples with quite distinct languages, aspirations, and customs. For example, Copenhageners think they are rather more cosmopolitan and urban than their Swedish colleagues who live in smaller cities and towns. They also think Swedes drink a lot of alcohol, but one suspects the reality is that because alcoholic beverages are relatively cheap in Denmark, a lot of Swedes go there to purchase beer and spirits and are far more likely to be noticeably inebriated in public in Denmark than are Danes in Sweden. There is also a reluctance to leave one's place of residence and to move across the Sound to be closer to a job.

This latter phenomenon is of importance when one tries to determine how successful the integration project has actually been. After all, a successful cross-border urban agglomeration must amount to more than cheap Danish beer and inexpensive Swedish clothing. Are increased commutation and other cross-Sound travel the best indicators? In this case the project would not be considered to be a great success. While car traffic across the bridge has doubled during the past 7–8 years, it is still only 12 000 cars per day. Many more, of course, use the train connection, but if one looks at the typical metropolitan region with its edge cities and suburb to suburb travel patterns the movement of people to the central city might not be much different from that within Øresundia, whether between Copenhagen and southern Sweden or between central Copenhagen and its outlying areas to the west and south. In this newer spatial configuration the best indicator of successful regional integration is probably the extent to which a specialization of activity has been introduced throughout the region and the degree to which firms on both sides of the Sound interact with each other. While I do not have data that relates to intra-regional specialization, it is clear from the functioning of initiatives such as Medicon Valley, the cluster of bio-pharmaceutical firms in the region, that close and active cross-Sound interaction has been developed. Another institutional indicator of close interaction is Øresund University, a cooperative initiative which includes the 14 institutions of higher education throughout the Øresund region.

Second, there has been considerable anguish over the difficulty there has been in creating a true 'Øresund identity' among residents on both sides of the Sound. Actually it has been easier to do this among Southern Swedes than it has among Copenhageners, perhaps because of the 'mouse and elephant' size differential between the two. But an outsider could ask whether this ephemeral and difficult to define identity is actually needed, as long as the institutions of an integrated space, such as Medicon Valley and Øresund University, function effectively.

These two institutional structures were crucial to the realization of the potential identified earlier in three key industrial sectors: life sciences, ICT and environment. Clearly life sciences is an impressive success. From 58 participants in 1997, there are now 138 firms involved. They exist in a highly interactive environment, with hospitals, universities and industry cooperating extensively. Specialties have been developed in research and treatment of cancer, diabetes, neurosurgery and the ICT dimensions, to the point that each is among the top three ranked in the EU. ICT has been slowly developing in other areas, such as mobile telecommunication, software and games. But environmental technology has been a disappointment. The original thinking was that advances would be made in this area and that firms would locate in the Øresund region, but firms have typically gained access to the technological developments and have then taken them to their home locations where they will be utilized in production. So the impacts on local production and employment have been far less than had been anticipated.

Beyond the Øresund project, it has generally been the case that the other elements in Copenhagen's strategic thinking in 1990 have been rather successful; in fact, virtually all of the recommendations of Initiativegruppen have been achieved. While not 'the' metropole of the north or 'the' bridge between Scandinavia and the EU or between the EU and the Baltic region, Copenhagen has managed to become 'one' of each, along with its main competitors Hamburg, Stockholm and Berlin. The airport at Kastrup has remained one of the primary advantages of the city, as it is the primary international hub for its principal airline, SAS. Its position in the Baltics was helped by the active intervention of its foreign minister on behalf of their membership in the EU, which generated considerable good will on the part of the three Baltic states and Poland.

Copenhagen's success with regard to its 1992 strategic plans is to a large extent due to the fact that it had a dynamic and effective leader in its Lord Mayor, who served until 1995, and because it was able to get the national government to see the wisdom of making the capital city a strong urban economy in the EU and to adopt the initiatives and give the financial support that would realize these plans. Again, effective governance proves to be of crucial importance.

Dresden
Geographic proximity and cultural affinity gave Dresden advantages over other cities in serving as a bridge between East and West. In certain respects this function was less fully achieved that had been anticipated at the beginning of the 1990s. First, the historic enmity between cities in Poland and the Czech Republic and Dresden's two main competitors, Munich and Berlin, dissipated quickly. Second, as Copenhagen discovered, for many companies and activities no bridge was needed; direct access to cities throughout the EEC, now the European Union (EU), was possible and efficient without need for an intermediary. Third, purchasing power in Poland and the Czech Republic, whether on a per capita basis or in the aggregate, was insufficient to provide a substantial market for goods produced in Dresden.

However, this strategic thrust was by no means a total failure. Dresden does participate in four types of EU funded projects that attempt to develop the economies of Central Europe. First are the four categories of tourism, environment, social, and economic development. Second, Dresden participates with Karlsruhe, Breslaw and Ostrava in City Center Development. Third, there are many cultural exhibitions and exchanges. Fourth is the locally important High Water (flooding) Protection. The floods of 2002 had dramatic impacts on Dresden, most notable being the damage to its library, and cities along the Elbe River immediately saw the wisdom of cooperation. For example, high water in Prague has its impact in Dresden three days later so an information system about water levels, rainfall, and so forth is being developed.

In spite of the softening effects of the decade of the 1990s on perceptions in Central Europe of Munich and Berlin, the shared mentality does have its impact today. Sister City relationships have been established between Dresden and Wroclaw, Oshava and St. Petersburg. Local officials stress that these are functioning, working relationships and not just exchanges of high school choirs as so often tends to be the case. While Dresden has not served as a first stop for migrants from Central Europe – they tend to go directly to cities such as Hamburg or Munich – there are many skilled workers and engineers from Poland and the Czech Republic working in technology-related industries in Dresden. This will be made all the easier with completion of the A17 autobahn that will bring Prague as close to Dresden as Berlin – about 150 kilometers of fast highway. Travel to Breslaw, 250 kilometers distant, will be made faster with another new highway. In addition to making personal travel quicker, these and other improvements in transportation will facilitate integration of production sites for automobile parts and the labor intensive production in some of Dresden's high technology industries. Local officials now speak of Dresden-Prague-Wroclaw as one of the many Euro-regions. So while not a complete success, Dresden has managed to realize much of what was anticipated after unification and the SEA with regard to its position as a bridge between East and West.

Dresden has had considerable success in building on its historic strength in light industry. Whereas its neighbor in Saxony has had success as a center of heavy manufacturing in sectors such as automobiles, Dresden has developed during the 1990s its micro-electronics, molecular engineering, micro-biology, and information and communications technology industries. Automobile parts manufacture has also developed well. In micro-electronics there are now about 25 000 employees in 750 firms, carrying out all aspects of the industry – research, design, and manufacture – in the Dresden region. This sector has been growing at about 20 per cent per year, and research and development and engineering in this and other sectors have become the driving force of the Dresden economy.

This expansion of high technology industrial activity has provided some of the stimulus that was needed to support growth of the service sector. Since 1990, employment in this sector has grown from 12 000 to 41 000, with much of this in manufacturing services such as software, accounting, insurance, and the whole array of business services. However, financial services remain a weak point in Dresden's economy. Partly, this is a lack of financial institutions and facilities, but it is also a reflection of the lack of a willingness to support risk taking. While this can be said to be true for all of Germany, the old mentality in Dresden has made it worse there. Those in a position to lend venture capital seem to expect that all of the projects will be successful, whereas in the United States three or four out of ten is acceptable. Clearly, this inhibits start-ups and the growth of newer and smaller companies. One positive feature in this sector is the fact that as large firms such as Siemens establish research and production facilities in Dresden, or elsewhere, financial services usually follow as a matter of course to meet the needs of these important and relatively low-risk clients.

The major disturbances do not appear to have thrown the plans of Dresden leaders off course. The opening to Central Europe had some positive impacts on Dresden and this was expected to be the case with the addition of ten new members, including Poland and the Czech Republic, in May 2004. The introduction of the Euro was considered to be primarily a psychological problem as it meant loss of the Deutschmark which East Germans had seen as a pillar of strength and stability for so many years. Outsourcing and the emergence of competition for low-skill workers from producers in China and elsewhere in Asia has led to the loss of jobs in sectors such as clothing and textiles and where firms are too small to be able to generate the efficiencies that meeting this competition requires. This hit employment for women especially hard. To off-set this negative effect, it is realized that low-income workers need access to low priced goods, and in reality these are being produced primarily in Third World countries and in emerging countries such as China and India. The stagnation of the German and EU economies has slowed growth in much of the Dresden economy, although its technology-related sectors have shown strong growth. One macro-economic factor that is of interest with regard to achievement of Dresden's plans is that in 1990–92 a strong upswing in economic activity was expected. What happened was not the broad-based expansion that was anticipated, but a boom that was concentrated in the construction industry, which was in part stimulated by some short-term tax changes. When these tax changes came to an end, so did the economic expansion. Relief, of a sort, was brought by another construction boom in post-flood 2003, which was again followed by stagnation. Real, sustained economic growth of the German and EU economies would be especially welcomed by the other than high technology sectors of Dresden's economy.

Hamburg

During the years following 1992, Hamburg achieved some advances and survived some negative experiences leaving the economy in a positive situation and as one of the strongest in Germany. For example, while much of the traditional bulk shipping traffic declined, Hamburg emerged as one of the principal ports for trade with China. As a consequence of this, Hamburg has developed as a headquarters and business office location for about 240 Chinese trading and transportation companies operating in the EU, as well as 120 Japanese and 60 Taiwanese firms,[11] and the harbor has also been improved, with its channel and the Elbe River deepened by over a meter and with new logistics infrastructure investments to handle this new cargo. This has been supported by conferences such as 'China meets Europe' as a way of asserting Hamburg's position. In this new role, Hamburg is ranked third among northern European ports, but is second in container traffic, and is the second fastest growing port in the world, behind Shanghai. Ship-building has all but disappeared, with only Blohm and Voss and a smaller shipyard remaining; food processing is a high cost activity that is slowly declining in importance; and the advantage the port gave to copper and other metal production has been eroded by logistical developments elsewhere.

In addition to the sea, Hamburg's land location was another key element in its 1992 strategic thinking. The desire to become the principal economic center in the Baltic region and in the EU-Nordic linkage has been largely realized. While Stockholm has its strength in the Baltic and as an economic focal point for the Nordic region, the relationship between Hamburg and Copenhagen has evolved to one of cooperative contact rather than of intense competition. Over

500 firms from Scandinavia have established offices in Hamburg. The other anticipated competition from a revitalized Berlin has not materialized. Berlin has remained an administrative-government center and has not developed into an important economic center. The reasons for this are principally the lack of skills of the local labor force and a variety of urban problems that are off-putting to investors. The long hoped for magnetic-levitation high-speed rail link that would reduce the travel time between the two cities from 90 to 60 minutes is a very costly venture and will probably not be realized for another couple of decades. Hence the division of labor between Hamburg and Berlin is likely to remain, and with it Hamburg's economic vitality.

Links to Central Europe have also developed as anticipated. The port is one of the largest for the trade of Hungary, Poland and the Czech Republic, and there is much economic and political cooperation between Hamburg and cities and *länder* of the former German Democratic Republic. Indeed, with the birth rate remaining low among Germans throughout the country, much of Hamburg's population growth during the late 1980s and through the present has come from immigrants from these areas to the east. A significant percentage of these new workers are young, between 18 and 30 years of age, bring needed skills with them, and add to the quality of the work force. As a consequence, Hamburg has not experienced the level of anti-immigrant sentiment that has been found in other cities in Germany, although it must be admitted that rapid growth of the immigrant population has had negative short-term impacts on the social structure and the social system in all parts of Europe including Hamburg. From this, one can conclude that the *drehscheibe*, or turntable, function of Hamburg in northern Europe, with links to the Baltic, Scandinavia, Central Europe and the EU is being fulfilled.

With Berlin's failure to develop as a powerful economic center, competition from other urban centers is principally limited to two German cities, Munich and Frankfurt. But the primary sectors of the Hamburg economy, aerospace and media, are holding up well and are not seriously threatened. Neither has the economy been negatively affected by the areas of turbulence that have marked this period of time. The opening to Asia has been very positive for shipping and logistics and office functions, and relations with Central Europe have developed well, but the weakness of EU and German economic growth puts a damper on activity in general and the recent strength of the Euro has posed a more specific threat to Airbus sales.

In general, it can be said that Hamburg did fairly well in realizing the objectives it set out for itself in the early 1990s. There were some structural shifts that seem to have been absorbed without a great deal of unemployment or dislocation; the areas in which progress has been slow are primarily in areas such as transportation infrastructure which are national rather than sub-national responsibilities. While it is a peripheral urban region, Hamburg has been rather successful in creating for itself a sub-region of the EU in which it can function as a major player. Fortunately, major industries such as media do not benefit from a spatially central location; shipping and logistics are not easily transferred to other regions once the rail, canal, and sea related infrastructures have been put in place and activities have been built up in relation to them; and aerospace, about which more will be said in the next chapter, is in some sense an activity which has been designated as one for the peripheral regions of Spain, south-west France and, of course, Hamburg. The city provides an interesting example of how a peripheral city can make the best of its location and the opportunities that come its way.

Munich

Munich's strategic plan was quite simple: continue to support the three principle sectors of the economy (media, insurance and electronics); promote technology-related training, education and production; implement some flagship projects; and work to resolve the problems attaching to economic growth (housing, industrial sites, and labor bottlenecks). Unification of the two Germanys was not expected to be a major event but the opening to the East was. As it turned out, turmoil in the Balkans and slow, even negative, growth in much of the rest of Central Europe reduced the economic significance of this region to the large and dynamic economy of Munich. The lack of purchasing power has kept this a marginal area for Munich, although some firms have moved their labor-intensive production there.

The housing and industrial site problems have not been fully resolved, but considerable relief was gained by expanding the Munich economy out into the surrounding areas. This has been facilitated by accomplishment of some of the flagship projects. Expansion of the airport has made its surrounding area one of the most dynamic of the Munich region and a prime location for much of the food-processing industry. The beltway, or Ring, around Munich has not been fully completed, but the rapid rail system, the S-bahn, has been extended to outlying areas. As would be anticipated, as soon as a community gains a stop on the S-bahn it becomes significantly more attractive to commuters and its growth is assured. This has made it necessary for Munich to cooperate as never before with the county of Oberbayern and, in contrast with a decade earlier, this latter entity has emerged to become a major partner of Munich in spatial planning initiatives and their funding. Some land has become available from no longer used military sites and also along the rail line from the west. In the course of the 1990s, Munich has been able to control growth within the city limits and thus has met the objective of minimizing the negative consequences of that growth.

In addition to cooperation or networking with Oberbayern, Munich has actively involved its university-level institutions of higher learning, research entities such as the Max Planck Institute (basic research) and the Frauenhof Institute (applied research) in further developing focused areas such as Martinsried for biotechnology and Oberpaffenhofen for aerospace, or city-wide structures for computer technology, telecommunications, medical research, and a variety of engineering and manufacturing industries. In addition to cooperation with Bavaria and Oberbayern, there is also some coordination that occurs at the federal government level, with Munich specializing in biotechnology and Karlsruhe getting the mandate for nanotechnology. It is both interesting and informative to note that in its brochure on the 'City of Knowledge,' which highlights Munich's areas of strength, the Department of Labour and Economic Development also presents the city's assets in universities, museums and exhibition centers, theatres and other performance centers and libraries.[12] A focus on culture, the arts and learning is, of course, nothing new in Munich as this initiative was begun by Maximilian I Joseph and Ludwig I in the first years of the 19th century with construction of the university and such cultural institutions as the Alte and Neue Pinoktek and the Glyptotek. Not all cities recognize the importance of cultural assets as an essential concomitant to the science and technology aspects of the economy. Proximity to the Alps and the high quality of life in Munich also always receive priority publicity.

Outsourcing of production to Asia and other low-wage places has contributed to the loss of perhaps 200 000 industrial jobs in recent years. One recent example is Völkl skis. The company has 550 employees in the Munich area, but has decided to move production of the low-price end of its product line to China, keeping the high quality production in Munich. In the process it will reduce its local work force to about 300. However, the strength of Munich's economy is its balance, with four or five major growth sectors, and the relatively steadily and rapidly growing United States is its primary export market, so it has managed to ride smoothly through difficult times for any one of them. In the aggregate, outsourcing in labor-intensive industries and slow growth in the German and EU economies has meant that the unemployment rate, while one of the lowest in Germany, has risen recently from 4.5 to 7.0 per cent, and currently over 70,000 workers are unemployed. Introduction of the Euro was a contributing factor as it tended to increase prices and to impose a burden on lower wage workers, both for their standard of living and for their jobs.

The service sector has retained its dynamism with continued top ranking for the city's media, insurance and some aspects of finance. It is also argued that with the Bertelsman company and its activities, book publishing is on a par with that of other major cities such as New York. The annual media fair is a natural place for intra-industry networking, but in the financial sector competition is too keen and there is very little contact among the major players. More will be said about this in Chapter 6.

Munich's leaders justifiably feel rather content with the economy that has been created. Not all of the credit goes to them as the roots of this success go back decades, if not centuries. The benefits of the consistent pursuit of a limited number of strategic objectives over an extended period of time is one important lesson that can be gained from the experience of Munich.

Seville

Seville's experience following the World's Fair in 1992 did not bring the benefits that had been anticipated, at least at first. The local economy was significantly slowed by the economic stagnation that characterized most of the EU economic space. With demand depressed or stagnant in the major export markets the negative impacts on local incomes, employment and economic growth put on hold most of the projected initiatives that had been part of Seville's strategic thinking in the period leading up to 1992. The Seville economy stagnated during the period 1993–1996.

Symbolic of this was the lack of development of the science and technology park Cartuja, which was the center piece of Seville's attempt to make a leap from traditional activities such as food production, marble and leather goods into the modern economy of research and development-based advanced manufacturing and services, without going through the intermediate stages. Cartuja was to take off immediately after the World's Fair closed, but it was not until the end of the decade that it began to realize the potential that had been seen for it. In 2000 a second, and more successful, attempt was initiated. Cartuja was to be a headquarters and research and development center for firms, many of which are small start-ups, with manufacturing to be done elsewhere. There was some evaluation of potential clusters, with environmental engineering and information-communications technology being the most promising. The idea was to make it into a 'context for collective learning,' as one official put it. So the Cartuja 'clusters' were set up to encourage active contact and collaboration among the firms located there. By 2005 Cartuja was occupied to its capacity, and officials consider it to be one of Europe's most successful science and technology parks.

Since Cartuja lacks space for expansion, another park linking the university and some technology firms is being developed in the South of the city, there is a food processing cluster, and a major aerospace park, Aeropolis, near the airport. The latter is linked to EADS, the European Aerospace and Defense System, and will assemble the Airbus 340M, a military version of the successful commercial aircraft. Transmissions are being made in Seville for Renault-Nissan. Avingo, a local environmental engineering firm, has just become the first Spanish company to be listed on the NASDAQ exchange in New York. These successes may not appear to be of major importance for many other cities, but one must remember the situation in which Seville finds itself. It is an urban economy far out on the periphery of the EU, it is relatively isolated from other major urban centers, and, given its concentration on traditional industries, it has had to reinvent itself as a modern technology-based economy.

A second aspect of Seville's planning that may show some success is its focus on a logistics center, based on the fact that the city does have a port on the Guadalivara River which can accommodate small ocean-going ships. The notion is that cargo from these ships can be transshipped via inter-modal facilities and then taken by truck or by rail to the rest of the EU. The difficulties are, of course, that most of the traffic will come in ships that are too large for Seville's facility and that very strong competition will come from Barcelona, Marseilles and Genoa-Turin, each of which will be able to handle all ships and are, given the fact that travel by ship is less costly than is travel to land, much closer to the ultimate destinations of these cargoes.

The other element in Seville's pre-1992 thinking was the effort to make something positive out of its peripheral location. It was to be the bridge to both Latin America and North Africa. But bridges turned out to have been of little substance. Seville simply lacked the economic weight, the corporate headquarters and the financial institutions to serve as a bridge to Latin America. Trade between the two was negligible and all there was to sustain this dream was nostalgia about the heroic past. With regard to North Africa, there was little economic activity there to generate much interest from the rest of Europe. The only country other than Spain to trade with this area was France, and that country had its own traditional linkages, linkages which did not include Spain or Seville. Furthermore, there were substantial cultural and economic differences that made cooperative ventures between Seville and North Africa difficult. With regard to the economies of the two places, Seville was fully engaged in the market liberalization programs of Spain and of the European Union, with the role of the state being reduced and with economic rationality and efficiency replacing protectionism and favoritism in decision-making. North Africa did not participate in these structural and procedural reforms so it was difficult to form close ties between public and private sector entities in the two economies. It did not take long for Seville's leadership to realize the folly of this notion of a bridging function for the city.

Between 1996 and 2005, Seville has made considerable progress toward achieving its leap from the traditional to the modern in its economic activity. Progress was not soon in coming nor, in retrospect, were all elements in the strategic thinking based on a realistic appraisal of the city's potential. This city provides us with a clear example of the need to avoid nostalgia and to base an economic strategy on an objective evaluation of the city's strengths and weaknesses.

COMMENTS IN CONCLUSION

Even the best formed plans can be made ineffective by a dramatic change in the underlying conditions in which an urban economy functions. Unfortunately, it is quite impossible to make accurate forecasts regarding the extensive array of political, economic and strategic events that can occur, so the planning process is best structured when some degree of flexibility and of uncertainty are incorporated into it. Some of the changes, such as introduction of the Euro, were easy to forecast, but others, such as the nature of the market in Central Europe and the strength of the emergence of economies such as China, were sure to catch many planners and city leaders off guard. When there is a high degree of uncertainty about the future, planning tends to be done with a shorter-term horizon than would otherwise be the case, and the city may deviate from what would be considered to be its optimal long-term path. As the ten cities in this study began the 1990s we have examined the expectations each had with regard to what it would anticipate and how its planning process would be designed.

The major events that had negative consequences for some of the cities were: 1) the failure of the market of the newly freed economies of Central Europe, 2) outsourcing of production to low-wage countries in Asia and in Central Europe, and 3) the economic stagnation of the EU economy. However, introduction of the Euro does not appear to have thrown any of the cities in the center off track, but peripheral cities, which are relatively more focused on extra-EU markets had some difficulty. Ineffective governance structures were especially difficult for the Italian cities, but it was up to them and their national government to tackle these.

Several of the cities considered the deterioration of their traditional manufacturing activity to be a blessing in disguise as this forced them to restructure their economies toward higher technology and skill activities, activities that while not part of their past were expected to be part of their future. Planners in Milan and Turin saw this future but had great difficulty in realizing their potential to participate in this new high technology economy, although Milan did much to enhance its position in traded services. Dresden is an example of a city that stuck with its historic strength, light manufacturing, with some success.

Most of the geographic restructuring was actually realized: the Öresund project was successfully implemented, Hamburg and Copenhagen both had some success in reaching out to the Baltic region, and Eurocities was especially important for Amsterdam, Barcelona and Lyon. The market of Central Europe was disappointingly slow in developing, but many cooperative ventures of firms in Dresden, Hamburg and Munich were initiated and show considerable promise. But Seville's aspirations to develop its ties with North

Africa came to little. Industrial clusters were developed in Barcelona, Copenhagen, Dresden, Lyon and Munich, and efforts are underway in Seville, while Hamburg, seeing its traditional port and shipbuilding decline, made the transition to the China trade and regional headquarters activity.

While much interest is devoted to the communications infrastructure of urban regions, for the cities in this study it was the transportation infrastructure that was most important. High-speed rail and international air have captured most of the interest here, but it was local or regional rapid rail services that have allowed Amsterdam, Barcelona, Copenhagen and Munich to restructure themselves spatially so as to develop their technology sectors in new industrial parks and close to their airports.

NOTES

1.   David Morley and Arie Shachar (eds), *Planning in Turbulence*, Jerusalem: The Magnes Press, The Hebrew University, 1986.
2.   David Morley and Arie Shachar, 'Epilogue: Reflections by Planners on Planning,' in Morley and Shachar, *Planning in Turbulence*, pp. 143–44.
3.   Morley and Shachar, p. 148.
4.   *Torino Negli Ultimi 50 Anni*, Turin: Camera di commercio, industria artigianato, e agricoltura di Torino, 2004, p. 47.
5.   Istituto Ricerche Economico-Sociale del Piemonte, *Relazione sulla situazione economica, sociale e territoriale del Piemonte 1988*, Turin, Rosenberg & Sellier, 1988, pp. 4 and 36.
6.   Aldo Enrietti and Renato Lanzetti, *La Crisi FIAT Auto e il Piemonte*, Turin: Istituto Ricerche Economico-Sociale del Piemonte, 2002.
7.   Andrés Rodríguez-Pose and Maria Cristina Refolo, 'The Link Between Local Production Systems and Public and University Research in Italy,' *Environment and Planning A*, Vol. 35, 2003, pp. 1477–92.
8.   Maurizio Maggi and Stefano Piperno, *Turin: The Vain Search for Gargantua*, Turin: Istituto Ricerche Economico-Sociale del Piemonte, 1999.
9.   See *Torino Negli Ultimo 50 Anni*, p. 172, for the national figures and Maggi and Piperno, p. 13, for the city comparisons.
10.   Maggi and Piperno, p. 32.
11.   *Hamburg, Business Centre for Northern Europe*, Hamburg: Hamburg Business Development Corporation, undated.
12.   *City of Knowledge*, Munich: Department of Labour and Economic Development, City of Munich, July 2003.

6. The ten cities and their planning for 2005–2015

One of the most striking changes that has taken place during the past 15 years is the fact that almost all internationally engaged cities are undertaking some form of strategic–economic planning. For some it is an explicit, formal exercise that conforms largely to the suggestions that were made earlier in Chapter 2; for others it is a less explicit continuation of implementation of a strategic thrust that has served the metropolitan region well for many years. Partly this is due to the recognition by each set of city leaders that action on their part is required if they are to avoid marginalization and stagnation of their economy for the next decade; in part, the publicity and experience sharing that has been part of the increased participation in entities such as Eurocities, Metropolis, and other international and national organizations of city governments has put strategic–economic planning on the desk of every city leader in the world. So the future is certain to be one of increased municipal action, planning, concern for urban competitiveness, inter-urban problem and experience sharing, and lobbying superior levels of government for funding of and authority to proceed with transportation, housing, city center renewal, education and training and all of the other things that are crucial to the well functioning and competitive metropolitan region.

For cities in Europe, while macro- and micro-economic and global and regional turbulence have not had powerfully disruptive impacts on all cities, each has been of some consequence on almost all of the cities. The coming decade promises to be equally turbulent so EU metropolitan regions will continue to be forced to make accommodations in their plans for economic activity due to events beyond their control. Obviously this calls for flexibility, adaptability, some attention to foresight, and a diversion of resources from the things they would very much prefer to do to things they must do.

The Euro has shown that its depreciation or appreciation can have an impact on urban economies that are tied to export industries such as aircraft production, to low wage and low profit margin production which can be done more cost effectively in Central Europe or Asia, and to the location decisions of major multinational corporations. The value of the Euro is largely a function of the relative macro-economic performance of Euro-land and the United

States and the generally held expectations about EU economic growth and the competitiveness of its industries. EU economic stagnation and alternating bouts of optimism and pessimism about the likelihood that it will be overcome have brought significant movements in the value of the Euro. So what EU city leaders have to look forward to is an extended period of uncertainty; always the enemy of effective planning.

The recent events in Madrid and London have put terrorism in the forefront of the agendas of all planners in Europe. While the events to date have had short-term impacts, any increase in their frequency could force the member countries of the EU to increase their intra-EU, as well as their extra-EU, border supervision and controls. If the logistics infrastructure of the EU becomes or is seen to be potentially a vehicle for explosives or chemical/nuclear elements, the movement of the past half century toward tighter economic integration, the creation of a true single market and the functioning of an economic and political union could be halted and forced into reverse. Of the many negative consequences of this, one is that urban economies would find their economic reach, the inter-urban division of labor and economic specialization dramatically reduced. Goods flows would become more time consuming and costly, individuals would become less willing to travel, especially to large metropolitan areas that are thought to be likely targets, and the drain of security measures on public finances would divert funds from initiatives that are aimed at enhancing the competitiveness of urban regions.

The evolution of trade and investment relations with the ten new members of the EU and with emerging economies in Asia, Latin America and, some day, Africa will continue to force a reconsideration of specific characteristics of economic vitality and the long-term viability of certain vulnerable economic activities. Finally, trans-Atlantic relations with the United States may become contentious if the US administration opts for isolationist, restrictive and quasi-protectionist policies as the answer to disappointing economic performance there. This will spill over beyond the bi-lateral relationship into areas such as negotiations within the World Trade Organization and relations in organizations such as the United Nations and the OECD.

None of these potential areas of turbulence can be predicted at this moment in time, but city leaders must continue to expect the unexpected and to establish local governance and planning structures that will allow for fairly agile policy and initiative responses. It is not at all certain that national governments will be in a position to do much on their behalf. Strategic–economic planning will be facilitated by the fact that the cities in this study have already made decisions about the basic continuing structures of their economies, so the planning that is currently being done is in the nature of quantitative expansion of existing activities rather than of meeting the challenge of qualitative restructuring, to use the terminology of Chapter 2.

CITIES IN THE CORE

Cities in the core are both advantaged and disadvantaged in that their economies are tightly integrated with those of other nations that are in close proximity. Each of the four cities in the core are close to important if not dominant trading partners. If the turbulences identified above are minimal in their impacts, these economies should benefit from continued interaction and the refining of the specialization of their economic actors. However if the reverse is true and, say, terrorism becomes more of a feature of daily life than it is today, then these urban economies should suffer disproportionately. Amsterdam, Lyon, Milan and Turin have all been very active in developing relations with contiguous economic space in neighboring countries. This will, of course, continue to be an advantage if terrorism remains an extraordinary and occasional, albeit horrible, event.

Close proximity to each other has meant that cities in the core find it easier to conceive of joint infrastructure projects that have the potential to bring economic benefit than would be the case if they were separated by hundreds of kilometers of space. High-speed TGV lines linking these cities were some of the first lines that were constructed. Lyon and Turin have exerted pressure on their national governments and the EU for a tunnel through the Alps. This project has yet to be realized, but this sort of thinking is common among cities in the core. The Milan-Turin TGV line is currently under construction. Airports of core cities, Amsterdam and Milan in this study, but, of course, Frankfurt as well, are well connected hubs that service the rest of Europe. Lyon had ambitions to develop such an airport, but the reluctance of both Paris Charles de Gaulle and Air France has made this impossible.

Finally, core cities have developed their service and decision-making functions in ways that have not been possible for cities such as those in this study that are situated in the periphery. The original study of DATAR that gave us the 'blue banana' used the density of these and other functions such as research, media, culture, education and so forth as the basis of its model. The passage of time and improvements in the technologies of communication, transportation and production have not reduced the importance of being an urban economy in the core rather than in the periphery. This has also been demonstrated by the literature on convergence and divergence within the EU that was reviewed in Chapter 3. The planning initiatives of the four cities in this section reflect the importance of a core location.

Amsterdam

The current approach to strategic–economic planning in Amsterdam is that of achieving a transformation of the economic activity of the urban region, rather than the expansion of existing activities that had characterized the approach of the past several decades. This is not quite the fundamental shift, that was discussed in Chapter 2, from a 'quantitative expansion' to a 'qualitative restructuring,' but is rather attaching different weights or priorities to existing strengths of the Amsterdam region. Logistics will continue to be a central element, as will the point-of-access and headquarters functions. Finance and business services will retain their important roles. But, as is the case with most of the cities in this study, Amsterdam will focus on 'creative industries,' such as advertising, media, information-communications technologies, and cultural activities. Additionally, there has been increased recognition of the importance of the flower and vegetable export activity with the notion of a Greenport linked, and situated in close proximity, to Schipol.

The creative industries are the fastest growing sector of the economy, at 20–30 per cent per year, but this is not entirely the result of a focused policy by government. One of the most important supports of the creative industries is a strong system of higher education, and Amsterdam is rich in knowledge-generating institutions. The city has made itself attractive to a young and cosmopolitan work force and once these workers are concentrated in residential areas with good restaurants, clubs and bars and impressive cultural assets (museums, concerts, dance, galleries, and so forth), serendipity takes over and, not surprisingly, creative people end up doing creative things. This seems to be indicative of the general approach that is being taken by current city leaders, in that there is less emphasis on taking specific actions to achieve a specific objective and more reliance on simply creating conditions or an environment which will be supportive of economic activity in general, albeit primarily that of a knowledge- or skill-based nature, and letting individual actors and market forces give specific shape to economic development. This approach has been welcomed and accepted by investors and the private sector, and excellent relations have been developed between local government and firms. There are strong and effective linkages between the institutions of higher learning and large firms, but much remains to be done to bring smaller firms into this environment.

As Amsterdam restructures its priorities, city leaders have found an increased value in membership in Eurocities. Many member cities are attempting to do things that are similar to Amsterdam's initiatives – expansion of the creative industries, better linkages between universities and small firms, and so forth. Study of the experiences of other cities is certainly beneficial. Eurocities is also increasingly important for a city such as Amsterdam as the EU gains in power and responsibility, since a budget line for cities will be introduced as of 2007, and as decision-making slowly evolves from a top-down model toward a bottom-up one. This is an indication of the extent to which the national governments have retreated in the face of the growing financial and policy responsibility of the EU and its offices.

In its effort to create a modern transportation and housing infrastructure that meets the needs of middle and higher income residents, or potential residents, Amsterdam has been blessed by the relative lack of a major manufacturing sector and the central city shipping facilities that have marked the waterfront of cities such as Barcelona. Because of this, there has been very little in the way of contaminated land and derelict structures that required renewal. It has been relatively easy and financially feasible to convert the waterfront areas to attractive office and residential uses.

While the problems of absorbing the Moroccan immigrants continues, another migration issue that confronts the city is the intra-national migration into Amsterdam to take advantage of its educational opportunities. Some of these young people stay in the metropolitan region after graduation but many leave for other parts of the EU or for the United States. In exchange, Amsterdam receives immigrants from the rest of the EU; they comprise about 10 per cent of the work force and most of them are relatively skilled workers. So the cross-border labor exchange does not really hurt Amsterdam.

Under the rubric 'Opting for Urbanity,' an effort is being made to link the center and its suburbs into a 'network city,' with cooperation in planning, allocation of functions such as sports facilities and cultural institutions throughout the metropolitan region. The transportation system will be improved with the hub of it being a restructured central train station with a bus station, the metro and water transportation attached to it. This coordinated planning initiative seems to be quite successful at this moment in time and if it continues to be so it would provide a useful example for other metropolitan areas to study. This cooperation is linked to a continuing decentralization of power with the national government having less importance to the cities in the Netherlands, with the exception of financial support for major infrastructure initiatives. Rural areas are no longer the force they were in the past with regard to policies and funding by the government in the Hague and, to some extent, the EU and Brussels have expanded their role concomitantly. Going beyond the Amsterdam metropolitan region, there is currently underway a 'rethinking the Randstat' process in which the functions of the three primary cities, Amsterdam, Rotterdam and the Hague, will be more clearly defined and differentiated. This should remove the normal efforts to compete for functions and facilities that can lead to inefficiency and duplication. Rotterdam will focus on its port activities and small offices related to logistics, the Hague will be defined more clearly as an administrative and government city and Amsterdam will specialize in headquarter and service functions.

Today, external factors of turbulence are having a negative impact on the Amsterdam economy. The slow growth of Germany is particularly telling, but the increased value of the Euro is changing the relationship, in terms of production and trade, with non-Euro Europe.

Lyon

Lyon began to develop its plan for economic development, *Le Schéma de Développement Economique* (SDE), in 1997, and in 2003 it announced that the SDE was to become known under the title '*Grand Lyon, L'esprit d'entreprise*' and the city advertised itself as '*Lyon-Ville de l'Entrepreneuriat.*' Under this rubric are almost 20 named associations from the Chamber of Commerce to those with initials that can be interpreted only by their participants, as well as financial institutions, and professional groups. The individual elements of the plan range from development of traditional sectors to identification of three poles of excellence to advancing the city's cultural assets. Each of the roughly 20 working groups has an identified leader from one of the participating institutions, usually the Chamber of Commerce, Grand Lyon (an umbrella organization for major entities in Lyon) or one of the major associations, a budget, and a set of actions to be put in operation. The deadline for completion seems to be 2007, although many of the groups will be finished by that date. All of this action is grouped under six major headings:

- *Lyon-Ville de l'Entrepreneuriat.*
  This consists essentially of a series of initiatives designed to encourage the formation and survival of new, and thereby small, enterprises. There is a special focus on traditional sectors, such as chemicals and textiles, as well as efforts to increase the interaction of these new firms, to make best practices known to them, to increase the skilled labor they require, and to look after their financial needs
- *Interaction and innovation.*
  Isolated firms tend not to be leaders in innovation. This section of the plan focuses on efforts to develop closer functional ties among firms and professionals with the objective being that of enhancing innovation and improving competitiveness and performance.
- *Reinforcement of the poles of excellence.*
  The three sectors that have been highlighted are biotechnologies, electronic games, and creativity in fashion. Each has an existing base in Lyon, with biotechnologies being the best established and the largest. Each of the three, obviously, has its own requirements for success.
- *Promotion of the metropolitan region.*
  Here the cultural, tourism and trade fair assets of the Lyon region are to be developed. In addition, there are efforts to make the city more congenial than it already is to entrepreneurs and foreign firms.
- *Managing and leading the region.*
  Further developments in the transportation infrastructure are planned, as well as some industrial sites and the area around the airport.

- *Enhancement of the general environment.*
  The focus here is on amelioration of the typical urban disamenities such as air, water and noise pollution.

It is of some interest to note that while Lyon has used the terms biocluster, electronic games cluster and environment cluster in the headings of its planning document, an explicit cluster approach has not been used. To the extent that the concept of the cluster is found in Lyon's approach, it is not so much a strategic approach to be implemented for key sectors, but rather a description for elements of that sector that are already in place. This suggests that Lyon's current strategic thinking is essentially a continuation of what was already being done than a break with the past in the search for something that would promise more success than was already being accomplished.

It is important to note that by 2005 one could say that Lyon had developed a more realistic understanding of its place in France and in Europe. Its airport will probably never become a much more significant hub than it now is,[1] it is unlikely to find that niche in financial markets it had sought, and projects such as the Lyon-Turin TGV will be long in coming, if at all, due to competing demands for increasingly stretched funding possibilities from Rome, Paris and Brussels. On the other hand, once comfortable with the realities of its 'second city' status, it can develop its potential along with other second cities such as Barcelona, Turin, and Manchester. Lyon's current plan seems to be structured in accord with this realization.

Lyon is only half way through its planning period, so it is too soon to pass judgment on either the plan or its execution. All of Europe's cities are being challenged by the elements of turbulence that were identified at the beginning of the previous chapter, perhaps more now than during the 1990s. In contrast with some of the cities in this study, Lyon does have an accurate sense of itself, a coherent strategic plan, a decade or more of real accomplishment behind it, and an apparently effective metro-wide structure for decision-making and initiative implementation. It would have to be judged to be one of the success stories of strategic planning in Europe.

Milan

After the *tangentopoli*-induced decade of inaction, Milan has begun to arouse itself. The first effort seems to have been an initiative to enhance Milan's capacity to be innovative, with support from the RITTS (Regional Innovation and Technology Transfer Strategies and Infrastructures) program of DG Enterprise of the EU.[2] The 'strategic programme for innovation' was initiated in 2002 and had seven 'Axes' or objectives, each of which has two or three specific measures that were to be implemented. The Axes are:[3]

- Support companies' R&D initiatives and technology transfer.
- Generate new entrepreneurship and new employment.
- Promote interventions for territorial diffusion of innovation.
- Strengthen the dissemination of information to SMEs and the spread of the scientific and business cultures.
- Support quality projects and SME internationalization.
- Simplify the relationship between companies and Public Administration.
- Strengthen local networks and European networking activity.

The bases for this initiative were several items that are common to many such projects, and which appear in the 'measures.' It is noted that the existing situation in Milan is one in which individual firms and actors are isolated, that structures are fragmented, and that coordination is lacking. Hence, one focus must be on creating linkages among entities and developing networks. Finland was held up as an example of a country which has been successful in creating an 'innovative milieu,' one with strong synergies, common objectives, an ability to identify quickly strategic lines of action, and a consistent focus on regional innovation. Another set of foci was small businesses, business start-ups by women, start-ups in general, and incubators. 'Best practices' will be identified and publicized, as will 'centers of excellence.' The approach of the innovation exercise is general in nature, rather than focused on two or three high priority sectors. It was explicitly a bottom-up program, with a clear understanding that the firms involved will have to meet the test of the market, and tries to avoid explicit direction from above.

Innovation is felt by most planners to be one of the key items in urban economic–strategic planning because of the rapid pace of change that is characteristic of technology, market access, demography, and urban competitiveness in general. So Milan's city leaders were right to begin their project with it. The next step for Milan was a formal strategic plan that was made public during the spring of 2005, and should be seen as a partner to the innovation plan.[4] As we shall soon see is the case with Barcelona, the documents that precede the Milan plan of 2005 itself discuss the process of strategic planning. In the eyes of the Milan planners, a strategic plan is: 1) an integrated activity involving a network of diverse policies and interventions, 2) oriented to produce innovation and change – it is a departure from the routine, 3) a political document which identifies both actions and actors, 4) dominated by the practical, 5) not a plan of land use nor does it have the 'force of law,' and 6) a process involving 'auto-reflection.' Although planners in a city, such as Munich, which has been on a successful course for decades might have reservations about the second of the six items, it is very useful for a planning process to begin with some thoughts about the process which is about to be undertaken.

The strategic plan focuses primarily on the urban environment of Milan and the basis for this next step is a realistic appraisal of the urban region's strengths and weaknesses. The specific problems or shortcomings noted by the leaders of Milan and its urban region are the following: 1) Milan combines a high level of per capita income with a low quality of life – the city lacks the comforts of living in a metropolis, 2) attention needs to be paid to urban amenities (culture, parks, and so forth), 3) there is no over-all strategy for the metropolitan economic space, Milan lacks international linkages and recognition, and 4) social exclusion has not been dealt with adequately. This concern for livability is not just one of making life good for the Milanese, but it is explicitly linked to the competitiveness of Milan as a major urban center of the EU, and indeed of the world.

Some of the city's leadership have noted that Milan is usually positioned at the bottom in studies of creative cities of Europe, and have tried to take inspiration from Richard Florida's work on the 'creative class' and from London's slogan 'Creative London,' and have proposed '*Milano Metropoli del'Industria Creativa*' (Milan: Metropolis of Creative Industry).[5] This is a strategic focus which is common to most cities, but unlike wanting to become a center of automobile or steel production or a major airport, it is a strategy that can be realized by all urban regions – the trick is, of course, in the execution and only the next few years will tell this story.

Finally, the planners envision the province of Milan as being identified with three distinct 'interpretative images' with regard to its territorial position. First, there is the 'city of cities' in which the several constituent municipalities are recognized and efforts are made to achieve a common vision and coordinated action. Second, the provincial territory is considered as being something more than just the sum of Milan plus the municipalities in the urban region and residents are urged to see the entire province as a place in which to work, live, study and establish personal and cultural relationships. Third, it is proposed that the Milan urban region link itself to neighboring regions such as that of Monza to create an east-west axis that could form the basis of a sort of 'third Italy' that would both benefit all constituent urban regions as well as add to Milan's role as a transportation, decision-making and 'new economy' hub in the EU.

Clearly, Milan is trying to get itself in a positive motion toward a future it sees as being appropriate to its potential and to its role or function within Italy, the Alpine Region and the EU. The city has had difficulty in the past in following through effectively on its plans. One could argue that the stakes are higher this time, as other competing urban regions are increasingly proactive and more is understood about what needs to be done. As is always the case with Italian cities, the crucial factor will be the degree to which effective local governance structures can be designed, put in place, and allowed to operate.

Turin

From a false sense of complacency in 1990 to ineffectiveness during the 1990s, Turin turned the corner and moved toward more effective strategic planning as it entered the 21st century. Local officials took great pride in announcing that Turin had become, on February 29, 2000, the first Italian city to adopt a Strategic Plan. It was a real plan, put forward by Torino Internazionale,[6] the agency with the mandate for this sort of planning, and one that was rather impressive in some ways. First, some information about the process of developing the plan itself. Before the planning process began there was a substantial report commissioned, *Towards the Plan*, in which an assessment of the Turin region's strengths and weaknesses were assessed and observations were offered about the contemporary situation of cities in the global economy.[7] The discussion of Turin's weaknesses was commendably frank, noting among other things: that suppliers to large firms seem to be cut out of the large firm system so that 'the diffusion of innovation is generally inferior to what it could be'; that while computers and biotechnology have been traditional strengths of Turin, industrial connections are being lost or are unable to grow; that only one third of the 14–29 year old population has a high school or university education (Rome, Milan, Bologna and Florence are between 35.5 and 40.1 per cent); that Turin does not have a metropolitan government; and that reading and attendance at cultural events was no better than the national average so that 'a metropolis that is asking efforts of inno vation on the part of its population is equal to an average which includes, in a representative sample, the tiniest rural villages.'[8] There was recognition of the need to overcome two 'FIAT legacies': first, that Turin had put all of its effort into one major industry rather than pursue a strategy of diversification and, second, the labor force which had been substantially increased with low-skill workers from the south of Italy for industrial jobs on the production line. The challenge was to encourage expansion of two to four high-skill industries while at the same time providing some employment for those who were losing jobs at FIAT.

The process of developing the plan was apparently quite comprehensive, with working groups involving 100 public and private entities having discussions in 60 meetings. There were dozens of workshops, conventions and seminars, and an apparently genuine effort to elicit comment and input from all sectors of the economy and society. The result was a plan with six 'strategic lines' which comprise the substance of the plan:[9]

- Integrate the metropolitan area in the international system – efforts at internationalization and transportation infrastructure from upgrading the local airport (Caselle) to local rail and road projects such as high-speed rail links to Milan and Lyon.

- Construct the metropolitan government – put in place structures to overcome fragmentation and to create a true urban governance system.
- Develop training and research as strategic resources – essentially improve the local universities, enhance research opportunities and support, highlight the health services sector, and promote vocational and other worker training.
- Promote enterprise and employment – through technology districts, efforts to improve technology transfer, support the use of innovative technology and growth of the information-communications technology sector, assist the development of more insurance companies, and support formation of Territorial Pacts (a recent initiative to involve multiple levels of government and the private sector in infrastructure and development projects[10]).
- Promote Turin as a city of culture, tourism, commerce and sports – with the 2006 Winter Olympics being the central point here, but also focusing on Turin as a city of cinema, the avant-garde in art, and making a bid for Turin to be designated a European City of Culture.
- Improve urban quality – with various beautification and renewal projects.

From the standpoint of urban strategic planning, there are several things about the Turin plan that are of interest. First, is the lack of central focus on the key sectors of the day – informational-communications technology, and bio-engineering. Both are mentioned in the plan but only as already existing activities that could receive additional support. Other sectors so highlighted are health services, aerospace, and automobile production. But none of them is put at the center of the strategy. This is in sharp contrast to most other city strategic initiatives. Second, the initiatives of the plan comprise a general support that will have impacts on all sectors of the economy. Some of the initiatives are focused on making the productive system in general more efficient – support of education, technology and training – but others are simply to make the city more attractive as a place for work, living and tourism. This suggests, thirdly, a lack of direction from the top with regard to the specific direction the Turin economy will take and an approach of support for the private sector where these decisions will be made and where developments will occur. The obvious question is, of course, whether the small- and medium-sized firms in the Turin region will be up to the challenge that is given to them.

Four years into the 2000–2010 Plan, Plan II for 2004–2015 is close to being introduced. It calls for no major change in direction from the original Plan but recognizes a need to promote interaction among the advanced sectors, rather than a set of vertical structures, and participation in the process will be greatly expanded from perhaps 100 individuals to 3000 or more. There is some concern that the first plan was rather too general, in spite of what was said above, in an effort to build broad support for it, and that some specificity and prioritization may be called for.

In an effort to generate this specificity, Invest in Turin and Piedmont, an agency that was established a decade ago to encourage inward foreign direct investment, is giving priority in its work to two sectors that are currently strong points of the regional economy, information-communications and auto-mobile research and development, and to three that have promise, life sciences, nanotechnology and logistics. In the latter one, the effort is to provide a link from the port of Genoa for shipping traffic from Asia through Switzerland to northern Europe. This, of course, conflicts with the notion in Lyon that they should be the primary linkage between the Mediterranean and the north. The local airport, Caselle, would be used for intra-European flights and Malpensa, between Milan and Turin, would be the inter-continental airport. It is clear that conflicting visions abound.

It is felt in Turin that the big projects of the turn of the present century, such as expansion of Caselle airport, getting the 2006 Winter Olympics and more active participation in Eurocities have 'put the city on the European map.' Building on this, the city has managed to be designated UNESCO Book City in 2006, to host the International Architectural Congress in 2007 and to be the International Design City of 2007. While these events may strike some as little more than local boosterism, they do have an impact on the self-perception of the residents of a city and they do give it some international recognition.

A final comment on Turin would be to take note of the effort by Confindustria Piemonte, (the Federation of Piedmont Industries), to promote the notion of change. An initiative has been launched with the name '*Gli amici del cambiamento*,' or 'the friends of change.'[11] Their approach is to give prior-ity to three aspects: research, infrastructure and the complex of local indus-tries. The specific initiatives of the program, the Turin-Lyon TGV, upgrading of the universities and the local research capacity and the airport, are less strik-ing than is the notion that the region of Piedmont and its largest urban econ-omy, Turin, must embrace the concept of change in the contemporary context of rapid change.

Turin gives much evidence of having developed an effective strategic plan-ning process, and the major objectives, while not yet realized, do have broad-based support.

CITIES ON THE PERIPHERY

The six cities that are situated less advantageously than those in the core, suffer from the negative aspects of elements that were highlighted in the introduction to the core cities above. While Dresden, Hamburg and Munich are well served by Germany's high-speed ICE rail network, the other peripheral cities, Barcelona, Copenhagen and Seville, have no such rail connections. Copenhagen and Munch are second tier airports, with the former being heavily dependent upon the continued independent operation of its major airline. There is little thought given to improving the transportation connections or joint initiatives by cities such as Copenhagen and Hamburg or Seville and Barcelona.

While no city can be assured that it will not be host to a terrorist attack, the peripheral cities do appear to have a lower risk of such disruption, although following the July 2005 attacks in London, and more recently the 'cartoon crisis,' Denmark was identified as a possible future target due to its contribution to the military force in Iraq. But a slow-down in the flows of goods could be hard on the ports of Hamburg and Barcelona and on air traffic for Copenhagen and Munich.

The strategic–economic planning efforts of the peripheral cities are primarily focused on trying to extend the reach of the city into some region that is even more peripheral to the core of the EU – the Baltic for Copenhagen, Poland and the Czech Republic for Hamburg and Dresden, the Balkans and Hungary for Munich, and North Africa for Seville. Only Barcelona is primarily focused on enhancing its economic linkages with the core of the EU, in this case with contiguous areas of France and through extraordinarily active participation in Eurocities, and United Cities and Local Governments.

Barcelona
Given the earlier discussion of the long experience of Barcelona with planning, it should be no surprise that this city has had the most impressive strategic–economic plan of the ten cities of this present period.

At the center of Barcelona's approach is its conceptualization of its metropolitan region and the way in which its constituent municipalities relate to each other, and especially to the principle city. In its plan, three models of urban regions are presented.[12] Paris is shown to be the central city of a 'mononuclear radial model,' with two-way linkages with each of the smaller, and subordinate, municipalities. London is the center of a 'bi-hierarchic radial model,' having direct linkages with a handful of medium-sized cities, each of which has further linkages with the smallest municipalities in the region. Barcelona is depicted as being at the center of a complex 'poly-nuclear reticular model' in which there are three major cities, with Barcelona presumably being 'head among equals'. There are also several intermediate cities and many more smaller ones. What is distinct about the Barcelona model is the fact that each of the participating municipalities has multiple linkages with others at the same or different levels. This graphic structure is reflected in the way in which the design and implementation of the plan are carried out. Based on the participation of the Plan of 1988, the association which supervises the design and implementation of the plan consists of 300 members including the usual economic, labor, university and NGO actors as well as representatives of eight of the metropolitan region's 36 municipalities. It is noted in the planning document that a dozen or more of the municipalities in the Barcelona region have also initiated their own strategic plans; obviously harmonization of vision and coordination of policies and initiatives is a high priority in this situation.

The Barcelona planners began, as was the case with Milan, by stating their understanding of the strategic planning process. The introduction to the plan states that a strategic metropolitan plan is not the same thing as one for a city; the city has a clear structure of governance whereas the metropolitan region has to seek to create such a structure – it must establish a consensus among municipalities that normally focus solely on their own individual development and future. In order that a common vision could be developed, five technical commissions were established, each of which focused on a separate critical theme. The part of the Plan that speaks to 'territorial coherence' emphasized the need to: '(c)reate suitable frameworks . . . for reaching consensus on decisions;' '(p)romote territorial planning that establishes links between mobility, accessibility and urbanism;' and '(c)reate mechanisms for the monitoring of territorial development that facilitate decision-making with a broad metropolitan space perspective.'[13]

The Plan itself begins with the most general objectives relating to the quality of life, the wellbeing of the citizenry and culture, and proceeds to very specific tasks that are to be accomplished.[14] The vision of the planners focuses on three main points: 1) to use innovation, creativity and knowledge to enhance the competitiveness of Barcelona, 2) to develop the region's productivity so as to promote sustainable development, the environment, and social progress, and 3) to assure the efficient management of the urban region. More specifically, on the basis of efficient management and governance the Barcelona Plan has three 'vectors of activity:' 1) 'economic development, based on sustainable criteria and employment,' 2) 'territorial model and mobility,' and 3) 'culture of good coexistence, social cohesion and cooperation.' Each of the vectors is presented with a set of 5–12 critical evaluations of the existing situation that generates the identification of problem area or shortcomings, which are then followed by a set of 5–11 relevant objectives. Each of the objectives has several identified policy initiatives or measures that are to be pursued. This approach to strategic–economic planning conforms closely to what was suggested in Chapter 2 of this book. Without getting into the extensive details of the objectives and responsibilities detailed in the plan, it can be noted that each of the policy initiatives appears to be reasonable and can be expected, in combination with the others clustered under that objective, to be effective in realizing that objective. Of course, the proof will be in the execution of the plan.

With regard to the direction that is being proposed for the economy of the Barcelona metropolitan region, it must be noted that of the ten cities in this study none, with the exception of Turin, has had to restructure its economy away from tradition manufacturing toward a 'new socio-economic model' to the same extent. The Barcelona region changed its economic structure from the textiles of the 19th century to automobiles and electric/mechanical appliances in the 1970s. With the replacement of the dictatorship of General Franco by democracy and with membership in the EEC, Barcelona emerged as a modern, services-dominated metropolitan economy.

The objective today is to foster another transformation of the economy into one of the urban regions in the EU which has most successfully managed to realize its potential in the high technology and knowledge economy of the 21st century. To accomplish this objective, universities are to be considered 'motors of development' and they, professional education and business schools are to increase their international perspective. The higher education sector is targeted to become an important export source. Barcelona is to focus on quality of life issues and will define itself as an 'open city,' presumably along the Richard Florida lines. Other initiatives are aimed at upgrading the transportation, housing, office and industrial infrastructures, improving local governance and plan coordination and inserting the Barcelona region more explicitly into the network of urban regions of the EU. One thing that is lacking is a focus on a small number of specific industrial sectors. Barcelona has already developed competitive strength in areas such as logistics, aeronautics, bio-pharmaceutics and electro-mechanical manufacturing, as well as a broad array of services such as finance, tourism and media. As was noted in Chapter 5, this activity was well established before the current plan was undertaken.

It should be clear from this discussion that Barcelona has taken a highly effective approach to strategic–economic planning. This was made clear to me, when I encountered frequent comments by those I interviewed in some of the other cities to the effect that Barcelona was, in this regard, a model for other city leaders to follow.

Copenhagen

The heart of Copenhagen's attempt to insert itself into the EU urban hierarchy continues to be its emphasis on education, Medicon Valley, some strength in mobile telecommunications and software, rapidly developing film and audio-visual activity, and its gateway function. Delocalization is not a bad word in Copenhagen as the jobs that have left have been replaced with better jobs and those workers who have been displaced have been generally successful in being retrained and employed in higher skilled positions. Perhaps the most impressive feature of the Øresund region is Øresund University, an umbrella institution that coordinates the activities of fourteen institutions of higher education in metropolitan Copenhagen and Skåne. This includes the universities of Copenhagen, Roskilde, Malmö and Lund, the Copenhagen Business School, technical universities, and two agricultural colleges. The initiative was begun in 1989, explicitly in response to the crisis that was having such a negative impact on the regional economy. Entities throughout the Øresund region have explicitly embraced the 'triple helix' model which develops and strengthens the actors of government, universities and companies. The consequence of this has been a set of platforms that support clusters of research entities and production firms in areas such as medical technology (Medicon Valley Academy), bio-pharmaceutical, nano-technology, culture-film, food processing, and environmental aspects of economic activity. There is a genuine collaboration across the sound with major universities, companies and science parks, such as Ideon in Lund and the Øresund Science Region which it founded, located on both sides, and with support from local governments at all levels. This degree of cross-border collaboration is unique in the EU and perhaps in the world.

In spite of the success of the Øresund regional integration project, there are three clouds on the horizon for the economy of Copenhagen. First, is the future of the airport at Kastrup. This is predicated on the continued success of SAS. If SAS should have difficulties, as is the case with so many airlines today, it is feared that it would merge with another airline such as Lufthansa, in which case a large portion of the intercontinental flights would be transferred from Kastrup to Frankfurt and Stockholm. To a considerable extent, because of the success of Kastrup, Copenhagen has developed, through its international functions, into a city that is far larger than is required for a country the size of Denmark (6 million inhabitants). With a reduced function for Kastrup, Copenhagen might begin a slow decline to a less impressive size and status. Amsterdam faced the same uncertainty when its primary carrier, KLM, merged with Air France. However, in this instance it was agreed that the two hubs would continue to have international and intercontinental flights with the Charles de Gaulle/Schipol division being set at 70/30 per cent, for the foreseeable future. It is conceivable that a similar arrangement could be made with regard to Copenhagen, should any such merger take place. Nonetheless, it is understood by all that Kastrup is central to the continued vitality of Copenhagen and the Øresund region.

A second concern is the education system and the level of educational attainment. While there is no crisis at hand, there is a general sense that the current generation is being less well educated than was their predecessor. Should this continue to be the case, the advantage Copenhagen has in knowledge-based industries would gradually erode. With this in mind, the Danish Prime Minister has declared that within the next decade Denmark, and Copenhagen, will become the best educated among its EU competitors. The strategic focus of the city administration is on the creative and innovative aspects of all sectors of its economy. This means that the advances in, say, information-communication technology and design, will be applied to areas as diverse as logistics, audio-visual, and the needs of elderly people. The understanding among city leaders is that there has been a history of inter-agency cooperation that will make feasible the extensive networking that this approach will require.

The third potential cloud on Copenhagen's horizon is the restructuring of government on a national basis that is underway. The objective is essentially that of being able to provide health care more effectively for all Danes. Structurally, this means that the county level of government will be significantly weakened and its powers will be divided between the national and municipal governments. In effect, the national government will pay for the hospitals and the municipalities will fund the patients. But this reform will spread out into all areas of policy. Two hundred and seventy five municipalities will be merged into 115, nationally, but Greater Copenhagen, a metro-wide structure, will become 25 municipalities. In effect, for Copenhagen, the restructuring will be similar to what Thatcher and Pujol did in England and Catalonia with regard to the largest cities in England and to Barcelona during the 1980s. In actuality, the consequence of this step is still uncertain and it has its adherents and its detractors within Copenhagen itself. The crucial aspect for the economy is the establishment of a Business Development Forum in each of five regions plus the island of Bornholm into which Denmark will be divided. Each Forum will be charged with promoting economic development within that region, with promoting the interaction of business, universities and government (the by now famous 'Triple Helix'), and with supporting that region's comparative or competitive advantage. Each Forum will conduct a benchmarking exercise and an analysis of existing and potential industrial clusters.

Detractors argue that the restructuring will give more power, even a veto, with regard to economic–strategic planning to municipalities and that this will make such planning virtually impossible as municipalities will argue over their own specific interests. The concern is that five or more years of strategic planning will be lost while the restructuring is working itself out and that this could prove to be disastrous for Copenhagen and the Øresund region. How could the Øresund region maintain its position in the EU urban hierarchy if so much time is lost? Furthermore, no one can be certain how this restructuring of responsibilities will affect cooperative initiatives such as Medicon Valley and Øresund University, initiatives that have proven to be of great importance to the economic vitality of the region. In response, supporters of the restructuring note that the regional councils that have been formed typically have 20 members, of whom only three represent municipalities and that unions, business interests, universities, financial institutions, employers, labor and other interested individuals dominate the entities. In the Copenhagen-North Sjælland region a business representative will probably be appointed the chairperson. Hence, they argue, the municipalities will not be able to dominate decision-making. The economic–strategic plan for the next decade has been developed by the metro-wide agency, HUR, and it is almost certain that this plan will be accepted by the new authority – if it is rejected they will have nothing and the five years of indecision the critics fear would indeed be realized.

Economic growth has been lower in Copenhagen during the past five years than it has in competing cities, such as Stockholm, Hamburg and Berlin – 2.5 per cent versus 5 per cent. As a consequence the focus is now on maximizing, or at least increasing, the rate of growth of output and incomes rather than on redistributing wealth. Officials discuss the desire to make Copenhagen an attractive city for high-skill workers, the mechanics of creating a regional innovation system, the positive consequences of being a creative city, and so forth. This is in clear contrast with the social-democratic strategy of earlier years. They speak of 'business angels,' or venture capitalists, who assist the establishment of start-ups and of promoting risk taking, although they recognize that to fail is in some sense to become 'branded' as a failure and that in small Denmark there is nowhere to hide or to start up again, as is possible in the US or in England.

Across the sound in Sweden, city leaders in Malmö have come to realize that the collapse of the ship-building industry in Skåne was, in the long term, the best thing that could have happened since it forced them to break with an economic past that was not going to be viable for the years to come. The university developed from a branch of Lund University and now has a specialization in the health professions. The planning process in Malmö was limited to upgrading the various districts of the city, enhancing the city's environmental attractiveness and economic sustainability, increasing the population density and improving the transportation infrastructure with the needs of commuters in mind.[15] With an investment in development of the water front, new residential areas and a landmark building Turning Torso by the architect Calatrava, Malmö is no longer a declining port city but an attractive town for commuters from Copenhagen as well as for workers in its own economic entities.

In summary, city leaders throughout the Copenhagen-Øresund region see no need for dramatic refocusing of their strategic-economic thinking. The focus will continue to be on education, innovation, maintaining their position as a key urban region in the north of Europe with its relationships with the Nordic and Baltic areas, the rest of the world, and the EU intact. The several technology platforms and structures such as Øresund university and its components are already established and are expected to provide the base of the regional economy for the foreseeable future. If Kastrup can maintain its major hub status and if the governmental restructuring is successful, Copenhagen and its region should have a reasonably positive next decade.

Dresden

Given the confused situation in which it found itself in the first years of the 1990s, Dresden has had a rather successful decade. The German magazine *Capital* has it ranked, in one of its most recent issues, as number 14 as an economic center and sees it as being headed for the top ten. It is second only to Leipzig in its rate of improvement in this annual ranking of 60 cities in Germany.[16] The article took particular note of the success Dresden has had in attracting high technology companies such as Infineon and AMD (Advanced Micro Devices). For the future, Dresden leaders plan to stay on course. One difference will be in the way the strategic plan is to be treated. In the early 1990s the plan that was devised, with its foci on technology, services and the bridge function, was not widely discussed or even understood. A small group of city leaders pressed for the initiatives, through the state apparatus, that would be required for the success of 'their plan.' Little was written down and the main focus seems to have been that of keeping firms in the Dresden region. Today, the plan is widely available in a report with a forward by the Mayor, Ingolf Roßberg.[17] It explicitly stresses the concept of *Kompetenzfeld* (competence field) and specifies four of them: 1) micro-electronics, information and communication technology, 2) new materials (polymers, ceramics and high-temperature super-conductors), 3) mechanical and plant engineering, automotive engineering, aviation industry, and 4) biotechnology. In a striking contrast, the current plan was presented to the City Council for its consideration and approval. This should ensure that all important actors and the general public will be fully informed of the substance of the plan and will, presumably, be on board.

In contrast to many cities, including Leipzig which used the consulting firm McKensie, Dresden's focus on competence fields was home-grown and grounded in historic strengths. However, these are in fact clusters and clusters are in the air everywhere so no terribly original thinking has been required. It is in the implementation of the competence field concept that Dresden has shown some good thinking. In the city government the economic development office has been restructured so there is a team with a person in charge for each competence field. This individual is charged with working actively with the firms involved and with coordination of relevant activities of other departments. Each competence field is to be structured with intra-city networks, a critical mass of activity, a focus on research and development, the infrastructure it needs, and an effort to do the complete line of activity from R&D to design to production in the Dresden region.

The intra-city network brings together the city, companies, educational institutions and the chambers of commerce and handwork. Their charge is with: 1) designing a cluster strategy and appropriate networks, 2) meeting the needs of small and medium-sized firms, in particular with regard to bidding successfully for public purchasing competitions and 'small firms in trouble,' 3) encouraging start-ups, 4) developing international contacts and marketing, and 5) treating labor force issues. This is very good on paper, but only time will tell how effectively these disparate entities are able to work together.

A research and development network has been established with seventeen members – firms, research laboratories, universities, and so forth. Each has to make a significant payment to participate so this is not to be an honorific exercise; in fact, it conducts projects, supports a student competition, is pressing for Dresden to be designated the '2006 City of Science,' and encourages joint projects between its members. This is always a very difficult thing to accomplish since firms are concerned with, among other things, proprietary knowledge but two of the largest companies have successfully developed the 'laser line mask.'

These initiatives in networking are, of course, designed to ensure that the competence fields take root in Dresden and are able to be successful in the long run. It is clearly understood that if this is done correctly the whole can, indeed, be greater than the sum of its parts.

The final issue that should be treated with regard to Dresden is the challenge for many cities in attracting and keeping a high-skill labor force and its young workers. Dresden's *Kulture und Kunst* are obviously powerful attractions to highly educated and to middle aged workers. Younger people, however, need something else. Dresden's leaders feel they have a strong asset for this component of the work force in the Tristen-Neustadt district just across the Elbe from the central business district. This is a district that has followed the path that has been taken in so many other cities: a derelict and high crime area with solid structures becomes attractive to young people seeking low rents, then come the funky shops, clubs and restaurants, then the young professionals looking for something fun to do at the week-end discover it, and then gentrification slowly develops. Neustadt certainly does not rival New York, Paris and London, but it may do the job for Dresden.

Dresden does seem to have taken an intelligent approach to the coming decade. The plan is clear and limited in its objectives, it is being publicly discussed and adopted, and several initiatives have been undertaken in an attempt to ensure that the desired results will be realized.

Hamburg

One of the central aspects of Hamburg's current strategic thinking is that of overcoming the general malaise that currently afflicts the German and EU economies. In a time of stagnation and decline of many of the regions of the EU Hamburg is focusing on the slogan of being a 'growing city.' The current population of the city proper is 1.7 million and 4.1 million for the metropolitan area, making Hamburg Germany's second largest city. The proposed growth in population is to come from the immigration of largely skilled workers, primarily from Central Europe, and this is to be linked with growth in both commerce and employment. This sort of expansion conveys a spirit or mentality of optimism and progress, in place of the gloom which pervades much of contemporary Germany. Increased revenues will allow for improvements in the quality of life of its residents and enhance Hamburg's position as a regional and international economic center. Economic growth should be more feasible since the Social Democratic-Green Party in the Senate has been replaced by the conservatives; both argue for more growth but the former imposed some constraints on behalf of the environment that are not supported to the same degree by the latter.

A second aspect is the focus on a set of 'competence clusters': aviation, IT and media, logistics, life science, nanotechnology, renewable energies, and trade with China. The strength of aviation is dependent upon that of Airbus, media is the major center in Germany, the China trade and logistics are growing rapidly, and with over 6000 firms involved in the information-technology sector it is the top center in Germany. The other sectors are less prominent but all have good growth potential. What links them all together in the need to maintain and enhance Hamburg's position in these technology-related sectors is the excellence and comprehensiveness of the metropolitan region's educational and training infrastructure. In addition to the University of Hamburg, there is the Hamburg-Harburg Technical University and several other publicly and privately funded institutions of higher learning with curricula focusing on scientific and commercial education. The extensive listing of universities, institutes and companies that are linked together can be seen on web-sites, such as that for the information-technology faculties of the University of Hamburg (www.HITeC-HH.de). It is from complexes of institutions such as this that the potential for life science, nanotechnologies, and energy will be realized. Life science will be focused not on pharmaceuticals, which in Germany are largely concentrated along the Rhine River, but on medical equipment and technology which evolves out of the local strengths in machinery and microelectronics.

The physical space of the Hamburg area will be enhanced by the Hafencity · initiative, completion of which will enlarge the area of the city center by about 40 per cent. Replacing a former docklands area, the objective is to construct a place for work (40 000 jobs), shopping and residence (12 000 inhabitants), rather than the almost exclusively residential Java Island of Amsterdam or the largely logistics nature of much of Barcelona's waterfront renewal. The most dramatic structure will be the Elbe Philharmonic concert hall, in addition to maritime-related museums and science centers.

Metropolitan area governance is a challenge for all urban regions and that of Hamburg is a unique situation in that *Freie und Hansestadt Hamburg* is also a *land*, or sub-national province, hence the cooperative structure that is being created must include the city, the *land*, and 14 neighboring municipalities in the provinces of Schleswig-Holstein and Lower Saxony. This development is still a work in progress but substantial achievement has already been realized. Early initiatives are a Metropolcard which enables one to visit a wide variety of facilities throughout the metropolitan region, joint exhibits, and recognition that no growth strategy will be successful without the participation of all relevant entities. Other initiatives and projects can be examined on the web-site www.wachsende-stadt.hamburg.dc.

Similar to Lyon and Munich, Hamburg has not undergone a formal strategic–economic planning process, but has rather made relatively marginal additions to a basic strategic thrust which has served it well for the past couple of decades. There are no major restructuring efforts, new industries or sectors to develop from the ground up, or fundamental repositioning of the role or function of Hamburg in the urban network of the EU. There is a new slogan, 'Hamburg – a Growing City,' but in terms of the two goals that were suggested in the discussion of strategic planning in Chapter 2 this is more in the nature of a 'quantitative expansion' than of a 'qualitative restructuring' of economic activity.

As a final observation, it is clear that there are enduring strengths in the economic outlook for Hamburg: the port and logistics are growing, there is adequate skilled labor – much of which is gained through migration from the east. However, there is some concern, as there is almost everywhere, about the quality of K-12 equivalent schooling. The primary potential threats are largely from outside: the China trade and Airbus must remain strong but there is little or nothing Hamburg can do about either. Also the rate of economic growth of the markets that feed the China trade and output in general are dominated by policy at the level of the national government in Berlin or the EU agencies in Brussels. As a result, city leaders are solidly optimistic but could see this optimism darkened by actions taken elsewhere.

Munich

While Dresden and Hamburg are ranked by *Capital* as numbers 14 and 4, respectively, Munich is considered to be the number 1 economic center in Germany and the only German city among the top ten (it is ranked number 10) when the same criteria were used to rank the 40 largest cities in the EU (including the ten new members).[18] This comes as no surprise to those involved with the economy in Munich. They are supremely confident about the current and future economic situation of their city. This makes the study of strategic planning in Munich a bit difficult, as the constant theme in interviews conducted there was that Munich is such an attractive city that no serious effort at such planning is needed. Munich has its quality of life, recreational and cultural assets, consistent focus on education and technology, and has beneficial relations with and support from both the county and provincial governments. An outsider, of course, wants to examine this situation so as to determine whether this optimism is warranted and what, if anything, the city leaders are actually doing to insure realization of this satisfying prospect.

At the level of the province, it should be noted that Bavarian Premier Stoibel has made the further development of clusters an official objective, with aerospace, bio-technology and genetics, media, and information-technology being specified for Munich.[19] In clusters, it is often very difficult to develop much interaction among the participants. In some sectors, such as aerospace and information technology, many of the major firms do work on government contracts. In this case the various levels of government are able to exert some pressure for a degree of interaction that would not otherwise be achieved. One initiative in this area is consideration of a magnetic-levitation (mag-lev) rail link from the airport to the city center. While this is not yet approved, if it is it would put Munich at the center of this developing technology. In bio-technology there is confidence that Munich can become the equal of Cambridge at the head of all European centers. There is state funding of both research and start-ups to support this objective and it is given in coordination with the Max Planck and Frauenhof institutes and the universities and technical schools in Munich that, while ranking only about 10–15 in Europe, are among the best in Germany.

In the private sector, electronics is dominated by Siemens and its many local suppliers, and its networking is locally intra-firm but also global in its extent. Auto manufacturer BMW has a research center in Munich with about 800 employees and the insurance company Allianz has a research center for risk analysis. But there are weaknesses here as private sector financing is difficult to get for long term projects, venture capital is difficult to obtain, and entrepreneurship, while its promotion is a city priority, is not something that as of yet characterizes the local business community.

The county, Oberbayern, is also supportive in funding and coordination of planning of the major flagship projects and the operations of the Messe (trade fare center), and is increasingly so as economic activity spreads from the city of Munich out to the surrounding areas. There is a pervasive understanding throughout the relevant government offices and in private sector entities regarding the crucial importance of the 'soft' factors such as cultural, recreational and educational assets in addition to the usually supported transportation, housing, and communication infrastructures.

Munich's plan for the future is essentially 'more of the same.' The natural attractiveness of the city and its surroundings combined with focused attention to the 'soft' factors makes city leaders optimistic and confident with regard to the city's economic future – one hopes not complacently so. More proactively, there are also continuing efforts to nurture the targeted clusters with the objective of making or keeping each ahead of the competition from other cities in Europe. Much is made of the success Munich had in attracting the headquarters of the European Patent Office, seen as giving recognition to the city's past, current and future predominance in research, engineering and technology. Looking to the rest of Germany, Munich does not consider Berlin to be a competitor as the labor force there is not nearly as well educated and trained as it is in Munich; however, Hamburg is serious competition in some sectors of the service industry, especially in media.

The 'soft' factors are of great importance in attracting and keeping both a highly educated and skilled labor force and the younger members of the labor force on whom the future so much depends. In addition to the 'high' culture assets, some of which have already been mentioned, the city has developed the facilities of the 1976 Summer Olympics as a major site for not only sporting or athletic activities but also for such 'pop' or *Jugend* (youth) culture events as the World Skateboarding Championships and music concerts and extravaganzas. The objective is to make Munich an 'Interesting City,' and knowledge and 'soft' factors have been described as actually being the Strategic Focus of the city.

Crime is not a problem, but a dark cloud on the horizon may be a growing gap between the skilled and unskilled, and perhaps unemployable, components of the labor force. The city is making some efforts at providing more low-rent housing and expansion of the public transportation system and it is hoped that this will make it somewhat easier for the 'excluded' to gain access to jobs and housing. The short-term cost of providing various services to a new immigrant population appears to be manageable as inflows of migrants seem to have stabilized.

Seville

The strategic–economic planning of Seville is taking place on two levels, by two different agencies. In 2000 the city council created an entity, Sevilla Global, which is the city's urban agency for economic development. As mayor Alfredo Sánchez Monteseirín put it: 'If Competitiveness, Cohesion and Freedom are the new policy values we must learn to balance, then Sevilla Global('s) challenge is to work upon the first of these goals.'[20] In addition to this planning at the metropolitan level, the state of Andalusia has adopted its own initiative which is aimed at 'innovation and modernization' of the state.[21] While Andalusia contains several major Spanish cities – Cadiz, Malaga, Huelva, Cordoba, and Grenada – this plan cannot be seen as one that is focused primarily on Seville; however, since Seville is the principle city of the state this initiative is certain to have its major impacts there.

The Andalusia plan aims at bringing together various entities from the worlds of higher and professional education, business, the public sector, and research and development with the objective being that of establishing a network of technological infrastructure that will stimulate the creation and sharing of new knowledge and technology. This will be used to promote a convergent economic development, social cohesion, an improved quality of life, and enhanced regional competitiveness. In addition to a very knowledgeable discussion of the nature of innovation and modernization and of the situation in Spain, the plan understands that the success of this initiative will depend upon: 1) the commitment of the government, 2) a coherent structure of policies and means of their implementation, 3) adequate capability and provision of resources, 4) broad participation among the members of the community so as to promote understanding and to minimize the natural resistance to change, and 5) regular adaptation of the plan through the course of its implementation. This sort of discussion and attention to factors that can facilitate or inhibit successful implementation is of great benefit to planners and to the planning process.

Following the discussions of innovation, the vision of the government and factors of success, the plan for innovation and the modernization of Andalusia presents what has become a standard list of policies aimed at promoting: 1) equal access to information technology throughout the state, 2) the development of business firms, 3) sustainability, the environment and energy, 4) cooperation and knowledge creation of firms and universities, 5) development of the society of information, and 6) 'intelligent' (public) administration. It is impressive that in addition to providing a long 'wish list' of policy initiatives and actions, the government also gives a statement of its commitment to provide €5.682 billion over the six year period 2005–2010, almost half of which is devoted to knowledge creation by firms and universities. The plan is devoid of any details as to which universities, urban regions, sectors, and so forth will be the beneficiaries of this funding, but this will presumably be allocated on a competitive basis. Seville should certainly be able to get substantial support for activities that are in agreement with its own initiatives.

Much of the work of Sevilla Global is devoted to promoting commerce and retail sales, renewal of industrial sites, creation of new industrial areas, and identifying new residential districts. As was noted earlier, this sort of land-use planning has implications for economic development but is something quite different from the strategic–economic planning that is the subject of this book. Nonetheless there are initiatives of Sevilla Global that are of considerable interest to us.

Prior to the innovation initiative of Andalusia, Sevilla Global had issued a study on 'the technologies of information and communication in firms in Seville.'[22] In this study it is noted that Spain is grouped with France and Italy as laggards in the North–South divide in the EU with regard to the implantation of information and communication technology, although with some business-related indicators, such as personal computers per 100 employees Spain is at the EU average. The situation for Andalusia is that it is a lagging region that is far below the average use of ICT within Spain, with the exception of firms using e-commerce and firms with web-pages. When looking at business firms in Seville, Sevilla Global considers five indicators of business use of ICT and presents the following classification: 1) firms fully integrated in the information society, 2) firms that are well along toward full integration, 3) firms that are just starting on this path, and 4) firms that are excluded from the information society. The writers of this study conclude that, in general, Spanish firms are moving from classification 3 to classification 4, but that firms in Seville are one step behind – moving from classification 4 to classification 3.[23] The positive aspect of this result is that Seville firms are seen to be in positive movement and are thought to be generally well placed to take advantage of the initiatives in the Andalusia plan on innovation and modernization.

The other dimension of Sevilla Global's approach to the city's economic future is its strategy to project Seville and its urban region into the rest of Spain and internationally.[24] The actions of promotion are quite standard, but what is more interesting is that the economic activity that is to be promoted is focused on six clusters: 1) leisure, culture and tourism, 2) advanced services, 3) food processing, 4) metal-mechanical, 5) logistics, and 6) transportation equipment. Much of the aforementioned land-use planning has been done in support of these clusters. An aerospace district has been established near the airport at which, among other things, the military version of the Airbus 340 will get its final assembly. A logistics district will be created north of the city which will link the port, just to the south of the city, to rail and trucking lines to the rest of Spain and into France and the rest of the EU. While this is in no way seen as competition to the major ports, Marseille, Genoa, Rotterdam and so forth, it may have some advantage for smaller vessels. As Cartuja has become filled to capacity a new center of technology and industry will be created in the city, similar to the Tony Gerland Center in Lyon. To the south of the city a new university and a technology park of 800 hectares will be established. Here is an excellent example of the explicit interdependence of land-use planning and strategic–economic planning.

In evaluating the success of the Cartuja '93 techno-park, Miguel Rivas Casado argued that, in contrast with the model of the 'suburban garden' which dominates much thinking about science and technology parks – a sort of university campus being the ideal – Cartuja is characterized by a 'radical centrality' and that this urban nature will serve as a guide for Seville's other efforts to develop its potential as a center of the new economy of knowledge.[25] As has just been demonstrated, the technology focus of Cartuja is also central to strategic thinking of decision-makers.

COMMENTS IN CONCLUSION

Whereas the previous two chapters looked backward to the experiences of the ten cities during the decade of the 1990s, in this chapter we examined how their city leaders are positioning them for the near future. The first thing to note is that every city has a project designed to shape the future of that city's economy. Second, many cities have embraced the notion of clusters being an essential component of a successful strategic–economic plan; however other city planners expressed reservations with regard to the way in which clusters would operate in their urban situation. Third, several of the cities have explicitly adopted the Triple Helix approach which integrates local government, universities and the private sector into a symbiotic whole that benefits each of the participants and promotes overall economic development. It has become clear that in all of the cities local authorities understand that a desirable future economy can be attained only if the city and its urban region act positively to adopt policies and to introduce initiatives and that they must pick up the slack, so to speak, now that national governments have reduced their own capacity to intervene. So the first years of the 21st century suggest that the near future will be one of increased local activism.

While the advantageous situation of core cities remains important with regard to the access to a large market, the advantages that come from a dense transportation network and the ease of engaging in cooperative ventures with other cities, several of the peripheral cities, for example Hamburg, Munich and Barcelona, have done extremely well in developing their economies in ways that would be considered appropriate to the requirements of the new economy of the first part of the 21st century. In many cities the focus has been on creativity and the 'creative class,' and this aspect of urban development does not necessarily privilege cities in the core. In fact, development of the creative assets of a city can work to off-set the inherent disadvantage of location on the periphery.

Examination of the planning documents of these ten cities reveals a very considerable increase in the knowledge among city leaders of the strategic–economic planning process, an understanding of its increasing necessity and a sophistication in policy formation that was absent in almost all of the cities in 1990. This must be taken to be a very positive development. At the same time, city leaders in most of the ten cities seem to have developed a more realistic understanding of the strengths and weaknesses of their particular city. This may just be a consequence of taking a more serious approach to looking at the future of their local economies. Some of the more ambitious linkage or network plans, such as Seville becoming a bridge between the EU and South America and Africa, have come to naught. In 1990 most EU cities saw themselves as the center of some significant economic space, but they soon came to realize that theirs was a not very exclusive, and hence rather useless, center. The planning process has become a far more open process, with dozens of committees, task forces, decision centers and so forth. This can become a bit cumbersome but once a plan has been agreed to it is far more likely to be realized than is the closed process that was found in some of the cities, such as Dresden in 1990.

Most of the cities have discovered the value to their economic development strategy of universities and other institutes of higher learning. They are now seen to be central to the development of the high technology clusters, creative milieux, learning regions, and other such structures that rely on a skilled and creative labor force. At the same time, in many of the cities there has been a growing concern over the adequacy of K-12 education.

On the dark side of these urban experiences are two perhaps increasingly important phenomena. In the post-September 11 period, questions of security have the potential of disadvantaging large centrally located cities, of slowing down the flow of goods among nations and of exacerbating ethnic and social tensions in cities with a high degree of multi-ethnicity. National governments may adopt policies through necessity that will have their primary negative impact on urban regions. The second dark element is somewhat related to the first – the difficulties cities will have in assimilating flows of migrants from non-EU countries. Amsterdam has had difficulty integrating the second wave of immigration, composed of low-skilled immigrants who do not come to the Netherlands with knowledge of the Dutch language, contrary to the first wave in the 1960s and 1970s. The experience of Turin with the long-run consequences of attracting low-skill, poorly educated migrants for the automobile industry is indicative of the potential for negative impacts tomorrow of apparently rational decisions made today. Xenophobia is often strongest in the rural regions of a country, but policies that national governments adopt to placate this sentiment may, again, have their primary negative impact on urban regions. Either of these two factors could create difficulties for city leaders in achieving the objectives of their strategic–economic plans.

NOTES

1. For a discussion of this in the context of French airport policy, see: Jean Claude Giblin, 'Les Aéroports Régionaux à la Veille de la Décentralization,' *Hérodote*, No. 114 (3), 2004, pp. 101–21.
2. Giorgio Monaci and Gabriele Pasqui, *Le politiche e gli strumenti di sostegno all'innovazione nell'area Milanese*, Milan: FrancoAngeli, 2002; and *Strategic Programme for the development and support of innovation and the growth of production activities in the province of Milan, 2002/2004*, Milan: Provincia di Milano, 2002.
3. *Strategic Programme for the development and support of innovation and the growth of production activities in the province of Milan, 2002–2004*, Milan: Provincia di Milano, 2002, pp. 11–12.
4. *Provincia di Milano: Un progetto strategico per la regione urbana Milanese*, Milan: Politecnico di Milano, Dipartimento di Architettura e Pianificazione, 2004.
5. Giorgio Lonardi, 'Creatività, Milano lancia il guanto di sfida,' *La Repubblica*, January 31, 2005, p. 36.
6. The documents can be found on: www.torino-internazionale.org.
7. *Towards the plan*, Turin: Torino Internazionale, 1998.
8. *Towards the plan*, pp. 21, 26, 54 and 56.
9. *The strategic plan of Torino 2000–2010*, Turin: Torino Internazionale, 2000.
10. See Francesca Governa and Carlo Salone, 'Italy and European Spatial Policies: Polycentrism, Urban Networks and Local Innovation Practices,' *European Planning Studies*, Vol. 13, No. 2, March 2005, pp. 265–83.
11. Pier Paolo Luciano, 'Ecco le tre chiavi del futuro,' *La Repubblica*, February 24, 2005, p. XI. See also *Nuove opera per il Piemonte che cambia*, Turin: Federazione delle associazione industriali del Piemonte, February 2003.
12. Barcelona 2000, *Plan estratégico metropolitano de Barcelona: Documento núm. 11*, March 2003 (there is an English language version of the Plan, but I primarily used the original as the English text is somewhat abridged).
13. Barcelona 2000 (English version), p. 37.
14. Barcelona 2000, p. 22–44.
15. *Implementation of the Comprehensive Plan Malmö 2000*, Malmö: Stadsbyggnadskontor, October 2004; and *Malmö 2005: Aktualisering och komplettering av Malmös översikesplan*, Malmö: Stadsbyggnadskontor, April 2005.
16. 'Die Hoffnungsträger,' *Capital*, February 2005, pp. 14–19.
17. *Wirtschaftsförderung 2003/Economic Report 2003*, Dresden: Wirtschaft und kommunale Amt, 2003, pp. 15–36.
18. 'Die Hoffnungsträger,' p. 19.
19. *Metropolregion München – das Kratzentrum Deutschlands*, Munich: Industrie- und Handelskammer fur München und Oberbayern, 2003, p. 18.
20. 'Mayor's Message,' http://www.sevillaglobal.es/acercade/alcade/index.html.en.html
21. *Plan de Innovación y Modernización de Andalucia*, Seville: Junta de Andalucia, 2004.
22. Sevilla Global, *Tecnologías de la Información y las Comunicaciones en la Empresa Sevillana. Un informe de Alproximación*, Seville: Sevilla Global, 2002.
23. Sevilla Global, p. 63.
24. Sevilla Global, *Estrategia de Promoción Exeterior para Sevilla y su ámbito metropolitano*, Seville: Sevilla Global, 2003.
25. Miguel Rivas Casado, *El Nuevo plan general de ordenación ante las actividades productivas: una valoración*, Seville: Sevilla Global, 2002, p. 6.

7. Lessons from the past and a look to the future

In this final chapter we will review the experiences of the ten cities over the past decade and a half, and then we will suggest what the future may hold for the city leaders who have to chart the courses of the economic development of their urban regions. The experiences of the ten cities in this study, which were presented in Chapters 4 to 6, enable us to gain an understanding of the degree to which city planners in each city adhered to what were referred to in Chapter 2 as the 'five components' of effective urban SEP. In Table 7.1 the five components are arrayed horizontally across the top and the cities are listed vertically on the left. It is, of course, possible that in spite of the interviews with city leaders and the examination of planning documents of each individual city the effort of local leaders with regard to one or more of the five components may have been understated. Any such misstatement is sincerely regretted.

This review of the recourse of each of the cities to the five components indicates that half of the cities included in this study, Amsterdam, Barcelona, Copenhagen, Lyon and Munich, have implemented all five of the components, but the remaining five have omitted one or more of them. Dresden did much better with its recent SEP than it did a decade ago. The process was open, involved all of the major entities in the urban region, and the resulting plan appears to be well suited to the potential of the local economy. However, since the plan has just been approved it is not yet clear how well local resources are being mobilized or the degree to which their performance will be monitored.

Hamburg is not changing direction in its economic trajectory, hence there has not been much involvement of local entities in the design of an SEP, nor is it therefore possible to determine how well the plan meets the aspirations of local actors. One suspects, however, that there is not much controversy with regard to that trajectory so the absence of significant participation in the process by local actors does not pose a problem. Since the future is most likely to be 'more of the same' in Hamburg, responsibilities of participants are well clarified, but the degree to which performance is monitored was not clear.

Milan has labored under the handicaps of the *tangentopoli* scandals of the early 1990s, a national government that has not been very decisive, and a regional governmental structure that does give primary position to clear lines

Table 7.1   Use of the five components of strategic–economic planning

The five components	1	2	3	4	5
The cities					
Amsterdam	x	x	x	x	x
Barcelona	x	x	x	x	x
Copenhagen	x	x	x	x	x
Dresden	x	x	x	?	?
Hamburg	x	–	–	x	?
Lyon	x	x	x	x	x
Milan	–	x	x	–	–
Munich	x	x	x	x	x
Seville	–	–	x	x	?
Turin	x	x	x	x	?

The five components of effective strategic–economic planning:

1. an objective examination of the urban region's strengths and weaknesses in relation to other competing regions
2. involvement of the general public and of all major entities in the region in an exercise that will make explicit the actual aspirations and concerns of local residents and entities
3. design of a strategic–economic plan that realizes the realistic aspirations and concerns that have just been identified
4. mobilization of local human resources in the context of clear responsibilities and lines of authority and with an understanding of who or which agency is in charge of the process
5. regular monitoring and evaluation of progress and performance

Note: 'x' indicates this has been done; '?' indicates uncertainty as to whether it has been done; '–' indicates this has not been done.

of responsibility. As a consequence the planning process has not been implemented as effectively as in most of the other cities. There is no evidence that a truly objective assessment of Milan's strengths and weaknesses was part of the process. Participation in the process appears to have been limited to what might be referred to as entities with standing rather than being open to the broader public. While the plan has specified a set of objectives, one has doubts as to whether an efficient structure of responsibilities and authority will be instituted, and the same must be said regarding the monitoring of performance by participants. The fact that an OECD Territorial Review of Milan was scheduled for several months later was an added incentive to get the SEP process organized properly.

The planning process of Seville appears to have been designed by a limited number of actors without involvement of the community at large, and there was little objective assessment of the city's strengths and weaknesses. The SEP itself is clear with regard to its objectives and the responsibilities of the entities involved are clearly specified. While the mechanism for monitoring of performance is not made clear, one has the feeling that due to the limited number of participants, performance that is not up to par will be noticed.

The other Italian city, Turin, has done a very good job of the first three components: an assessment of the city's strengths and weaknesses was done, rather broad participation in the process was achieved and the resulting plan is clear in its objectives. Given the pressing need to refocus the local economy away from traditional manufacturing to activities that will be more promising in the future, there was urgency to this process that was not as strong in other cities. Thinking in Turin was dominated by the fact that the Winter Olympics were scheduled for early 2006. This provided the city with the incentive to realize the physical infrastructure initiatives that had been planned as well as putting the SEP process under added scrutiny by the community as a whole. The primary uncertainty that remains is the degree to which effective monitoring of performance will be accomplished.

The experiences with SEP of these ten EU cities provides us with examples of how the process should be done for maximum effectiveness as well as what sorts of glitches can insinuate themselves even in a well designed plan. The contrast between these focused, proactive initiatives on the part of city leaders stand in stark contrast to the confusion and indifference that marked the actions of their counterparts around 1990. On the basis of these experiences we can make several observations with regard to effective strategic–economic planning.

OBSERVATIONS FROM THE EXPERIENCES OF THE TEN EU CITIES

As has been noted earlier, during the winter and spring, 2005, I interviewed city officials, academic researchers, representatives of entities such as the chamber of commerce with regard to the strategic–economic planning experiences of their urban regions. In addition I was able to accumulate a large number of planning documents, studies, and data that have given me what I believe to be a solid understanding of what these ten cities have been doing with regard to SEP. On the basis of this information I can offer five observations that are most relevant given the topic of this chapter:

- City leaders can indeed have major impacts on the economic lives of their cities through effective strategic–economic planning.
- The turbulence of macro- and micro-economics and of regional and global economic and political events such as regional economic integration, introduction of the Euro, EU economic stagnation, the opening up to Central Europe, emergence of new competitors from China, India, Brazil and other emerging economies have made planning initiatives more difficult. But many cities have risen or fallen in relation to comparable cities, in large part due to the actions of their city leaders.
- Effective governance and strong leadership with a clear and widely accepted vision are essential for a successful experience with SEP.
- Today's activity of comparative advantage may well become tomorrow's problem area. Low-skill, poorly educated workers employed in traditional manufacturing may not be employable in the technology-related economic activities that will be the base of the urban economy of the near future. This will result in the usual varieties of urban social pathologies such as exclusion, unemployment, crime, deteriorating housing, and so forth.
- Regular examination of the aspect of a city's economic development over time is important if rising tax burdens and deteriorating quality of urban life are to be avoided.

The remainder of this section of the chapter will be devoted to amplification of these observations from my examination of the experiences of these ten urban regions.

Leaders Can Have Impacts

Plans, decision-making structures, assignment of responsibilities, review procedures, and so forth all exist on paper; what makes for effective implementation, however, is the quality of the leadership that is provided by the individual who is ultimately in charge of the effort. All participants must have the understanding that none of their colleagues will be allowed to be slack in carrying out their responsibilities. What quality leadership means for any individual city depends upon the governmental and administrative context in which it functions. For example, it was very important for Lyon that Raymond Barre was mayor during much of the 1990s, because of the importance of the national government in Paris in the distribution of funds and the empowerment of local authorities. Mr. Barre was not only well regarded in Lyon, he was also considered to be a powerful figure in Paris. Without his clout in the national government, developments would have been less positive for the city. For Turin in the early 1980s and Milan a decade later local governments were racked by corruption scandals and the chief executive of the city government has to be held responsible for this. These two corruption scandals halted any initiatives by local government until recently since the residents understandably demanded that the municipal books be put in order and some assurance of honest performance of duties could be gained. Turin was fortunate enough to have a respected mayor in office during the mid-years of the 1990s and his actions have resulted in what appears to be a potentially successful strategic–economic planning process, beginning with the city's successful bid for the Winter Olympics in 2006.

In each of the ten cities, students of local government can identify mayors or urban region chief executives who were effective and who sparked effective planning exercises and economic expansion, and, of course, others whose administration supervised a period of stagnation. This is not to suggest that a charismatic and competent mayor can turn around any city, but it seems to be closer to the truth to suggest that this sort of leadership is the *sine qua non* of a competitive city and of efforts to enhance that competitiveness.

Effective Governance

While leadership is essential to effective strategic–economic planning, little can be accomplished without a structure of governance that is equally effective. Cities that have had long experience with planning, such as Amsterdam and Barcelona, or that have had in place an approach to economic development that is consistent and successful, such as Munich and Lyon, are examples of cities with effective governance. Responsibilities are clearly assigned, lines of reporting are defined, squabbling among various metropolitan units and agencies is minimal, and so forth. An example to the contrary is given by the US city of Buffalo, New York. In the early 1990s, following adoption of the Canada–US Free Trade Agreement, Buffalo had designed a strategic plan that was based on realization of the potential benefits from the agreement. But when the municipal leaders met, they included representatives of two counties, two airport commissions, four bridge commissions, the chamber of commerce, the Western New York Development Agency, the city and perhaps one or two others – with no single individual having the authority over the others to ensure that the plan could be effectively implemented. Buffalo has continued to stagnate ever since.

In some instances in which cities have seen a spatial expansion of the location of corporate production and distribution facilities into contiguous areas, such as Munich and Barcelona, it has been necessary to create metropolitan-wide cooperation and governance structures without which no effective action would be possible. In other cases, cities such as Hamburg and Dresden had to reach out to other sub-national or national entities if they were to realize the potential benefits of the liberalization of interaction throughout the extent of their economic reach. In these structures, there must be a clear net benefit to all of the participating municipalities if they are to continue their engagement – this participation cannot be seen merely as a way of making the central city more competitive on the vague promise of some spin-off or spread benefits to come to other municipalities at some future date.

Turbulence

The major elements of turbulence that have had the potential to affect negatively the performance of the ten cities have been enumerated. The importance of this turbulence for any individual city was largely determined by the economic structure and specialization of that city. Since the German economy has been so sluggish throughout the period of this study, cities such as Dresden and Amsterdam, for whose economies the German market is of such great importance, have been particularly hard hit by macro-economic stagnation. Munich and especially Hamburg are linked to aerospace production and as long as Airbus finds the global market to be receptive they are far less affected by the state of the German or EU economies. But for these latter cities the exchange value of the Euro can pose significant problems if it appreciates and Airbus loses sales to Boeing because of this. The opening to Central Europe has the potential to increase demand of some 15 EU products, but this region has also become an attractive place to relocate some production from cities in the west. Manufacturing centers such as Turin and Barcelona have lost production facilities to locations in Central Europe. While both Hamburg and Dresden were able to develop important logistics and economic relationships especially with Poland and the Czech Republic, Munich was disappointed in the economic impact of the opening to the East due primarily to the weakness of the demand for Munich-produced goods there.

Passage of the SEA had very positive impacts on both of the Spanish cities, coming as it did so soon after Spain became a member of the EEC. Barcelona in particular was able to position itself as a key participant in the European urban structure and to use membership and the SEA as vehicles for the transformation of its economy following the isolation of the Franco years.

Increased competition from Asia has had a broad-based negative impact on industries such as ship-building, steel, motor vehicles, electronics and consumer goods. Hamburg saw its ship-building industry virtually disappear but both it and Amsterdam became regional centers for Chinese offices related to logistics and marketing. Munich lost much of the production of Völkl skis to China, but has been able to retain production of the high quality and high price end of the product line as well as the headquarters; this can be seen as a response that is typical of that of many EU urban regions – the low-skill activity is lost to Asia but the high end, design and headquarters functions remain in Europe. Cities which have traditionally been centers of the textile industry, such as Barcelona and Dresden, have lost this activity to producers in Asia and other low-wage countries.

So macro- and micro-economic and global and regional political turbulence have had their impacts on the ten cities studied, but the specific impacts are dependent upon the economic structure and specialization of that individual urban region. This is, of course, as should be expected.

Today's Comparative Advantage can Create Tomorrow's Social Pathology

The clearest example of this is to be found in Turin. During the post-WWII years, FIAT greatly expanded its production of motor vehicles. The labor force needed did not require much more than a certain amount of physical strength and coordination. The cheapest way to get this labor was to import workers from the south of Italy – from Sicily and other provinces in the Mezzogiórno. This strategy was successful for several decades, until the rise of competition from more efficient producers in the rest of Europe and then in Asia. Since the beginning of the 1990s production by FIAT in its Turin facilities has steadily fallen, leaving the metropolitan region of Turin with a large force of largely uneducated workers with skills that are not suited to the modern production system of the industrialized world. The result is that today 60 per cent of Turin's workers lack a high school education, many of whom are of an age that reduces the attractiveness of further training. A large number of essentially unemployable workers poses obvious threats to the fiscal viability of a city, to public safety, to the reputation of the city, and to the ability of the city to find a place for itself in an increasingly skill-intensive modern economy. So it can be seen that the elements that give a city its economic strength or competitiveness at one moment in time can turn around to be the factors which hamper the city's effort to be competitive at a later date.

This phenomenon is experienced by all regional economies as they evolve along with the economic environment in which they exist. The shift from agricultural production to manufacturing continues to be eased by massive protectionist measures of one sort or another through the Common Agriculture Policy using the argument that no society can be dependent upon other, potentially antagonistic, nations for its basic sustenance; the same argument does not carry water when it is applied to the shift from manufacturing to services, and especially to high-skill services. Thus, when designing a strategic–economic plan for the next decades, city leaders must be aware of the need continually to upgrade the skills of their labor force so as to avoid the development of competitiveness reducing social pathologies. Cities such as Munich and Lyon that have pursued for decades a strategy of production based on science, technology and research have been largely able to avoid this potential problem, since their labor force is, as a matter of course, continually being upgraded.

Regular Examination

As a final observation from the study of ten internationally engaged cities in the EU, I would note briefly that once a plan has been adopted regular monitoring of progress, difficulties, new insights, and so forth is absolutely necessary. The failure of one activity to be carried out as intended will have negative impacts on the ability of other objectives to be realized. Both an engaged leadership and effective governance can help greatly in assuring that the expected progress is being made in all areas, that the individuals assigned the tasks are able to do the work, and that necessary modifications to the plan can be identified and implemented. Too much is at stake, in regard to the economic livelihoods of the metropolitan region's residents, to allow favoritism and ineffective performance to be tolerated. The recently adopted plans of these ten cities have not been in operation long enough for observations to be made with regard to this aspect of the SEP process.

THE STRATEGIC–ECONOMIC PLANNING CHALLENGES OF THE FUTURE FOR CITY LEADERS

The experiences of the ten cities with various aspects of turbulence in the environment in which their SEP initiatives were implemented, which were examined in Chapter 5, showed that some but not all turbulence had negative impacts on the planning process. It was primarily the macro-economic stagnation of the EU economy, the weak expansion of that of Central Europe and outsourcing of production to low cost countries, in Asia and Central Europe, that had the most significant impacts. Trade relations with North America were positive throughout the period, and the introduction of the Euro and its depreciation and then appreciation had an impact on selected cities, such as those in which Airbus is a major part of the economy. The micro-economic impacts of deregulation of financial markets and the slow relaxation of controls on mergers and acquisitions and other aspects of competition policy do not appear to have had significant impacts on the performance of the ten urban economies.

Nine Questions about the Future

We cannot know what the next decade will have in store for Europe's major urban economies, but it would be safe to assume that the degree of turbulence will be at least as great as it was during the past 15 years. The final subject to be dealt with in this book is an examination of the likely elements of turbulence that will confront these city leaders and to possible impacts they will have on their ability to plan for the economic future of their economies. These will be presented as a series of nine questions.

Will the EU economy be able to generate growth or will it continue to stagnate?

There is ample reason to believe that the relative economic stagnation of the past 15 years will be extended into the foreseeable future. One does not have to be a free market purist to understand that the EU economy is in dire need of reforms that will enable its economic actors to function with flexibility, adaptability and initiative. As will be argued below, one response of the EU economies to economic stress has been to slow the integration process and to give legitimacy to protectionist forces. In mid-March 2006, French newspapers gave full coverage to the effort of French Prime Minister de Villepin to ease the hiring and firing procedures for young workers, which has been met with protests at universities and lycées throughout the country. The objective of this reform is to make firms more willing to take on young workers, among whom the rate of unemployment is in excess of 25 per cent. However, a century or more of distrust of the actions of employers and government make it difficult to introduce any changes to labor practices, and makes it difficult to present this reform as a choice between continued high unemployment for young workers and a very unsatisfactory entry into the work force and lower unemployment with more opportunity for inter-job movement.

This resistance to change and to becoming more responsible for one's own economic future is mirrored in actions by EU firms. In the spring of 2005, the Italian economy was clearly in difficulty with high unemployment, low growth and low productivity. When Confindustria, the Italian employers association, met to deal with the situation, the first proposal they had was that the government had to come up with a new policy. For better or worse, it is inconceivable for this to have been the response of industry in the United States where, it must be noted, productivity and growth are relatively high and unemployment is relatively low.[1]

Europeans are understandably tired of having Anglo-Saxon economists lecture them on the virtues of what the continentals refer to as *le capitalisme sauvage*, but there is an undeniable logic to market-based decision-making in the context of a global economy in which little if anything can be sufficiently controlled or managed so as to accommodate the existing and unchanging institutional structures and processes that were created, dare one say ossified, at a time when Europe stood atop that global economy.[2] But the follow-up to adoption of the 'Lisbon agenda' that was to promote reforms that would make the EU the most competitive regional economy by 2010 has, at mid-point, been judged to have been a failure. Two economists, Jean Pisani-Ferry and André Sapir, have just issued a report that criticized the member nations for failing to provide for any method for assessing progress, for failure to identify countries that have ignored the recommendations, for failure to provide adequate funding, and for assigning junior rather than senior civil servants to the initiative.[3] Growth, job creation and productivity all continue to lag six years into the decade.

The final handicap for the EU economy is the demographic phenomenon of the aging of the EU population that is projected to continue for several decades. Low rates of natality, increased longevity, resistance to increasing the retirement age and a pay as you go approach to retirement benefits are all combining to create a situation in which the steadily increasing expenditures for retirement and health care are matched by a reduction in the component of the population that will bear the burden of the required taxation. The obvious difficulty historically emigrant societies are having in welcoming and assimilating young immigrants from non-European nations may well be matched by young EU workers making the economically rational decision to emigrate, themselves, to North or South America, to Australia and New Zealand or to some other nation with a more promising economic future.

There is little that city leaders can do to change labor, competition or industrial policy at the national or EU level, but each urban economy has the possibility of bringing its local firms and labor together and creating an environment of cooperation, facilitating the movement of workers from one job to another through improving both contacts between firms and workers and information about jobs and retraining opportunities, and avoiding the harsh combination of Anglo-Saxon flexible processes and continental institutional rigidity. Failure to act in a way that will move the local economy in the direction of one that can respond to the decline of existing economic activities will condemn that economy to a future as unpromising as is that of most of the EU national economies.

What will be the future value of the Euro?

The future value of the Euro is, of course, quite impossible to forecast, in part because the course of its movement in the years since its adoption as an internationally traded currency has shown little relation to economic variables. After falling from $1.18 in 1999 to $0.83 in 2000, the Euro then soared to over $1.34 only to settle at about $1.20 at present. During this recent rise the EU economy performed rather poorly. The new European Central Bank has kept its primary focus on any tendency toward inflation, so EU interest rates have been maintained higher than would otherwise have been prudent policy. But where it goes during the next decade is dependent upon so many unpredictable events, such as the other items of turbulence being discussed in this section of the chapter, that it would be foolhardy to suggest even the direction in which it might move. But it is easy to argue that there is little to suggest that the Euro will appreciate very much if at all during the foreseeable future. Macro-economic stagnation, the stress which attaches to enlargement, and the diffi-culty in implementing effective governance either at the level of the EU or in most of the national capitals all suggest a weak rather than a strong Euro. At the moment of this writing, in the spring of 2006, there is even discussion of the inability of Italy to remain in the Euro system for the next five years. While ardent Euro supports might say 'good riddance to the Italians' the mere possi-bility of such an event would make governments, banks and individuals reluc-tant to move their funds from other currencies such as the dollar to the Euro, and its actual occurrence should extend the period of uncertainty further into the future.

While a gradual depreciation of the Euro might be welcomed by some city leaders, the wiser ones will hope for stability and no dramatic developments in the market value of the Euro. Neither uncertainty nor instability will do any of them any good. One major change in exchange rates which is both reason-ably likely and of benefit to EU urban economies is the gradual appreciation of the Chinese Yuan. Should this occur, there would be some marginal benefit to low-wage manufacturing activities in cities throughout the industrial world. At best, this would give a bit more time for the ultimate restructuring that faces these economies and it must be remembered that these industries are not the ones on which city leaders want to base their economies. On the other hand, the International Monetary Fund has argued that the adjustment of imbalances among major economies will require a significant depreciation of the dollar over the next few years, an event that would have the opposite impacts on EU urban economies.[4] This would be especially troublesome given the importance of the US market for the goods produced in these economies.

Will the emerging economies of China and India, and other low-cost economies continue their expansion?

These two nations have led the way in terms of successful transition toward being sophisticated economies that are linked to the most rapidly growing aspects of the global economy. Each has significant problems relating to regional economic imbalances, rural to urban migration, urban congestion and housing, health care, and so forth. China has set out on a path that at least in its initial stages is based on low-cost low-skill labor, while India has chosen to highlight its low-cost high-skill labor. This is not to say that each of them will remain primarily on the present path. But from the standpoint of the ten EU urban economies it is clear that the challenge posed by just these two Asian competitors is presenting itself on both the high- and low-skill labor fronts. The recent initiatives to restrain Chinese exports of textiles and shoes are symptomatic of the defensive response that has been so typical of the EU and its member nations. Trade-related adjustment mechanisms such as appreciation of the Chinese and Indian currencies will lessen the threat but not only are they likely to remove it, but similar challenges are sure to be presented by other nations eager to emulate the successes experienced by China and India.

The competition from production sites in China and India has caused significant dislocation and restructuring in certain vulnerable industries throughout the EU. Some cities such as Hamburg have managed the adjustment rather well while others have pressed for protectionist measures. The latter may result in some short-term relief but only at the cost of allowing economic actors to postpone the restructuring that will be required sooner or later, with a process that will only be even more painful and costly. Far-sighted city leaders will understand the nature of this challenge and the need for some creative thinking about the transition of their own economy from its traditional strengths to the activities that will allow it to thrive in this new world in which their vitality will have to be earned and not assured by their entrenched position in traditional markets. So the extent to which the evolution of the economies of China and India pose serious difficulties to the ten EU cities is to some considerable degree dependent upon the decisions made by their leadership. Neither success nor disaster is predetermined.

What of Latin America and Africa – will they stabilize and emulate China and India?
Both continents are rich in resources and have ample populations of low wage, trainable labor. With capital extremely mobile, and with firms and investors always looking for a new location for profitable investment, the primary hindrance for economies in both Latin America and Africa is political stability under conditions of democracy which can assure the rule of law, transparency, the right to withdraw capital and profits, and the other conditions that are considered the *sine qua non* of national economic transformation and growth. Sadly, the legacy of a century or centuries of colonialism have left these countries reluctant to accept the latest round of inducements to open their borders to the benefits of globalization. However, there are many indications that some countries in Latin America are making the transition from nationalist dictatorships to more democratic political systems and market-based economic decision-making; sadly, Africa has yet to give much evidence of this movement. But if Latin American and African countries successfully integrate themselves into the present international economy with all of its exigencies, the major urban economies of the EU should expect the current challenges which are emanating from Asia to be extended well into the fore-

seeable future. Fortunately, they will have had experience with the emergence of Asia as a competitor in many areas of economic activity and the emergence of the two remaining continents should be feathered in gradually and over an extended period of time. Nonetheless, it will be incumbent on city leaders to understand that this sort of adjustment process is going to be something with which they will have to deal and will have to build it into their strategic–economic planning process. If this is done, the emergence of economies in Latin America and Africa should not cause them significant difficulty.

How will the economies of Central Europe develop and relate to the rest of the EU?

The turbulence that has been experienced to date that is based on EU membership of the countries of Central Europe has had its impacts, both negative and positive, on the ten urban economies studied here. The growth of market demand in this region has been disappointing to firms in Munich, but both Hamburg and Dresden have had positive experiences in developing longer term relations with contiguous and other areas in Central Europe. However it must be noted that the farther the city is from the old border between East and West the weaker are the impacts, of either sort. As the infrastructure develops and it becomes a more attractive place in which to locate economic activity, and as Central Europeans gain a more realistic understanding of the consequences for their economies from EU membership, the positive impacts should be more noticeable than the negative ones. Markets will expand, jobs will be created in economies from which there have been sizeable flows of migrants to Germany, Italy and the rest of the earlier 15 member countries. But it is likely to continue to be the case that these impacts will be felt primarily in urban economies in Germany and the Nordic members.

Will the US continue to reconfigure itself and maintain its healthy growth or will it enter a period of stagnation?

In stark contrast with the economies of the EU, US economic performance has led the industrialized world since 1990. It is common to attribute this superior performance to the ability of its economic entities and actors to reinvent or to reconstitute themselves as, sometimes rapidly, changing economic circumstances require. The most prominent negative aspect of the US economy is inept economic policy on the part of the federal government which has resulted in a burgeoning national debt that is fed by an irrational policy of tax cuts in the context of a major military conflict and other spending increases linked to, among other things, major weather-related disasters. Trade performance is disappointing in part because of the freedom US firms have to transfer production of goods out of the US to low cost alternatives in countries such as China, rather than using the US as an export base. This is sustained only by the willingness of foreign governments in countries with substantial trade surpluses with the US to place the dollars gained in that trade in US capital markets, especially in US Treasury obligations.

The dark cloud on the horizon for the US is the possibility that these foreign governments may wish to transfer their funds out of US dollar assets to something else. There are of course some factors that make this unlikely. First, there is a lack of alternative places to put those funds. Not even the much touted Euro could absorb the enormous amount of funds that would have to be accommodated. Second, any move away from the dollar would cause the exchange rate to fall and would reduce the value of the remaining funds still in dollars. Third, few countries would like to see the dollar fall significantly as this would increase the competitiveness of goods produced in the US, leading to a reduction in their trade surplus and a disinvestment in production facilities in these other countries in favor of investment in the US. Thus, we have a 21st century example of the notion of John Maynard Keynes to the effect that if one owes one's banker £1000 one has a problem, but if one owes one's banker £1 000 000 then one's banker has a problem.

Will market liberalization continue to progress or will its challenges drive the major economies back to protectionism?

Different economies react to economic recession or stagnation differently. Canada tends to seek closer relations with its largest trading partner, the US, while the US tends toward protectionism. The US current account deficit for 2005 exceeded $800 billion and after several years of lack of attention to this situation and of fiscal irresponsibility Congress is now weekly considering introduction of some new protectionism measure. In the EU, readers of newspapers and business/economic magazines are fed a steady diet of items with regard to the reluctance of one member country or the other mounting resistance against some cross-border investment or take-over of some domestic bank or utility. Recently, EU Commissioner for the Internal Market, Charlie McCreedy, was quoted saying that the Commission lacked the policy instruments to battle against the protectionist pressures of its members.[5] With continued EU economic stagnation more likely than not, one can only anticipate continued protectionism and pressure to slow down or reverse the process of realization of the potential of the 'four freedoms' that have been reaffirmed in every major EU agreement since the Treaty of Rome.[6]

Given the likelihood that the EU economy will continue to experience relative stagnation, pressure from protectionist forces should continue and the major urban economies of the EU should anticipate that they will be affected. Both foreign and local firms will find the EU an attractive place for investment in the production of goods destined for the EU market. In this case, the recent expansion of EU membership to 25 countries would be advantageous as it has increased the size of the internal market. However, the EU would become a decidedly less attractive location for production for the world market, as, among other things, imported inputs would be more costly and access to foreign markets would be less free. Since all major EU urban economies, including the ten included in this study, have, to varying degrees, based their economic expansion on integration of their industries into world markets, increased protectionism would bring impacts that would impose significant costly restructuring in urban economies. Local political leaders would have few options other than accepting this policy reality and doing whatever adjustments are required. This could make it necessary for most cities to redesign their SEP.

What will be the continuing impacts of the concern for terrorism and national security?

The consequences of the need to respond to the threat of terrorist action against nation states are similar to the consequences of imposition of a tariff or some other barrier to trade. To protect their residents from terrorist acts national governments put up impediments to the free flow of goods and people. This makes some goods less tradable, it imposes the cost of additional time or transportation, it makes the delivery of goods less reliable, it increases the time and cost of travel for individuals and it reduces the flows of some categories of travelers, such as tourists, whether because of fear or the inconvenience of security checks or the reluctance to pay for a passport, in the case of travelers between the US and Canada for example. One effect of this is on the prices of goods traded, with imports now increasing in cost. This in itself will result in individuals moving to a less preferred indifference curve, in the terms of micro-economic theory; their welfare will be reduced. A second effect is to make the economy operate at a reduced level of efficiency, since specialization and exchange will be constrained. This is in effect a movement of the production possibilities curve toward the origin. Again, when the new equilibrium has been attained individuals will be on a lower indifference curve on which their welfare will be reduced. National governments can introduce new technologies and new procedures that will reduce these impacts, but the uncertainty about making commitments to transactions or investments over the long term will still be there. The companies involved may also be able to introduce programs in cooperation with governments that will reduce the negative impacts on their own activities. However, given the uncertainties with regard to both the timing and nature of possible future terrorist actions there will always be a residual cost and inconvenience that will remain as long as those who wish to pursue these actions are in a position to do so.

The consequences of this policy response on urban economies will be that of making both their exports and imports used in the production of goods for both domestic and external consumption more costly. Therefore, activities that sustain the local economy may be less viable in the new security conscious economic environment. This is an issue over which city leaders are not likely to be able to exert any pressure or control, so the premium will be on the ability of them to envision what is in store for their economy and to build a response to the challenges of terrorism into their SEP as early as is possible.

Edwin Mills has concluded that the new environment of terrorism will drive some economic activities away from tall buildings in central business districts and even away from large densely populated urban centers to suburbs and edge cities. This could reverse the effort to limit sprawl and could give an advantage to personal automobiles rather than to mass transportation.[7] Edward Glaeser and Jesse Shapiro argue that even within a large city such as New York areas that are thought to be high-risk, downtown for example, will lose out to others, such as mid-town or even to New Jersey just across the Hudson River, that are thought to be relatively low-risk.[8]

Terrorism, while horrific in its aftermath, can be thought of as being just another risk with which decision-makers must contend. As has been noted on more than one occasion in this book, the cities that get the policy response right first will be the ones to be successful in achieving their economic objectives.

What will be the impacts of continued technological advance?

There are two things that are certain about technological advance: 1) it will continue its pace of rapid development, because of its own logic and because of the interest so many economic actors have in its continued advance, and 2) its consequences will be, except in the most general and least useful way, impossible to predict. In other words, this is a classic situation of high uncertainty. Unfortunately, in this context a premium is placed on the ability of an economy and its primary actors to react, adapt and adjust in the shortest possible time. Every urban economy is in a highly competitive position and delay in adjustment usually means that the other competitor gets the prize. Equally unfortunately, these are values in which the EU has always been deficient in comparison to its North American and increasingly its Asian competitors. On the other hand, it is not at the level of the national economy that the technology game is being played. Nations can provide a favorable macroeconomic climate, although this seems to be a potential yet to be realized in the EU, and they can make constructive investments in the transportation infrastructure, but as was noted in the discussion of Porter's diamond in Chapter 3, it is at the level of the cities and urban regions that the crucial decisions will be made and the congenial and competitive environment will be created. It is this understanding that motivated the writing of this book. As the burden for decisions and policies devolves to lower levels of government, city leaders must come to realize the responsibilities that have been placed on their shoulders and must develop effective ways to plan their responses.

The anticipated consequences of technological advance were detailed in Chapter 3 – new industries, new ways of producing goods, demands for labor with specialized skills, and new demands on infrastructure and governance, among others. Analogous to the demand of the 'new international economics' for pre-emptive action to foster the development of an industry, a passive, *laissez-faire* approach will not work if a city's competitors do not adopt the same approach.[9] City leaders must do what they can to facilitate the movement by the firms in their economy into new and promising activities and they must periodically take stock of the openness of their economy to new ideas and new ways of doing things. They can do this by supporting improvements in the local educational system, by fostering a spirit of creativity, by establishing institutions devoted to innovation, research and entrepreneurship (risk taking), and by sponsoring forums and networks through which the individuals who should be interacting with each other can be encouraged to do so. The only guarantee involved here is that of marginalization of the urban region's economy if nothing is done.

FINAL THOUGHTS

In this book I have argued that a strategic–economic planning exercise is of vital importance for cities concerned with their competitiveness and their economic future. An effective plan will result in the most efficient utilization of the available resources or assets; it will mobilize the community and key individuals around a common set of desired results and means to achieve those results. The methodology offered here will facilitate that process. It also indicates how carefully that strategy must be determined and what specific means are attached to that strategy or set of strategies. Finally, it suggests how finely nuanced the plan will be for each individual city. There is no single approach that works for many or all cities, and local authorities should avoid following the pact, so to speak, with the latest trend in thinking about competitiveness and economic development. If done properly, the results can be very positive and will be invaluable for a city trying to navigate through the sea of globalization-induced threat, challenges and opportunities to create the economic future to which its residence realistically can aspire. The experience of each of these ten urban regions has differed in essential ways from those of the others, but a study of them should be of benefit to city leaders throughout both the industrialized and the developing world.

NOTES

1. Chris Giles, 'A productivity prescription: how the US has pulled away from Europe and Japan,' *Financial Times*, January 25 2006, p. 12.
2. The situation of the French economy was analysed, with a conclusion that was perhaps a bit overly positive, in Peter Karl Kresl and Sylvain Gallais, *France Encounters Globalization*, Cheltenham, UK and Northampton, MA, USA: Edward Elgar, 2002.
3. George Parker, 'EU's economic growth strategy heading for failure, report says,' *Financial Times*, March 15 2006, p. 2:1.
4. Krishna Guha and Shererazade Daneshkhu, 'IMF eyes dollar depreciation to resolve global imbalances,' *Financial Times*, April 20 2006, p. 1:3.
5. Giussepi Sarcina, 'McCreevy: contro il protezionismo? Dateci più poteri,' *Corriere della Sera*, March 11 2006, p. 21:3.
6. 'Freedom fried,' *The Economist*, February 11 2006, pp. 11–12.
7. Edwin S. Mills, 'Terrorism and US Real Estate,' *Journal of Urban Economics*, Vol. 51, 2002, pp. 198–204.
8. Edward L. Glaeser and Jesse M. Shapiro, 'Cities and Warfare: The impact of Terrorism on Urban Form,' *Journal of Urban Economics*, Vol. 51, 2002, pp. 205–24.
9. Paul R. Krugman (ed.), *Strategic Trade Policy and the New International Economics*, Cambridge, MA, USA: MIT Press, 1990.

Bibliography

'Die Hoffnungsträger,' *Capital*, February 2005, 14–19.

'Freedom fried,' *The Economist*, February 11, 2006, 11–12.

'Mayor's Message,' http://www.sevillaglobal.es/acercade/alcade/index.html. en.html

http://europa.eu.int/growthandjobs/index_en.htm

www.competitiveness.org.

www.competitiveness.org/

www.torino-internazionale.org.

Anderson, Hans Thor and Christian Wichmann Matthiessen (1995), 'Metropolitan Marketing and Strategic Planning: Mega Events. A Copenhagen Perspective,' *Danish Journal of Geography*, **95**, 71–82.

Balchin, Paul N., David Isaac and Jean Chen (2000), *Urban Economics: A Global Perspective*, New York: Palgrave, 48–53.

Barcelona 2000, *Plan estratégico metropolitano de Barcelona: Documento núm. 11*, March 2003.

Boldrin, Michele and Favio Canova (2001), 'Inequality and Convergence in Europe's Regions: Reconsidering European Regional Policies,' *Economic Policy*, **32**, April, 207–53.

Boschma, Ron A. (2004), 'Competitiveness of Regions from an Evolutionary Perspective,' *Regional Studies*, **38** (9), 1101–14.

Britton, John N.H. (2003), 'Network Structure of an Industrial Cluster: Electronics in Toronto,' *Environment and Planning A*, **35**, 983–1006.

Brunet, Roger, *Les Villes 'Européennes'*, Paris: DATAR, May, 1989.

Bunnell, Timothy G. and Neil M. Coe (2001), 'Spaces and Scales of Innovation,' *Progress in Human Geography*, **25** (4), 569–89.

Burton, Jack (1990), 'Denmark: A Bridge to the North, *International Management*, June, 70.

Camagni, Roberto (2002), 'On the Concept of Territorial Competitiveness: Sound or Misleading?,' *Urban Studies*, **39**, 2395–411.

Cappelen, Aadne, Fulvio Castellacci, Jan Fagerberg and Bart Verspagen (2003), 'The Impact of EU Regional Support on Growth and Convergence in the European Union,' *Journal of Common Market Studies*, **41** (4), 621–44.

Casado, Miguel Rivas (2002), *El Nuevo plan general de ordenación ante las actividades productivas: una valoración*, Seville: Sevilla Global.

Castells, Manuel (1988), *Proyecto Cartuja '93, Seville: La Sociedad Estatal Expo '92*.

Christensen, Otto (1988), 'Er vi klar til det europæiske hjemmemarked?,' *Børsen* (Copenhagen), March 15.

Ciccone, Antonio (2002), 'Agglomeration Effects in Europe,' *European Economic Review*, **46**, 213–27.

City of Knowledge, Munich: Department of Labour and Economic Development, City of Munich, July 2003.

Daniels, P.W. and J.R. Bryson (2002), 'Manufacturing Services and Servicing Manufacturing: Knowledge-based Cities and Changing Forms of Production,' *Urban Studies*, **39** (5–6), 977–91.

de la Fuente, Angel (2002), 'On the Sources of Convergence: A Close Look at the Spanish Regions,' *European Economic Review*, **46**, 569–99.

Dresdens Wirtschaft in Zahlen, Dresden: Stadtverwaltung, Amt für Wirtschafsförderung, 1991.

Emerson, Michael, Michel Aujean, Michel Catinat, Philippe Goybet and Alexis Jacquemin (1988), *The Economics of 1992*, Oxford: Oxford University Press.

Enrietti, Aldo and Renato Lanzetti (2002), *La Crisi FIAT Auto e il Piemonte*, Turin: Istituto Ricerche Economico-Sociale del Piemonte.

Evans, Graeme (2005), 'Measure for Measure: Evaluating the Evidence of Culture's Contribution to Regeneration,' *Urban Studies*, **42** (5–6), May, 959–83.

Florida, Richard (2002), *The Rise of the Creative Class*, New York: Basic Books.

Florida, Richard and Irene Tinagli (2004), *Europe in the Creative Age*, London: Demos.

Gardiner, Ben, Ron Martin and Peter Tyler, 'Competitiveness, Productivity and Economic Growth across the European Regions,' *Regional Studies*, **38** (9), 1045–67.

Gertler, Meric S., Richard Florida, Gary Gates and Tara Vinodrai (2002), *Competing on Creativity: Placing Ontario's Cities in North American Context*, Toronto: Ontario Ministry of Enterprise, Opportunity and Innovation, and the Institute for Competitiveness and Prosperity, November.

Giannetti, Mariassunta (2002), 'The Effects of Integration on Regional Disparities: Convergence, Divergence or Both?,' *European Economic Review*, **46**, 539–67.

Giblin, Jean Claude (2004), 'Les Aéroports Régionaux à la Veille de la Décentralization,' *Hérodote*, **114** (3), 101–21.

Giles, Chris (2006), 'A productivity prescription: how the US has pulled away from Europe and Japan,' *Financial Times*, January 25, 12.

Glaeser, Edward L. and Jesse M. Shapiro (2002), 'Cities and Warfare: The Impact of Terrorism on Urban Form,' *Journal of Urban Economics*, **51**, 205–24.

Governa, Francesca and Carlo Salone (2005), 'Italy and European Spatial Policies: Polycentrism, Urban Networks and Local Innovation Practices,' *European Planning Studies*, **13** (2), March, 265–83.

Graham, Stephen (2001), 'Information Technologies and Reconfigurations of Urban Space,' *International Journal of Urban and Regional Research*, **24** (2), 405–26.

Guha, Krishna and Shererazade Daneshkhu (2006), 'IMF eyes dollar depreciation to resolve global imbalances,' *Financial Times*, April 20, 1:3.

Hamburg, Business Centre for Northern Europe, Hamburg: Hamburg Business Development Corporation, undated.

Hamburg – Ein Wirtschaftszentrum der EG, Hamburg: Handelskammer Hamburg, 1989.

Hamburger Wirtshaftspolitik im vereinten Deutschland, Hamburg: Senat, 1990.

Hat München als Produktionsstandort noch eine Zukunft?, München: Wirtschaftsamt, December 14, 1989, 4–5.

Howells, Jeremy R.L. (2002), 'Tacit Knowledge, Innovation and Economic Geography,' *Urban Studies*, **39** (5–6), 871–84.

Hutchins, Mary, 'Appendix 1: The meaning and measurement of Urban Competitiveness – Technical paper,' in Michael Parkinson, Mary Hutchins, James Simmie, Greg Clark and Hans Verdonk (2004), *Competitive European Cities: Where do the Core Cities Stand*, London: Office of the Deputy Prime Minister, 80–105.

Implementation of the Comprehensive Plan Malmö 2000, Malmö: Stadsbyggnadskontor, October 2004.

Istituto Ricerche Economico-Sociale del Piemonte, *Relazione sulla situazione economica, sociale e territoriale del Piemonte 1988*, Turin, Rosenberg & Sellier, 1988, 4 and 36.

Jacquemin, Alexis and Lucio R. Pench (eds), *Pour une Compétitivité Européenne*, Brussels: De Boeck & Larcier, 1997.

Johansson, Börje and John M. Quigley (2004), 'Agglomeration and Networks in Spatial Economies,' *Papers in Regional Science*, **83**, 165–76.

Kitson, Michael, Ron Martin and Peter Tyler (2004), 'Regional Competitiveness: An Elusive yet Key Concept?,' *Regional Studies*, **38** (9), 991–9.

Kresl, Peter Karl (1989), 'Variations on a Theme: The Internationalization of 'Second Cities': Chicago and Toronto,' in Earl Fry, Lee Radebaugh and Panayotis Soldatos (eds), *The New International Cities Era: The Global Activities of North American Municipal Governments*, Provo, UT, USA: Brigham Young University, 185–98.

Kresl, Peter Karl (1991), 'Gateway Cities: A Comparison of North America with the European Community,' *Ekistics*, **58** (350–51), September–October, 351–56.

Kresl, Peter Karl (1992), *The Response of Urban Economies to Regional Trade Liberalization*, New York: Praeger.

Kresl, Peter Karl and Earl Fry (2005), *The Urban Response to Internationalization*, Cheltenham, UK and Northampton, MA, USA: Edward Elgar, Chs. 2, 4, 6 and 7.

Kresl, Peter Karl, and Sylvain Gallais (2002), *France Encounters Globalization*, Cheltenham, UK and Northampton, MA, USA: Edward Elgar.

Kresl, Peter Karl and Balwant Singh (1995), 'The Competitiveness of Cities: The United States,' *Cities and the New Global Economy*, Melbourne: The Organization for Economic Cooperation and Development and The Australian Government, 425–46.

Kresl, Peter Karl and Balwant Singh (1999), 'Competitiveness and the Urban Economy: 24 Large U.S. Metropolitan Areas,' *Urban Studies*, May, 1017–27.

Krugman, Paul (1994), 'Competitiveness: A Dangerous Obsession,' *Foreign Affairs*, March–April, 28–44.

Krugman, Paul (1993), *Geography and Trade*, Cambridge, MA, USA: MIT Press.

Krugman, Paul R. (ed.) (1990), *Strategic Trade Policy and the New International Economics*, Cambridge, MA, USA: MIT Press.

Lambooy, Jan G. (2002), 'Knowledge and Urban Economic Development: An Evolutionary Perspective,' *Urban Studies*, **39** (5–6), 1019–35.

Lever, William F. (2002), 'The Knowledge Base and the Competitive City,' in Iain Begg, *Urban Competitiveness: Policies for Dynamic Cities*, Bristol: The Policy Press, 11–31.

Lonardi, Giorgio (2005), 'Creatività, Milano lancia il guanto di sfida,' *La Repubblica*, January 31, 36.

Luciano, Pier Paolo (2005), 'Ecco le tre chiavi del futuro,' *La Repubblica*, February 24, xi.

Maggi, Maurizion and Stefano Piperno (1999), *Turin: The Vain Search for Gargantua*, Turin: Istituto Ricerche Economico-Sociale del Piemonte.

Malecki, Edward J. (2004), 'Jockeying for Position: What It Means and Why It Matters to Regional Development Policy When Places Compete,' *Regional Studies*, **38** (9), December, 1104–08.

Malmberg, Anders (2002), *Kluster dynamic och regional näringslivsutveckling*, Östersund, Sweden: Institutet för tillväxtpolitiska studier.

Malmö 2005: Aktualisering och komplettering av Malmös översikesplan, Malmö: Stadsbyggnadskontor, April 2005.

Markusen, Ann (1996), 'Sticky Places in Slippery Space: A Typology of Industrial Districts,' *Economic Geography*, **72** (3), July, 294–310.

Maskell, Peter and Gunnar Törnquist (2001), *Building a Cross-Border Learning Region*, Copenhagen: Copenhagen Business School Press, 11 and 43.

Matthiessen, Christian Wichmann (1990), 'Vesteuropa 1990,' *Geografisk Tidsskrift*, **90**, 45–6.

McFetridge, Donald G. (1995), *Competitiveness: Concepts and Measures*, Ottawa: Industry Canada.

Metropolregion München – das Kratzentrum Deutschlands, Munich: Industrie- und Handelskammer fur München und Oberbayern, 2003.

Mills, Edwin S. (2002), 'Terrorism and U.S. Real Estate,' *Journal of Urban Economics*, **51**, 198–204.

Mommaas, Hans (2004), 'Cultural Clusters and the Post-industrial City: Towards the Remapping of Urban Cultural Policy,' *Urban Studies*, **41** (3), March, 507–32.

Monaci, Giorgio and Gabriele Pasqui (2002), *Le politiche e gli strumenti di sostegno all'innovazione nell'area Milanese*, Milan: FrancoAngeli.

Morley, David and Arie Shachar (1986), 'Epilogue: Reflections by Planners on Planning,' in Morley and Shachar, *Planning in Turbulence*, Jerusalem: The Magnes Press, The Hebrew University, 143–44.

München und der Europäische Binnenmarkt, München: IFO-Institut für Wirtschaftsforschung, August 1989.

Negry, Cynthia and Mary Beth Zickel (1994), 'Industrial Shifts and Uneven Development,' *Urban Affairs Quarterly*, **30** (1), September, 27–47.

Ni, Pengfei (2003), 'China Urban Competitiveness: Theoretical Hypothesis and Empirical Test' (English text), Beijing: Chinese Academy of Social Sciences.

Ni, Pengfei (2003, 2004 and 2005), *Blue Book of City Competitiveness*, Nos. 1, 2 and 3, Beijing: Social Sciences Documentation Publishing House.

Nuove opera per il Piemonte che cambia, Turin: Federazione delle associazione industriali del Piemonte, February 2003.

Oerlemans, Leon A.G., Marius T.H. Meeus and Frans W.M. Boekema (2001), 'Firm Clustering and Innovation: Determinants and Effects,' *Papers in Regional Science*, **80**, 337–56.

On the Road to 2015 (1988), Amsterdam, Ministry of Housing, Physical Planning and Environment.

Parker, George (2006), 'EU's economic growth strategy heading for failure, report says,' *Financial Times*, March 15, 2:1.

Parkinson, Michael, Mary Hutchins, James Simmie, Greg Clark and Hans Verdonk (2004), *Competitive European Cities: Where do the Core Cities Stand*, London: Office of the Deputy Prime Minister.

Pla Estratègic Econòmic I social Barcelona 2000, Barcelona: Ajuntament de Barcelona, 1990.

Plan de Innovación y Modernización de Andalucia, Seville: Junta de Andalucia, 2004.

Polèse, Mario (2005), 'Cities and National Economic Growth: A Reappraisal,' *Urban Studies*, **42** (8), July, 1429–51.

Pollard, Jane and Michael Storper (1996), 'A Tale of Twelve Cities: Metropolitan Employment Change in Dynamic Industries in the 1980s,' *Economic Geography*, **72** (1), January, 1–22.

Porter, Michael (1990), *The Competitive Advantage of Nations*, New York: The Free Press.

Porter, Michael (1995), 'The Competitive Advantage of the Inner City,' Harvard Business Review, May/June, 55–72.

Provincia di Milano: Un progetto strategico per la regione urbana Milanese, Milan: Politecnico di Milano, Dipartimento di Architettura e Pianificazione, 2004.

Rantisi, Norma M. (2004), 'The Ascendance of New York Fashion,' *International Journal of Urban and Regional Research*, **28** (1), 86–106.

Rodríguez-Pose, Andrés (2001), 'Is R&D Investment in Lagging Areas of Europe Worthwhile: Theory and Empirical Evidence,' *Papers in Regional Science*, **80**, 275–95.

Rodríguez-Pose, Andrés and Maria Cristina Refolo (2003), 'The Link Between Local Production Systems and Public and University Research in Italy,' *Environment and Planning A*, **35**, 1477–92.

Rondinelli, Dennis A., James H. Johnson, Jr. and John D. Kasarda (1998), 'The Changing Forces of Urban Economic Development: Globalization and City Competitiveness in the 21st Century,' *Cityscape: A Journal of Policy Development and Research*, **3** (3), 71–105.

Sarcina, Giussepi (2006), 'McCreevy: contro il protezionismo? Dateci più poteri,' *Corriere della Sera*, March 11, 21:3.

Seminatore, Irnerio S., *Torino 2000*, Paris: Institut du Futur, Université de Paris VIII, undated.

Sevilla Global (2002), *Tecnologías de la Información y las Comunicaciones en la Empresa Sevillana. Una informe de Alproximación*, Seville: Sevilla Global.

Sevilla Global (2003), *Estrategia de Promoción Exeterior para Sevilla y su ámbito metropolitano*, Seville: Sevilla Global.

Shen, Jinafa and So Man-shan (2004), 'Measuring Urban Competitiveness in China,' *Asian Geographer*, **19** (1–2), 71–91.

Simmie, James (2004), 'Innovation and Clustering in the Globalised International Economy,' *Urban Studies*, **41** (5–6), May, 1095–112.

Smith, Richard G. (2003), 'World City Topologies,' *Progress in Human Geography*, **25** (5), 561–82.

Sobrino, Jaime (2002), 'Competitividad y Ventajas Competitivas: Revisión

Teórica y Ejercicio de Aplicación a 30 Ciudades de México,' *Estudios Demográficos y Urbanos*, **17** (2), 311–61.

Sobrino, Jaime, 'Competitividad territorial: ámbitos e indicadores de análisis,' Mexico City: Centro de Estudios Demográficos y de Desarrollo Urbano de El Colegio de México, unpublished paper.

Sobrino, Luis (2003), *Competitividad de las Ciudades en México*, Mexico City: El Colegio de México.

Strategic Assessment: The use of Telecommunication as an Element of Competitive Strategy by the City of Amsterdam, Amsterdam: Cambridge Systematics Inc., 1989.

Strategic Programme for the development and support of innovation and the growth of production activities in the province of Milan, 2002/2004, Milan: Provincia di Milano, 2002, 11–12.

The strategic plan of Torino 2000–2010, Turin: Torino Internazionale, 2000.

Torino negli ultimi 50 anni, Turin: Camera di commercio, industria artigianato, e agricoltura di Torino, 2004.

Torrani, Pier Giuseppe, and Giuseppe Gario (1987), 'A Metropolitan Process Analysis Experience: The Milan Project,' Milan: Istituto Regionale di Ricerca della Lombardia.

Towards the plan, Turin: Torino Internazionale, 1998.

Vickerman, R.W. (1997), 'High Speed Rail in Europe – Experience and Issues for Future Development,' *Annals of Regional Science*, **31**, 21–38.

Vreire, Mila and Mario Polèse (2003), *Connecting Cities with Macroeconomic Concerns: The Missing Link*, Washington: The World Bank, 8–11.

Wagner, Herbert (1992), *Rede von Oberbürgermeister Dr. Herbert Wagner beim CDU-Wirtschaftspartei-tag*, Dresden: Office of the Mayor, May 22 and 23.

Webster, Douglas and Larissa Muller (2000), *Urban Competitiveness Assessment in Developing Country Urban Regions: The Road Forward*, Washington: The World Bank, July 17, 9–13.

Wirtschaftsförderung 2003/Economic Report 2003, Dresden: Wirtschaft und kommunale Amt, 2003, 15–36.

Wolfe, David A. and Meric S. Gertler (2004), 'Clusters from the Inside and Out: Local Dynamics and Global Linkages,' *Urban Studies*, **41** (5–6), May, 1071–93.

Index